SCAFFOLDING LITERACY INSTRUCTION

SCAFFOLDING LITERACY INSTRUCTION

STRATEGIES FOR K–4 CLASSROOMS

EDITED BY

ADRIAN RODGERS

AND

EMILY M. RODGERS

WITHDRAWN

HEINEMANN • Portsmouth, NH

Heinemann
A division of Reed Elsevier Inc.
361 Hanover Street
Portsmouth, NH 03801–3912
www.heinemann.com

Offices and agents throughout the world

Library of Congress Cataloging-in-Publication Data
  Scaffolding literacy instruction : strategies for K–4 classrooms / edited by Adrian Rodgers and Emily M. Rodgers.
     p. cm.
  Includes bibliographical references and index.
  ISBN 0-325-00654-7 (alk. paper)
  1. Language arts (Primary). 2. Language arts—Remedial teaching. I. Rodgers, Adrian.
II. Rodgers, Emily M.
LB1528.S2862 2004
372.6—dc22   2004004128

Editor: Kate Montgomery
Production: Elizabeth Valway
Cover design: Linda Knowles
Cover photo: ©Arthur Tilley/Taxi/Getty Images
Composition: Argosy
Manufacturing: Steve Bernier

Printed in the United States of America on acid-free paper
08 07 06 05 04 RRD 1 2 3 4 5

We dedicate this book to students, yours and ours,
who challenge our assumptions about teaching,
who scaffold our learning as we scaffold theirs,
and with whom we love to work.

CONTENTS

FOREWORD

There are insistent demands today that the teaching of reading and writing in the primary grades become more effective. *Scaffolding Literacy Instruction* offers a direct answer to the often asked, perplexing question of "How?". The contributors of this book suggest that the answer lies in transforming how teachers interact with children during literacy instruction.

Traditional views of literacy instruction focus on the teacher as a sole provider of new information and modeler of correct performance. The student receives the new information and attempts to replicate what the teacher says and does. The interaction is one-way: the teacher talks; the student receives.

In *Scaffolding Literacy Instruction,* Adrian Rodgers and Emily Rodgers provide a collection of writing that proposes an alternative approach to literacy education. The authors suggest that the teacher's role is to construct a scaffold to support students' growing understanding and ability to resolve problems they encounter while reading and writing text. The term "scaffolding" is used to describe the support that helps the student complete tasks that would be unattainable without assistance. Thus, students share responsibility for completing an activity with the teacher. The interaction is two-way: the student does what he or she can do; the teacher helps with the rest.

The contributors of this book draw extensively from theory, classroom research, and practice to show the powerful impact of scaffolding on students' literacy learning. More than thirty years of writing and thinking from Jerome Bruner, Courtney Cazden, Marie Clay, John Dewey, Lev Vygotsky, and David Wood have contributed to the development of instructional models and techniques presented in this text. From the realm of practice, the authors provide rich descriptions of ways to manage independent learning and specific techniques to scaffold instruction in reading, phonics, word solving and writing from kindergarten through grade four.

This book is comprehensive in that the teachers whose stories are brought together are diverse. They vary in race and gender, and in the grade levels and areas of literacy (i.e., reading, writing, phonics) they teach. They practice in inner-city and suburban communities, and in public and private schools. The children whose school and life experiences are revealed are also diverse. They vary in race, gender, ability levels, and social and emotional development.

I will not forget the story of Corina, a mixed-race child, who came to understand herself and who she was becoming by reading and discussing many books about children with whom she could relate with her teacher. The scaffolding occurred in the kinds of opportunities the teacher created, the kinds of children's literature she offered, and in the conversations and writing in which she and Corina engaged.

The rich and far-ranging chapters in *Scaffolding Literacy Instruction* respond to teachers' concerns and frequently asked questions about their practice.

- What does it mean to scaffold children's learning?
- What does scaffolded literacy instruction look like?
- How do I meet the learning needs of all the students, especially those with learning problems?
- How do I help children work independently?
- How do I effectively scaffold writing activities for students with mild disabilities?
- What are some effective ways to teach phonics within a comprehensive literacy program?
- How can I support and extend students' use of strategies for word solving so that they understand what they are reading?
- How can peers scaffold one another's learning?
- What do I have to know and understand to support scaffolded literacy instruction?
- What difference is scaffolded instruction likely to make in teachers' and, ultimately, students' knowledge, skills, attitudes, and behavior?

The comprehensiveness of the stories told and questions answered will appeal to classroom teachers, special education teachers, reading teachers and teacher educators.

Scaffolding Literacy Instruction makes a significant contribution to literacy learning and teaching in three ways. First, it represents great diversity in children, their ages and their cultures, in the classrooms in which the teaching occurs and also in the backgrounds of the teachers who are involved. Despite their differences, the teachers whose stories are told share certain values about teaching. They respect children and their diversity. They provide a safe environment in which all children feel supported. They believe that scaffolding students' learning will help them become independent learners.

A second distinguishing feature of *Scaffolding Literacy Instruction* is that the authors and teachers featured in the book hold high expectations of children's ability to learn to read and write, and have confidence in their own ability to teach to those expectations. Children who struggle to learn or question their own ability are less likely to succeed when taught by teachers who have low expectations and believe that some children won't learn because they do not have enough brainpower or don't come from mainstream cultures.

Finally, one of the strongest aspects of *Scaffolding Literacy Instruction* is the use of narratives and teacher-student conversations to illustrate effective practice. The metaphors by which teachers live, the ways they think about their work, and the stories they recount tell us profoundly about what is going on in their lives and the lives of the children with whom they work every day. The stories provide an important way to think about teaching and learning (*obechenie*) and also give us an understanding of the critical role scaffolding plays in helping children reach their full potential.

Scaffolding Literacy Instruction comes at a good time. Editors Adrian Rodgers and Emily Rodgers have succeeded in combining an approach to teaching literacy, consistent with a Vygotskian perspective, with lively stories and conversations from teacher educators and practitioners working with diverse children in a variety of settings, grades, and schools.

After more than a decade of effort aimed at improving literacy instruction, there is a growing acknowledgement that in the final analysis it comes down to a matter of how teachers perceive and relate to children during instruction. There can be no effective substitute for recognizing children's learning potential and using sound judgment to differentiate instruction to meet the needs of diverse learners. The ability to provide this support lies in the teachers' language during interaction, which enables the teacher both to scaffold students' performance within the literacy activity and, through this, to provide a basis for them to know more and perform more effectively. In a time when learning to read and write has become an absolute necessity for success in school and life, *Scaffolding Literacy Instruction* provides needed direction and reassures us that teachers can make a huge difference in the educational, social, and emotional lives of our children.

—Carol A. Lyons

ACKNOWLEDGMENTS

All scaffolding is teaching but not all teaching is scaffolding. With that notion in mind, we invited educators whom we knew were investigating scaffolding to share their understandings with us in this volume. We are deeply grateful for their insights about scaffolding; their ideas are provocative and, at the same time, grounded in the classroom.

Emily especially wants to recognize and thank Rebecca Kitchen, the linchpin for the Reading Recovery project at The Ohio State University. Becky, a former teacher herself, keeps the office running smoothly and efficiently, and we are extremely appreciative of all that she does to help us complete projects on time. Other colleagues at Ohio State, including Gay Su Pinnell, Mary Fried, and Patricia Scharer, enrich our lives both professionally and personally. We also would like to acknowledge the work of Professors David Wood and Marie Clay; both are tremendous influences on the way we think about scaffolding. Deborah Cole, a teacher in Prince Edward Island, has helped us think more deeply about how children learn and we have benefited from her professionalism and dedication to her students.

Adrian is grateful to his students, particularly the EDT 660 students he worked with in the fall of 2002 at the University of Dayton's Capital campus. Their questions and observations regarding scaffolding were a great impetus for this book. A development grant from the School of Education and Allied Professions at the University of Dayton provided him with the support necessary to conceptualize and plan this book.

We deeply appreciate the efforts of Debbie Bowman, who helped us edit our manuscript prior to submission, and Leigh Peake, at Heinemann, who identified great people to help us with writing what we had learned. Kate Montgomery at Heinemann was a joy to work with, and our thanks also go to the committee of reviewers she assembled that provided us with such helpful comments.

SCAFFOLDING LITERACY
INSTRUCTION

1 | THE ROLE OF SCAFFOLDING IN TEACHING

EMILY M. RODGERS
ADRIAN RODGERS

In this volume, we began with a working definition of scaffolding. By "working definition," we mean that we rely on scholarship to point us in a direction that will help us understand the process without relying on bookish theory. Instead we transform the more obscure parts of theory to make it practical and useful.

DEFINING SCAFFOLDING

In Russian, there is a single word for the concept of teaching and learning: *obuchenie*. Until the 1970s, there was no English equivalent, perhaps because up until then we had not identified such a process. Instead, in research and in practice, teaching and learning were viewed as separate processes: we had theories about teaching and in the classroom we taught and then tested learning.

In the mid-1970s a new perspective emerged. Around that time, studies of interactions between parents and their children began to flourish, and Western researchers became familiar with Vygotsky's theory of learning and the notion of a zone of proximal development. In these parent-child studies researchers observed a different kind of process, one in which teaching and learning were intertwined. Wood, Bruner, and Ross (1976) famously described these helpful interactions between parent and child as "scaffolding," coining a term they define as a process that "enables a child or novice to solve a task or achieve a goal that would be beyond his unassisted efforts" (90).

The analogy of a scaffold is a useful one because it describes the process by which teacher and child interact as the child moves toward independence. A worker constructs a scaffold to work on an area of a building that is out of reach. The scaffold is only temporary and is removed when the work is finished. It can be put together and taken down quickly, as the need for assistance arises.

In terms of learning, the teacher is responsible for constructing the scaffold to support the child. It is only a temporary means of support and is removed when it is no longer needed. Perhaps most important, a scaffold is not used when assistance is unnecessary, just as you would not normally see a worker using a scaffold to work on easy-to-reach areas.

In studies of parent-child interactions that followed in the 1970s and 1980s, researchers observed parents working in partnership with their children to complete a task that was beyond what the learner could do without help. For example, in 1978, Ninio and Bruner observed scaffolding in the context of storybook reading in which mothers tended to work together with their children, usually providing more support when the child needed help reading and less help when the child was experiencing success. Even though it might have been the child's turn to read a page, the parent would step in and help when the child ran into difficulty.

Courtney Cazden, in 1983, observed this same kind of interaction going on between mothers and their children in the context of learning an oral language. The mothers that she studied seemed to know almost intuitively how and when to support their children's attempts to talk. Anyone who has overheard a parent conversing with a toddler will know how these interactions go. Emily, one of the authors of this chapter, recalls being in a bookstore and overhearing a child in a stroller say loudly, and it seemed urgently, "Ba, ba" to his mother, who was standing behind him. Without even pausing to glance at the child, the parent responded, "Did you drop your blanket on the floor? I'll get it for you." The mother's response not only supported what the child was trying to say but even extended his language, providing an exquisite example of scaffolded learning. (And the mother was right, the blanket was indeed on the floor!)

We see these kinds of parent-child interactions all the time in everyday life: the parent holding a child's two hands to help with the next step or running alongside the child's bike to help steady it. In all these examples, the parent who is the teacher seems to be operating from the question: "What can my child accomplish with assistance?" We are not surprised when we see these interactions because we expect them between parents and their children.

This is a vastly different process from the one we are accustomed to experiencing in classroom settings where teaching and learning are viewed as separate processes. As teachers we tend to ask ourselves, "What can this student do independently?" Unlike the way parents view learning, teachers do not usually operate from the notion "What can this student accomplish with assistance?" Instead we evaluate what they can do independently. In fact, our whole evaluation process in schools is geared to report what students can do on their own.

The early studies on parent-child interactions offer us a challenge. If parents are easily able to assess a learner's present cutting edge and then respond with just enough help to complete a task, can teachers do the same in classrooms? What does scaffolding look like in the classroom?

ALL TEACHING IS NOT SCAFFOLDING, BUT ALL SCAFFOLDING IS TEACHING

If that heading seems more like a riddle, keep reading and we'll sort this statement out together. Scaffolding is not synonymous with teaching, even though we have come to use the two terms interchangeably. Scaffolding is our English equivalent of obuchenie; it is teaching and learning. It implies a whole new way of looking at what we do in the classroom, how we make decisions about whether to help, the amount of help to give, the timing of giving the help, and the end goal of instruction. It is quite possible to teach without scaffolding learning. Let's look at an example.

Deborah teaches first grade. She has set up centers in her room where students can sort magnetic letters, listen to a book on tape, write a story, select books from their book boxes to read with a buddy, read independently, or work with the teacher. Today she is working with a small group of students who are reading at about a low-average level for her class. The students each have a copy of the same book, *Sally's Red Bucket* by Beverly Randell (1996), and they are taking turns reading. Deborah listens and makes teaching points whenever the students encounter difficulty.

Deborah is aware that finger pointing can help a student know where to look when reading, so as they take turns reading, she prompts each student to "read with your finger." She is consistent with this teaching and takes care to remind each student to remember to point to the words. Deborah also knows that sloppy finger pointing can get in the way of reading, so she doesn't allow students to point on top of the words or to slide a finger under the words. Deborah also insists that students in this group point while reading because it allows her to see that they really are looking at the words and not just reading the story from memory.

We would probably all agree from this description that Deborah is teaching; specifically, she is teaching the students in this group to match their utterances while reading. If you were to walk by Deborah's classroom and see them working together in this way, you'd probably conclude that Deborah is indeed teaching her students. But is she scaffolding their learning?

Remember that the definition of scaffolding is that it is a process that "enables a child or novice to solve a task or achieve a goal that would be beyond his unassisted efforts" (Wood, Bruner, and Ross 1976, 90). Therefore, in order to know whether or not Deborah is scaffolding her students' learning, we need to know what the students can accomplish on their own. As it happens, Deborah's students no longer need to finger-point while reading. They can track print and match one-to-one without the prop that the finger provides. They rarely insert extra words or omit words when reading. In fact, Deborah's insistence that they point while reading was having the opposite effect on their reading. Instead of helping, the finger pointing was interfering with learning how to phrase words and read fluently, forcing the reading to sound choppy and the reader to read word by word because the eyes had to slow down to match the finger's pace. Deborah knew what to teach and how, but the timing of the help did not match the children's present way of working; they were beyond it. She was teaching but she was not scaffolding learning.

Let's draw an analogy from a typical parent-child interaction to show how unhelpful assistance can be if it is offered when it is no longer needed. A parent has been helping with bike riding by holding the bike and running alongside to help with balance. Suppose that even after the child is able to balance the bike, the parent continues to hold on to the bike, running alongside. Not only would we think it not helpful to continue providing support after it is no longer needed, we would probably view the unneeded help as getting in the way of continued learning and even preventing further development. We might even wonder why the parent couldn't see that the child no longer needed assistance.

If scaffolding learning is so easy and straightforward outside the classroom in everyday learning situations, why does it seem to be so difficult to carry out in the classroom? The challenge probably has to do with the differences between what has to be learned in school and at home. Even though, for example, learning to walk or learning to talk are both complex actions, we feel well equipped to help children learn, perhaps because we are very familiar with what has to be taught. On the other hand, becoming literate is not so straightforward. Researchers do not agree on what has to be learned or how to teach it. No wonder scaffolding literacy learning is so challenging.

PRINCIPLES OF SCAFFOLDING

In the remainder of this chapter, we identify and discuss principles of scaffolding literacy learning in the classroom. These principles are summarized in Figure 1–1 and discussed in the sections that follow.

Principles of Scaffolding Literacy Learning
• Scaffolding is informed by careful observation.
• Respond to what you see the child actually trying to do.
• Teach today's child.
• Put the right book in the right child's hands.

An important principle of scaffolding learning is that teaching is informed by close observation of the learner, not by basing teaching on a preplanned scope and sequence of skills to be learned. Parents, for example, are often very knowledgeable about what their children can do and what they are presently learning how to do. This is particularly true when the children are still babies and very dependent on parents. On any given day, most moms or dads can tell you whether their baby is able to roll over independently, coo, babble, or string words together in a sentence. They know if the baby is able to crawl or stand alone for a few moments, a full minute, or only with the support of the coffee table.

How do parents come to be so informed about their children's development? Some information may come from secondhand sources like a babysitter or some other caregiver, but much of this knowledge comes from firsthand, close observation of the learner in action. These observations are important because they form the basis for decisions about the amount and kind of help that parents provide.

Of course, observing twenty active seven-year-old students in a classroom presents a different set of challenges than observing one child at home. Teachers need tools for recording the observations that will inform their teaching. Ross, a fourth-grade teacher, shared with Emily his procedure for systematically recording classroom observations. He developed a matrix, similar to the example in Figure 1–2, that provided him with a place to record his observations of individual children's use of reading strategies over time. In the example, Ross recorded observations for just one child, Niesha.

FIGURE 1–2
*Matrix to Record
Observations of
Independent Reading*

Niesha	10/7	10/14	10/21	10/28	11/4	11/11
Matching 1-1	1-1 off on every pg but didn't notice	1-1 off on multi-syllable words before I "Bec-fore"	usually	no lapses	no lapses	
Reads with fluency	choppy	word by word even on easy books	more phrased on easy books	easy books are phrased	re-reads for better phrasing	
Uses meaning	Checks pictures consistently	attempts are always meaningful	++	++	✓	
Uses first letters	neglects 1st letter got \ train out \ driver	no	no	fixed 2 errors flowers/g-g/sc garden	usually cake cookies	
Monitors errors	didn't notice mismatch	can had "That's not had"	notices mismatch visual flower plant	noticed "can't be" "lady" because "woman" of the "w"	doesn't notice mismatch beyond 1st letter would looks walked likes	
Self corrects errors	no evidence	no evidence	corrects 1-1 when its off but not dog puppy	fixed when errors were known see here	fixed when errors ignored she didn't info visual initially	
Rereads at difficulty	yes - goes back to top of page	yes doesn't but know how to solve	yes	does this quickly	++ goes only a few back to words to reread	

Ross has a matrix like this for each child in his class and has assigned days for recording his observations of students during independent reading. He will observe Niesha during independent reading time once a week and write anecdotal comments about her reading strategies. On Mondays, once the children are assigned to work at their centers, he pulls out the four matrices for the children he planned to observe that day and makes sure to observe those students and take notes during the independent reading block. On Tuesdays, he observes another five children, and so on.

Ross has written reading behaviors in the first column of the matrix that he wants to be sure to observe. He selected these descriptors because they fit with what Niesha is currently working on in reading. He is using the same matrix with three other students who are working on the same things as Niesha.

The observations that are recorded can be brief, as they are in Figure 1–2, perhaps with a few examples that provide some evidence of what the student was doing and as a memory prompt at a later date when you review your notes. The matrix also provides a bird's-eye view of change over time. We can see for example that between October 7 and November 11, Niesha's reading of familiar, easy books became more phrased and fluent (no doubt because Ross was teaching her how to read in a phrased, fluent way) and that she brought one-to-one matching of speech and text under control by October 28. We can imagine how a helpful matrix like this not only helps Ross track his students' learning, but perhaps more important, informs his teaching, providing some measure of assurance that his teaching will be on the child's cutting edge of learning. You can construct matrices like these in different ways to suit your preferences and needs.

Another way to structure the matrix is to simply have one matrix for the entire class, with each child's name in the column on the left. The blank spaces are then used to record the date of the observation and anecdotal comments about strategy use observed at that time. The advantage of using one matrix for the whole class is that you only need to bring one sheet of paper around with you during your observations. In this case, you will probably want to use eleven-by-seventeen-inch paper to have enough room to record your notes on each student. A disadvantage is that without the headings to prompt your observations, you may overlook particular strategies, and your observations may not be as systematic.

Respond to What You See the Child Actually Trying to Do

You would probably think it cruel if you saw a baby struggling to roll over while the parent stood by, withholding help. Imagine what you would think if the parent justified not helping by saying, "He should be able to roll over by himself by now, so I'm not going to help." We not only expect parents to help, but we also expect them to provide the help at the right time when it's needed, when the child needs assistance to complete a task or a part of a task that is beyond present capabilities.

The same principle applies to learning in the classroom. Even though you might think that a student should know a particular concept because you have taught it several times already, the fact that the student still does not know or understand is a clear signal that you should continue to provide support. It may also indicate that you need to examine how much help you are providing (is it enough?) and the kind of help you are providing.

Taking a running record of a child reading aloud is an excellent way to sort out what a child can actually do from what you think that child can do or ought to be able to do. This assessment tool, devised by Marie Clay (2002) and described in detail in her book *Running Records*, requires you to be a neutral observer of a child's reading. While the child reads, the teacher systematically records each reading behavior, noting accurate reading, substitutions, omissions, rereading, and self-corrections. The teacher can quickly calculate whether the text is at the child's frustration, instructional, or easy level, and by analyzing the child's errors the teacher can infer what sources of information (meaning, structure, or visual) the child is using or neglecting. This information can point the way for teaching.

Barbara, a first-grade teacher, had been directing Ronnie to use meaning as a source of information to help him at difficulty while reading. When he came to an unfamiliar word, she would usually ask him, "What would make sense?" to help him solve the word. Ronnie was not making much progress in reading, though, so Barbara decided she needed to check up on her assumptions about Ronnie as a reader. She took several running records and then examined the substitutions that Ronnie had made. Barbara found that Ronnie almost always incorporated meaning into his attempts, but he neglected to use visual information. For example, when he read *Nick's Glasses*, he said, "Have you looked under the cat" instead of "Have you looked behind the television?", substituting *under* for *behind* and *cat* for *television*. (In the story Nick is looking for his glasses, and this particular page shows Nick lifting up a cat that is sitting on top of the television.) As Barbara examined all of Ronnie's substitutions, she quickly uncovered a pattern of Ronnie using meaning and structure but neglecting visual information at difficulty.

Taking a running record revealed to Barbara what Ronnie was actually trying to do while reading. Instead of teaching him to use meaning, because he usually did anyway, she realized that she needed to teach him to notice the visual mismatch between his attempt and the letters in the words. Instead of saying to Ronnie as she might have done in the past, "Where else might Ronnie look?", which would direct him to use meaning again, she instead said, "It could be *cat,* but look at this letter here" (pointing to the letter t in *television*). This teaching point was really scaffolding Ronnie's reading because it was directing him to check a source of information that he had been neglecting: the letters. Taking a running record provided Barbara with a way to step back from her assumptions about Ronnie as a reader, to see what he was able to do and what he needed to learn how to do.

Teach Today's Child

The pace of a child's learning is extraordinary, particularly for young children who are emerging into literacy. Not only is the pace of learning fast, it is also variable from one child to another. Any parent who has had more than one child can attest to the different paths that each child takes on the way to independence. While we might be able to identify particular milestones that a child will achieve on the way to learning a particular skill, as Ross did in the matrix example shared earlier, we cannot predict the timetable for reaching those milestones.

Teaching decisions therefore must be based on what a child is presently able to do, not on what the child was able to do a month ago. In fact, if you are basing your teaching on what the child was able to do in the past, you probably are not working on that child's cutting edge. This is an especially important concept for teachers who use leveled groups in their classes if the group membership has remained unchanged for eight, ten, or twelve weeks.

Put the Right Book in the Right Child's Hands

This principle has to do with the "what" we teach. It may seem that much of what we teach is defined by people outside the classroom, such as curriculum developers at the state level who identify grade-level standards that must be met or consultants at the school district office who make decisions on materials that will be used in the classrooms. Even so, much of the decision making about what gets taught on a daily basis is rightly in the hands of teachers.

Deciding which books students should read is often challenging if you are trying to match books to students' abilities. If, on the other hand, you teach in an environment where everyone in the class reads the same book at the same time, you may have less to worry about. In this environment, it is also more likely that the book being read will match only a few students' needs and that it will be too hard for some or too easy for others. In either scenario, too easy or too challenging, it will be extremely difficult if not unlikely that you will be able to scaffold the students' reading.

A book that is too easy offers few opportunities for learning. More than likely there will be few if any challenges, and the student will be able to read it accurately without any errors. Errors provide the grist for the mill, the opportunity to notice some new kind of information that has as yet gone unnoticed, and the opportunity for self-correction. Some errors have to be present for new learning and scaffolding to occur. On the other hand, too many errors will mean the text is too difficult for the reader, and there is little chance that learning will occur. Clay recommends that accuracy rates on running records should be between 90 and 94 percent for texts to be in the instructional range. Below that the texts are too hard and above that the texts are too easy (Clay 1991). Matching children with books that are easy enough to read with just a few challenges to offer is perhaps one of the hardest teaching decisions to make, but it is a vital one because all scaffolding depends on it. It won't matter that you know exactly how a student is presently reading or what sources of information they use and neglect. You won't be able to scaffold learning if the book you choose is too difficult.

With our working definition of scaffolding established, in the remaining chapters we share case studies of teachers scaffolding student literacy learning in the early grades. Each chapter contains a set of features that we think will make this book useful for teachers seeking to hone their teaching practices. Chapters

- open with a vignette related to the chapter content as a way to sketch the scene.
- provide strategies for scaffolding literacy learning.
- feature teachers' voices through the use of teacher journals, interviews with teachers, and detailed descriptions of how teachers scaffold student's learning.
- include a select reference list for further reading.

The chapters illustrate scaffolding in a variety of settings familiar to every teacher, from the classroom to one-to-one settings to children working together in pairs. We present strategies to scaffold learning in each setting. In addition, we highlight various types of learners, from the so-called average to the child who has fallen behind his peers to the child with a mild disability. We also provide tools for scaffolding young children's knowledge of phonics and their understanding of story structure, and we describe how children's literature can be used to create a classroom climate where learning can be scaffolded.

Teachers face a multitude of learners every day. The challenge seems to be organizing literacy instruction in various ways (whole class, pairs, one on one) in order to better differentiate instruction for diverse learners. This volume will provide specific strategies for teachers to do just that. Few authors have the expertise to describe strategies for all these settings. This volume, because it is a collection of case studies, brings together many teachers' voices and experiences on scaffolding literacy learning, providing a breadth of expertise that just isn't available in a single authored resource.

NEXT STEPS FOR TEACHERS: RECOMMENDED READING

Berk, L. E., and A. Winsler. 1995. *Scaffolding Children's Learning: Vygotsky and Early Childhood Education*. Washington, D.C.: National Association for the Education of Young Children.

Bodrova, E., and D. J. Leong. 1996. *Tools of the Mind: The Vygotskian Approach to Early Childhood Education*. Englewood Cliffs, NJ: Prentice Hall.

Brady, S. 1994. *Mindful of Others: Teaching Children to Teach*. Portsmouth, NH: Heinemann.

Hogan, K., and M. Pressley, editors. 1997. *Scaffolding Student Learning: Instructional Approaches and Issues*. Cambridge, MA: Brookline.

Petrick, S. E. 1995. *Beginning Writers in the Zone of Proximal Development*. Hillsdale, NJ: Lawrence Erlbaum.

Rogoff, B., and J. W., editors. 1984. *Children's Learning in the Zone of Proximal Development*. San Francisco, CA: Jossey-Bass.

Soderman, A K. 1999. *Scaffolding Emergent Literacy: A Child-Centered Approach for Preschool Through Grade 5*. Boston: Allyn & Bacon.

Vygotsky, L. 1978. *Mind in Society: The Development of Higher Psychological Processes*. Cambridge, MA: Harvard University Press.

2 | IMPLEMENTING MANAGED INDEPENDENT LEARNING IN KINDERGARTEN

The First Twelve Days

BARBARA JOAN WILEY

Eric is an experienced and well-respected first-grade teacher. His principal and colleagues often compliment him on his exceptional classroom management skills. The students almost always do as they are asked, and hardly anyone can recall a discipline problem in Eric's class in his fifteen years at the school. Eric manages his classroom in what some might call a very traditional style. The only noticeable difference from days gone by is that students don't sit in small desks in rows. Otherwise, everything else seems much the same. All students cover the same material at the same time, with Eric leading the class in their learning, usually from the front of the classroom.

Although Eric seems like an accomplished teacher, he is unsatisfied with his style of teaching. He wishes that he had the flexibility to work with students in small groups or even individually from time to time. He knows he can best accomplish this by setting up centers in his room, but he wonders how he will ever be able to effectively manage his students' learning. It's easy to imagine the chaos that might ensue. How will students know what they should be working on? How will he be able to ensure that everyone is productively engaged and really learning? It's also easy to imagine that with such uncertainty and lack of structure, discipline problems will probably abound. Although every spring Eric vows he will set his classroom up with centers the following year, he just can't see how he will be able to do it all, so instead he settles for the same organization that he has always used.

Irene also teaches second grade and is just as experienced as Eric. She incorporated centers in her classroom for the first half of the school year but is now having serious reservations about her decision. It seems she is constantly telling students what they should be doing next and she worries that little is being accomplished at the centers while she works with a small group of students. The children are not getting along at the centers, and without her presence, they argue over the materials. Irene feels as though she is spending all her time resolving disputes and trying to get the children to work on their own. At the end of the day, the only learning she can be sure about is what happens in the guided reading group time. Irene feels frustrated and thinks that she is only reaching a small number of her students each day.

Gordon is having more success. After just three months of using centers, he is excited about his students' learning, and he notes that they seem to enjoy their center activities. Not only is he excited about what he is teaching, he also sees that his students are learning far more than he could have ever taught them as a whole class. Gordon's students are working fairly independently now, but he thinks they spent too much time in the first couple of months learning how to use centers and to work independently at them. He resolves that next year he will teach them how to work independently sooner.

Like many elementary school teachers, Eric, Irene, and Gordon want to differentiate instruction to meet their students' needs, and they see how centers will allow them to do just that. They just aren't sure how to get the students working independently at the centers so that they will be able to work with small groups of students at the same time. In this chapter we'll learn how Andrea does it. We'll follow her through the first twelve days of kindergarten and see what happens at the centers. Rather than learning about a particular kind of management style, we'll see how Andrea manages to scaffold the children's independent learning so they can manage themselves at the centers within just a few short weeks.

INTRODUCING ANDREA

Andrea stands at the classroom door welcoming her students. It's the fifth day of kindergarten, and today a new student, Zachary, joins their class for the first time. After welcomes, introductions, and settling in, Andrea asks another student, Samantha, to show Zachary around. They grab hands and begin the tour. Andrea calls out after them, "Be sure to show him the workboard and how we learn at centers." The child who is guiding calls back, "I know all about the workboard and I know how we figure things out at centers." As Andrea watches, the children move confidently into the classroom, and she hears, "And this is the workboard. This tells how we learn in kindergarten."

Andrea's school is part of the Literacy Collaborative, a cooperative partnership of schools and universities committed to the research and development needed to ensure literacy success for all students. As her school's literacy coordinator, Andrea provides professional development to the teachers in her school for half the day. She spends her mornings assisting and coaching teachers, organizing the school's bookroom, ordering supplies, analyzing assessments, and much, much more. Throughout the year she offers afterschool classes to help the staff teach reading, writing, and word study.

In the afternoons, she is a half-day kindergarten teacher. She uses the Literacy Collaborative framework for literacy lessons that consist of a number of elements that provide many opportunities for reading, writing, and word work (Fountas and Pinnell 1996). Andrea knows that good management is built in from the first day of school. According to her, those first days are important. "My goal is to teach routines and to get the kids actively engaged. It's not so much what they get done, but that they know what to do and they're doing it!"

I videotaped Andrea and her students during the first twelve days of school and then once a month throughout the rest of the year. I transcribed the videotapes, kept observational notes, collected artifacts of teacher and student work, and conducted informal interviews throughout the year. The children welcomed me and I soon came to be known as the lady with a camera and a notebook. Andrea welcomed me too as someone to talk to and reflect with after lessons and after school. We would ask each other questions that started with "Why do you think" and "What if."

In this chapter, I will describe the classroom environment in which Andrea and her children work and share the daily schedule they follow. Next, I will focus on centertime (also called MIL, or managed independent learning), the time during the day when the children work independently in centers and the teacher teaches literacy to small groups of children. I will give particular attention to how the centers were introduced to the children during the first week of school. Finally, I will look closely at how Andrea taught the students to work independently in the centers.

BEGINNING THE YEAR: ESTABLISHING CLASSROOM GOALS

Andrea's goal for her students is independence—independence in both behavior and learning. "I always think about independence, even if it's only walking down the hall and stopping at the end to wait for me. If I lead the line and they rely on me, more will go wrong when I'm not there." Learning is important to Andrea, and she teaches this value to her students. "I build a sense of community. We are here to learn. They must listen to my voice and do what I say. I want them to be actively in charge of their own learning." Andrea skillfully sets up her classroom and plans a schedule that teaches for independence from the very beginning of the year.

Classroom Environment and Daily Schedule

The classroom is set up with young children in mind. In the front of the room by the chalkboard, there is a large group area where the children can sit on a rug in front of the teacher's chair, as seen in Figure 2–1. Close by is a workboard, a large chart made of heavy cardboard with the names of the children in heterogeneous groups across the top and drawings of the centers they are to visit in rows underneath. The rest of the classroom is divided into centers, small areas in the room where the children can work and play independently. The tables in the room serve a dual function. At centertime they become part of the center, and at whole-group time they become a writing surface when needed.

There are eight centers in Andrea's room: ABC, writing, reading, math, listening, art, pocket chart, and a multipurpose center:

- ABC: The ABC center contains activities related to letter and word study. Andrea's ABC center has a table with a nearby shelf to hold supplies and on which a big book, chart, or sample product can be displayed. At the ABC center, children are asked to be involved in open-ended inquiry or to complete a task. For example, early in the year, the children sorted magnetic letters as an inquiry activity. During the first week of school, they worked on alphabet puzzles as a closed-ended task. Some days the children are asked to complete two or three activities related to letter and word study.
- Writing: The writing center consists of a table with a can full of sharpened pencils and a plastic container that holds crayons. Blank paper and finished writing products are stored in nearby plastic tubs. This center is open-ended. At the beginning of the year, for example, the children are asked to write their first and last names and then draw a picture with crayons. During the second week of school, the children are asked to write their full name, draw a picture, and write words to go with their picture.
- Reading: The reading center and the large group meeting area are in the same location in the classroom. This carpeted area is framed on one side by a long, low shelf that holds two shelves of plastic tubs full of children's literature books the children can choose to read. On another side of the area is a bookcase that displays books that are open to reveal their front and back covers. These books are colorful, inviting, and often ones that have been or will be chosen for read-aloud time. On the third side of this open area are the big books. The children are encouraged to also read these books during their independent reading time. During this time they often partner up with a friend, get a pointer stick, and read together.
- Math: The math center is located on a table with a shelf of drawers and cubbies nearby that hold math supplies such as plastic cubes, wooden cubes, counters, coins, and more. The tasks at the math center are often closed-ended. For example, one week early in the year the children were asked to sort forms by shape and color.

- Listening: The listening center is in a corner of the room close to an electrical outlet. It contains a tape recorder, headphones, and a tub with multiple copies of a book and its accompanying audiotape that will be listened to that day.
- Art: The art center contains a semicircular table pushed against the back wall and surrounded with chairs. Various art supplies are stored on the table, which the children will use to complete the project for the day.
- Pocket Chart: The pocket chart center is located in the corner of the room. At this center the children are asked to read the chart, poem, or song that is placed in the chart. They may also do some letter and word study.
- Multipurpose: The multipurpose center is a table. Often the children color and read easy-to-read books called Keep Books™ that have been purchased as part of the school's home/school project. Later in the year, the children will also be reading from their browsing bags at this center. Browsing bags are simply plastic bags containing books from previous guided reading lessons. Each child has a bag labeled with his or her name from which they choose the books they want to reread. The bags are stored on the shelf by the windows in the classroom.

FIGURE 2–1
Andrea's Classroom

Daily Schedule

Typically the daily schedule in Andrea's room moves from reading to writing contexts that contain word study activities. The day begins with independent reading and moves to reading aloud and then to shared reading. At the beginning of the year during independent reading time, the children look at books or retell familiar stories they have heard before, such as *The Three Bears* or *Mary Had a Little Lamb* or ones newly introduced in kindergarten. One or two of the children read simple texts during independent reading time. During read-aloud time Andrea chooses from a selection of children's literature books to read aloud to the class. Periodically during the reading,

Andrea stops to discuss what is happening in the story or the children may interrupt to share what they are thinking. In this fashion, the teacher and children are making meaning together. For shared reading Andrea uses enlarged texts. As they read the books together, Andrea helps the children to take on the strategies they need to become readers. Next comes workboard and centers.

In the beginning of the year, Andrea uses a workboard to monitor the time that children spend in the centers. As soon as the children are able to work independently in these centers, Andrea teaches reading to small groups of students.

Interactive writing and then independent writing follow centertime. During interactive writing time, the teacher and children create a piece of writing together, sharing both the negotiation of the message and the writing of the text. During independent writing time, the children practice independently what they have learned during interactive writing. As the children write independently, the teacher often sits with a low-progress student and guides the student's writing in a kind of one-on-one interactive writing session. At times, this slot in the day becomes a writing workshop where Andrea provides a minilesson; the children write as their teacher conferences with individual students, and they later share their writing with the whole group. Then it is time to go home. Andrea modifies the schedule only slightly to accommodate the first days of school (see Figure 2–2).

FIGURE 2–2
Schedule of Daily Events:
Andrea's Half-Day
Kindergarten

Schedule of Daily Events: Andrea's Half-Day Kindergarten
12:00–12:05   Independent Reading
12:05–12:25   Reading Aloud
12:25–12:35   Shared Reading
12:35–1:35   Centertime/Guided Reading
1:35–2:30   Interactive Writing and Independent Writing
or
Interactive Writing/Writing Workshop
2:30   Dismissal
Specials are scheduled on Wednesdays.

Day One: Assessment

On the first day of school when one-half of the class attends and on the second day when only the second half of the class comes, during centertime Andrea individually assesses children's early literacy achievement using Clay's Observation Survey (Clay 1993). The other children explore blocks, cubes, and books during this time. Andrea sets high expectations for her students. Even on the very first day of school, they are asked to play independently while taking care of their own needs for a long period of time.

From Day One, her expectations regarding behavior are stated explicitly. Any breach is quickly addressed and extinguished with clear, concise, polite language: "You have to choose the books, the blocks, or these cubes now. That's your choice right now. Not those other things. Thank you."

Day Two: Workboard Introduced

On the second day of school for each child, the whole class is there and they are introduced to a simplified workboard as shown in Figure 2–3. Andrea begins the introduction by meeting with the children in the large group meeting area. The children are sitting on the floor, and Andrea is standing beside the workboard displayed on the wall. Andrea says to the class, "Now we're going to learn how to work in kindergarten. This is going to be called our workboard. Every day, you're going to get a chance to do workboard. Workboard is going to be so much fun because you're going to do a lot of different things."

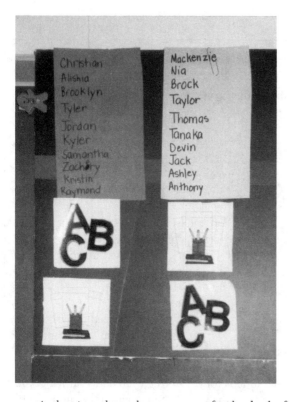

FIGURE 2–3
Simplified Workboard

Andrea introduces the two centers for the day by first telling the children about the drawings of the centers, or icons, as she points to them on the workboard. Then she shows the children where each center is by moving to the center and explains what they are to do there. In her explanation, she alerts the children to potential problems before they happen (see Figure 2–4).

FIGURE 2–4
*Introducing the ABC and
Writing Centers*

ABC Center

Teacher: Now are you ready? [Points to the ABC center icon.] I'm going to show you where the ABC center is. Watch me go to the ABC center. Don't get up. Turn your head. This one right here is called the ABC center. Say that with me.

Teacher and Children: ABC center.

Teacher: Everybody today will get to come to the ABC center and do you know what to do at the ABC center? You do puzzles. So today when you come to the ABC center you get a chair, sit down, and take out your ABCs. Then guess what you do? Take them all out and put them all back in. You're going to do one, two ABC puzzles. Do one and then two. OK? Not three, not four, not five. How many are you going to do?

Children: Two!

Teacher: Excellent!

Writing Center

Teacher: Then this is the writing center. Are you ready to find out what you do at the writing center?

Children: Yes!

Teacher: You come over and you sit down. Oh no, there's no paper. Are you ready to find out where the paper is?

Children: Yes!

Teacher: The paper is over here. So, today when you come to the writing center the first place you have to go is right here to get your paper. Once you've got your paper you'll walk back over and sit down and write something. Do you know what you start with?

Children: Color.

Teacher: Your name. Oops, do you know what you need to write your name? Pencil. OK, here I go, I've got my pencil. If you don't remember how to write your name, look what I've done. [Walks over to bulletin board.] You can walk over here and find your name. Let's pretend that I'm Zack. I'll go over and look for Zack. When you find your name you use two hands to pull it off the wall. It pulls right off because it's got Velcro on it. Isn't that neat? What am I going to do first?

Children: Draw.

Writing Center *continued*

Teacher: No, not draw. Write my name first using pencil. [Andrea copies Zack's name from the model on to the paper.] I'm done with my name. Guess where I put it? It will be stuck right up there on the wall so that it will be there the next time I need it. Now I've got my name done. Next, you color a picture using the crayons. So at the writing center you write your name and color a picture.

After finishing directions, Andrea returns to the large group area and asks the children to look again at the workboard as she reminds them of the meaning of the icons; she then explains that some children will go to the ABC center first and some will go the writing center first. After asking, "Are you ready to find out which one you go to first?" she reads the list of names that is above the first column as the children stand up. She then sends the children standing to the ABC center as she points to the icon and says, "You are all going to this one first and do your puzzles. Everyone else stay on your bottoms." She then reads the names of the students in the second group and sends them off to the writing center.

The first group goes to the ABC center, where they assemble two puzzles, and then to the writing center, where they write their first and last names (using a model) and draw a picture. The second group goes to the writing center and then the ABC center. The children work at each center until they are finished and then move to their second center. They spend about fifteen minutes in each center, while their teacher offers support as needed. In the writing center she helps, especially with last names, by offering words of encouragement like, "Now you can try your last name. It's right there on your name card, so try it." As the children begin to finish with a center, she monitors the movement between centers. For example, her conversation with Zack when he finishes with the writing center and needs to move to the ABC center sounds like this:

Did you write your name and draw your picture? You're all done. You can put it in the finished basket. Where are you going next? Do you know what it's called?

The first day of centertime, or MIL, with the whole class goes smoothly. Andrea makes sure the children know what to do and she also makes sure those things get done.

When centertime is over, the children meet on the rug for a group sharetime with their teacher to evaluate centertime. During sharetime, Andrea and the children have the opportunity to take care of any problems that occurred during MIL. Andrea may sort out confusions, reteach if needed, or reinforce routines she wants to establish. For example, today she congratulates the children who worked at both centers. Children need to learn what is expected of them. When they know what to do, they can monitor their own behavior and in so doing become independent. In this first full day of MIL, Andrea helps the children get the process going.

Days Three Through Twelve

In the days that follow, Andrea instructs the whole class in the workboard routines that the children try out in centers with teacher support. Andrea expects the children to learn the procedures of looking at the workboard, going to their first center, checking in with the teacher for help to read the workboard, following the workboard sequence to their next center(s), and getting a book to read on the rug when they finish. Figure 2–5 documents some typical language that Andrea uses to teach these routines.

Andrea's Language That Teaches Routine

FIGURE 2–5
*Andrea's Language That
Teaches Routine*

Day	Focus	Language
1	Make choices	"You have to choose the books, the blocks, or these cubes. That's your choice right now. Not those other things. Thank you."
2	Follow sequence	"Are you done? Where are you going next?"
3	Follow directions	"I will be checking to make sure that only the kids that are supposed to come to the block center come to the block center."
4	What to do when finished	"Are you all finished? This is the workboard and you have to do what's on here. . . . You're all done? You can get a book."
5	Look at the workboard	"What do you need to do to start workboard? What do you have to look at? We have to look at the workboard. So, let's turn and look at the workboard. Eyes over here so you know where to look."

By Day Twelve the children in Andrea's class are moving independently through four centers in ninety minutes and Andrea is able to work with small breakout groups. The children are using a much more sophisticated workboard, as shown in Figure 2–6.

In just twelve weeks, new kindergartners have moved from playing at the center of their choice to following a workboard as they time themselves and move through four centers in about forty-five minutes.

ACHIEVING CLASSROOM GOALS: LEARNING FROM ANDREA

Andrea makes the organization and management of independent centertime look easy, but it's not. It requires skillful teaching. I frequently hear other teachers ask, "How can I create a classroom environment that supports children

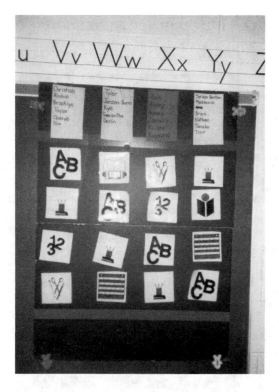

FIGURE 2–6
Sophisticated Workboard

working independently while I teach small groups?" An analysis of the data from Andrea's classroom can help us learn how a teacher can support young students in becoming independent learners during MIL. I observed that Andrea scaffolded her students' learning by

- using explicit language
- giving feedback
- employing problem-solving language
- providing successful challenges

She emphasized two areas of knowledge: (1) what to do (understand and follow routines), and (2) how to learn (be active and self-managed). As I marveled at the smooth, organized way Andrea and the children functioned during centertime, I began to wonder exactly how Andrea had established these two areas of understanding.

WHAT TO DO: TEACHING AND LEARNING WORKBOARD ROUTINES

I noticed that many of the early interactions during MIL focused on understanding the routines surrounding the organization and use of the workboard (see Figure 2–7).

Implementing Managed Independent Learning in Kindergarten: The First 12 Days

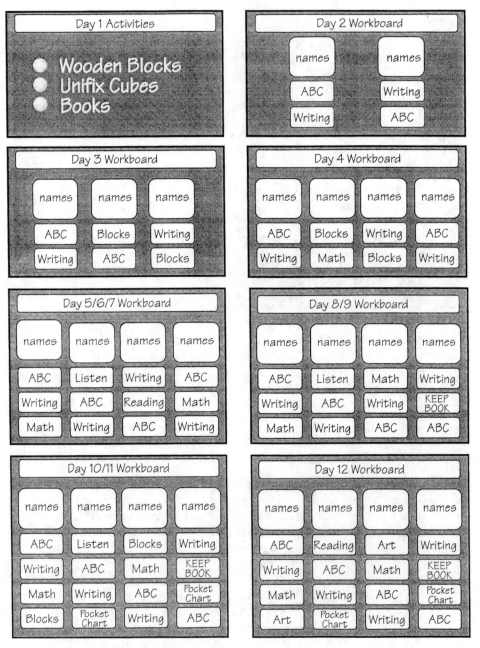

Day 1 Activities
• Wooden Blocks
• Unifix Cubes
• Books

Day 2 Workboard

names	names
ABC	Writing
Writing	ABC

Day 3 Workboard

names	names	names
ABC	Blocks	Writing
Writing	ABC	Blocks

Day 4 Workboard

names	names	names	names
ABC	Blocks	Writing	ABC
Writing	Math	Blocks	Writing

Day 5/6/7 Workboard

names	names	names	names
ABC	Listen	Writing	ABC
Writing	ABC	Reading	Math
Math	Writing	ABC	Writing

Day 8/9 Workboard

names	names	names	names
ABC	Listen	Math	Writing
Writing	ABC	Writing	KEEP BOOK
Math	Writing	ABC	ABC

Day 10/11 Workboard

names	names	names	names
ABC	Listen	Blocks	Writing
Writing	ABC	Math	KEEP BOOK
Math	Writing	ABC	Pocket Chart
Blocks	Pocket Chart	Writing	ABC

Day 12 Workboard

names	names	names	names
ABC	Reading	Art	Writing
Writing	ABC	Math	KEEP BOOK
Math	Writing	ABC	Pocket Chart
Art	Pocket Chart	Writing	ABC

FIGURE 2–7 *Workboard: The First Twelve Days*[1]

[1]You can find out more about how to use KEEP BOOKS® in your classroom by visiting www.keepbooks.org.

Andrea taught the procedures of workboard through explicit language and feedback.

Explicit Language

Andrea uses explicit, direct language when she teaches the children about the workboard. For example, when introducing the workboard for the first time, Andrea lets the children know what they will need to do sequentially. She tells them that they will need to find their names and then complete the activity represented by the picture on the center card. Then they will look below that card to find their next center activity. After teaching the children about the use of the workboard and modeling what to do in each center, Andrea reviews with the children how to use the workboard and then sends them off to centers using explicit language that is supported by pictures (icons). Her review both shows and tells the children what to do:

> OK, are you ready to find out which one you're going to first? [Reads names.] These children are going to the ABC center first and then to the writing center. [Points to the center icons in order.] So three kids stand up. [Reads names while children stand.] You are all going to this one first [points to ABC center icon] to do your puzzles. Everyone else stay seated.

It is important to note that Andrea teaches the children what they are expected to do in a center before they are asked to give it a try. In order to model center activities effectively, Andrea thinks through the activity first just as she did to explain the workboard. She asks herself, "What are the sequential steps I need to do to effectively complete this task?" At the same time, she anticipates problems and addresses them when modeling before they ever happen. Then Andrea actually moves to the center, gathers the children around her, and demonstrates the activity using real objects. For example, on Day Three, Andrea took the class to the block center, built a structure, and put the blocks away, all the while providing the children with a think-aloud that put the process into words.

While she's modeling, Andrea helps her students to prioritize her directions by using the marker words, "This is important." This contextual cue alerts her students to pay particular attention to what she is going to say (Dorr-Bremme 1990). For instance, after modeling at the block center, Andrea reminded the children to build only one structure so that they would have enough time to go to all three of the centers that day with the words, "That will be important to remember so that you'll have enough time at your next centers."

Andrea's goal for herself in the first few days of school is to be sure her students know what the workboard is and how to use it. When asked how she decides what to say when she teaches the children to understand and use the workboard, Andrea said,

As a teacher, I ask myself, "How can I make my life easier?" And the answer is to teach my students to be independent. I think about what they need to know, in what order, and how I can teach it to them. I plan and visualize in my head. When I share my sequential thinking with the children, it becomes easier for them, too!

Andrea knows that she will gradually move from this explicit directive teacher-language to less directive teacher-language used to convey meanings. In this fashion, the talk in her classroom will become "a powerful tool through which minds meet and children begin to use language to think" (Lyons 2003, 51).

Feedback

The feedback or follow-through portion of the teaching-learning cycle is particularly strong during MIL in Andrea's classroom. This helps her students to know and follow the routines. She anticipates problems, which prevents inappropriate behavior. Andrea says, "I stay on top of them from the beginning. It's another way to make my life (and theirs) easier." For example, when the children finish all centers, they are expected to get a book to read. On Day Three Andrea reminded the children that they should not be using chalkboards or engaging in other activities after finishing the cycle of centers, and gave the following feedback: "I said you could get a book to read now 'cause you're done. When I see everyone's reading I'll know that workboard is over and it's time to move on to interactive writing."

When children's behavior strays from what is expected, Andrea quickly gives feedback that tells explicitly (1) what needs to be stopped and (2) why it needs to stop with (3) polite language. This is how she keeps inappropriate behavior from becoming a habit. She helps by teaching the children a new pattern of behavior to replace the old (Lyons 2003). For instance, when a group of educators[1] were observing in Andrea's classroom, they heard the following comments:

- "Stop moving because I'm ready to get started. OK?"
- "Brock, eyes over here. I'll wait because I don't feel I have your full attention. Quickly, Brock, because I want to keep going. I've got things we've got to do today. Thank you."
- "Come sit up here, please. Do you know why? Because you are talking now and I am talking and it's not nice to talk when I'm talking. You have to be quiet because I'm going to talk about something really important."

After school, the educators debriefed what they had heard and decided that like MIL, Andrea makes discipline look easy, but it's not. Their conversation focused on providing explicit direct language, rationales for actions,

---

[1]Educators observing in Andrea's classroom included Melodie Bernhard, Cherie Colopy, Peg Daugherty, Michelle Dixon, Carol Hallett, and Wendy Kelsey.

and polite language. This is what they felt made the difference. Andrea's direct language tells the children exactly what she expects them to do (e.g., "Stop moving." "Eyes over here." Come sit up here."). The children in Andrea's room don't need to play a guessing game to figure out what she wants of them. Comparing her language to another teacher's in a nearby school who, when noticing a child shaking her head rhythmically from side to side when she should have been looking and listening, said, "I'm worried you won't get smart." This child may be uncertain as to what her teacher wants. She has to make an inference to interpret what the teacher means. She might think her teacher doesn't feel she is capable or that she doesn't want to learn when what her teacher really wants is for her to hold her head still and look forward. In order to act appropriately, children need to know what is expected of them. Andrea's explicit language, "Put it where it belongs," can be compared to another teacher's vague language, "Would you like to put that away?" In responding to this vague question, children might think that they have a choice and are not certain whether the teacher wants them to put the item away or not (Delpit 1988). Andrea's clear and concise language makes it easy for her children to achieve her expectations. When I watch Andrea in action, I am amazed at how she makes the complex look simple. No extra energy is wasted and confusions are avoided.

Andrea often tells the children why they are expected to behave as she requests. Her rationales are related to knowledge and learning (e.g., "I'm ready to get started." "I've got things we've got to do today." "I'm going to talk about something really important."). By paying attention to behaviors that affect learning, Andrea is helping the children to prioritize what is valued in this classroom. More time and attention in Andrea's classroom is given to thinking and learning, not to behavior systems with stars and rewards or to misbehavior and punishment. Additionally, by providing students with reasons for her expectations, Andrea is teaching for self-regulatory behavior. Children have self-regulatory behavior when they do what is expected of them without being told or watched. Two or three weeks into the year, once rationales are established and internalized, Andrea no longer offers reasons to accompany all of her behavioral requests. Andrea and the children have established a culture of understanding regarding what it means to be a student in Room 103.

When addressing behavioral issues, Andrea doesn't change her calm, caring tone of voice. She continues the conversation with succinct requests that are framed with the mannerly language of "please," "thank you," and "okay." A community of respect has been established. This respect is both between teacher and student as well as between student and student. As Andrea says, "We are all participants, there is an equal share for everyone. The children want to be a part of our class. If they are asked to leave, it is a very sad day." Andrea's students are respected. This kindness helps them to love learning. They don't want it interrupted with misbehavior. They know that they all have the right to learn in this classroom.

Along with "please" and "thank you," Andrea has other cueing phrases that help her children to achieve behavioral expectations. You'll often hear her counting backwards. This means it's time to listen and learn. On Day Four, the following words were uttered: "Five, four, three, two, one. Quickly sit down, Devin. I want to get started. You're still standing. [Devin sits down.] Thank you." Or, Andrea might say, "Put your hands on your head if you can hear me." Or, "I'll stop because I don't think I have your attention." She may even sing a song, "If you're ready and you know it, cross your legs. . . ."

Andrea knows that children are eager to please and that they will do what is expected of them if they:

1. know what the teacher wants
2. know why the teacher wants it
3. are treated respectfully

It is for this reason that from Day One, Andrea's expectations are stated clearly, rationally, and politely. Andrea implicitly follows a path that leads to successful management. She has internalized a list of important maxims that guide her actions and interactions in the classroom (see Figure 2–8).

FIGURE 2–8
*Successful Classroom
Management Thinklist*

Successful Classroom Management Thinklist

- Establish routines by teaching procedures.
- Stop unwanted behavior with clear, concise directives.
- Tell students why you are asking them to stop a behavior.
- Use polite, mannerly language.
- Be consistent and fair.
- Create a community of learners by being respectful.
- Value thinking and learning.

Andrea's way of giving feedback to her students is neither authoritarian nor permissive. Instead she has found a democratic, middle-of-the-road balance. She has set up consistent boundaries for everyone, and they know they are all on an equal playing field. Likewise, discipline in her room is neither a power struggle nor a free-for-all. Rather, Andrea is teaching for self-regulatory behavior. The children know where to go and what to do, and this internalization frees them and their teacher to concentrate on content.

Interestingly, on Day Five, I noticed a dramatic shift in the discourse. Andrea did not spend as much time telling the children to "Look this way" or "I feel you're not listening." Because the children had internalized her expectations, Andrea was free to scaffold individual children's academic needs. Instead, I heard comments such as, "Does your *r* look like mine?" and "I bet you can go home and show your mother *the* tonight!" This is the payoff. When the students know what to do, the teacher is free to teach them how to learn.

HOW TO LEARN: TEACHING AND LEARNING TO BE PROBLEM SOLVERS

Andrea's interactions are also driven by her theory of learning. She has appropriated Clay's definition of reading to use as her definition of learning. She believes that learning is "a message-getting, problem-solving activity" (Clay 1966, 6). Andrea helps her students become active problem solvers who monitor their own behavior, search for solutions, and check on themselves. To promote these behaviors, Andrea uses problem-solving language and provides challenges that students can meet with reasonable effort.

Problem-Solving Language

Through her language, Andrea helped her students realize that uncertainties became problems to solve. On Day Three, before MIL, Andrea talked with the children about the need to make a sign to solve the issue of center identification:

> Did you know that before you come to school there's another kindergarten class here in this room? They did the workboard the other day just like we did. But they had a problem. Someone in their class got the ABC center mixed up with the writing center. They came up with a wonderful idea. They decided that to help them remember that this was the ABC center, they would write a sign and put it on the table. The sign says, "ABC center." So now they'll remember. They won't get confused or think that this is the writing center. They'll know it is the ABC center.
>
> Now we have a problem. Because we have a sign on this table but we don't have a sign on that table. And I have trouble sometimes remembering what each table is supposed to be without a sign. I think that it is a fantastic idea today to help the other boys and girls remember that this is the writing center. Before we start workboard today we are going to write a sign to help us remember that that is the writing center.

Many of Andrea's conversations with her students were peppered with process words that focused on finding the problems, solving the problems, and checking the answers.

Interactions that focus on problem solving support independent learning (see Figure 2–9). By using such words as "look," "try," and "finish," Andrea demonstrates the type of language her students need to guide their thinking (Bodrova and Leong 1996). Children can begin to understand more fully the ramifications of such operations as monitoring, searching, and checking when they have a term for the strategic behaviors.

During sharetime, the most frequently addressed issue across the first five days of school was that of getting to both centers. With such language

Problem-Solving Interactions		
Monitor: Find the Problem	Search: Solve the Problem	Check: Check the Answer
"Eyes over here. Look this way. Eyes over here so you know where to look." (Day Four)	"But you're going to have to try it. You can't just say, 'I can't do it' 'cause then you'll never learn." (Day Two)	"She made a mistake and she went back and fixed it. That's what kindergarten is all about." (Day Two)

FIGURE 2–9
*Problem-Solving
Interactions*

as, "Some people didn't go to both centers," Andrea was building the understanding that the children need to regulate their behavior and keep the process going. Andrea knows that for her students to be problem solvers, they need to first notice (or monitor) that there is a problem for them to then solve. On Day Four at sharetime, Andrea celebrated that a child used the workboard to find out where to go next.

> Boy oh boy, did workboard go well today. Do you know what I saw today? I saw somebody in our class, after they finished their first center, walk over to the workboard. They looked at the workboard to figure out where they were supposed to go second. When they figured that out, they went to their center. I was just so impressed because that's what kindergartners should do during workboard. If you don't know where to go, you can slip and look at the workboard. Exactly right. That will help you get to both centers.

As Andrea says, "I think it's more important to get the children actively engaged in problem solving than it is to keep a record of what center each child goes to each day like some teachers do. Our lives here in this classroom revolve around problem-solving activities."

Successful Challenges

Andrea planned centers that offered just the right amount of challenge to help get the processing going. A successful challenge is a task that is a bit more difficult than a child can do alone, but one that they can successfully achieve with support. Support may come from such things as explicit directions, a more capable other, or a chart that becomes a reminder. If the work in a center is too easy, the children will not be required to grapple with problems and will likely become disengaged; learning will suffer. If it is too difficult, again they will not engage with the problem and are likely to stop trying (Vygotsky 1986). Balance is required, so Andrea designed workboards that had many familiar activities with only one or two new things to learn each day. In Figure 2–10, I show how Andrea constructed center activities from Day One through Day Twelve that are grounded in the known but become increasingly more complex.

Day	Known	New
1		<ul><li>Wooden blocks</li><li>Unifix cubes</li><li>Books</li></ul>
2		<ul><li>ABC: two puzzles</li><li>Writing: write full name and draw a picture</li></ul>
3	<ul><li>ABC: two puzzles</li><li>Writing: write full name and draw a picture</li></ul>	<ul><li>Blocks: build one thing</li></ul>
4	<ul><li>Writing: write full name and draw a picture</li><li>Blocks: build one thing</li></ul>	<ul><li>ABC: free explore with magnetic letters</li><li>Math: sort bears by color</li></ul>
5/6/7	<ul><li>Blocks: build one thing</li><li>Math: sort bears by size and color</li></ul>	<ul><li>ABC: make words with magnetic letters</li><li>Writing Center: write full name, draw a picture, and write words</li></ul>
8/9	<ul><li>Writing Center: write full name, draw a picture, and write words</li><li>Math: sort shapes by shape and color</li></ul>	<ul><li>ABC: practice name and "the" with wipe boards</li><li>KEEP BOOK®: read and color a book with the word "the"</li><li>Listening: picture book</li></ul>
10/11	<ul><li>Writing Center: write full name, draw a picture, and write words</li><li>Blocks: build one thing</li><li>Listening: picture book on tape</li><li>KEEP BOOK®: read and color a book</li></ul>	<ul><li>Math: patterns using unifix cubes</li><li>ABC: sort magnetic letters</li><li>Pocket chart: point and read chart; highlight known word "the"</li></ul>
12	<ul><li>Writing Center: write full name, draw a picture, and write words</li><li>Math: patterns with unifix cubes</li><li>ABC: sort magnetic letters</li><li>Pocket chart: point and read chart; highlight known words</li><li>KEEP BOOK®: read and color a book</li><li>Listening: picture book</li></ul>	<ul><li>Art: make an American flag with construction paper</li></ul>

FIGURE 2–10 *Managed Independent Learning Moves from Known to New*

Additionally, Andrea tried as frequently as possible to link the center activities to learning that was going on during other parts of the kindergarten day. An example of this connection occurred on Day Five when the children were asked to make words with magnetic letters at the ABC center. After suggesting that they make their names, which they had been practicing in the writing center since Day Two, Andrea asked, "Can anyone think of something else they can find letters to that they can make?" The children thought of the word *the* that they had highlighted on Day Five in the big book *Huggles Goes Away* during shared reading. They had also seen the word *the* in the color song they had read and sung on Days Three and Four. They realized that they could copy it from the Color Song chart or from the word wall where it had been placed on Day Four. Later in the first month of school, they would be asked to find the word *the* in the color song on the pocket chart.

Center activities are also carefully planned so that they offer just the right amount of challenge. The move is again a gradual one from known to unknown. Andrea offers just the right amount of support to ensure student success. The introduction and organization of the writing center is a good representative example. On Day Two Andrea introduced the writing center by teaching the procedures the children needed to understand to work in the center. First she showed them the location of the center and where to find paper, pencil, and a name card that they could copy. She then modeled what they would be expected to do there. She finished the directions by summarizing what they were to do at the writing center. "So, at writing center, you write your name and color a picture." On Day Three she established accountability for the writing center by looking at three papers and commenting on how they had remembered to write their name and draw a picture. "Wow, see how she wrote her first and last name in pencil and did her picture in crayons. She was a good listener. She followed directions." She finished up sharetime by saying,

> It's important for you to know that all of the work that you do at writing center, guess what I do after school, I go through and look at every one to see if you followed directions. I look at all of them. I do. I look at all of your fantastic work. So, it's important that you do your very, very best work.

On Day Four at sharetime, Andrea addressed a concern she had noticed in the writing center that day. She talked with the children about the need to work industriously so that it would be possible to get to both centers. "You can't go too slow and you can't go too fast either. It's kind of tricky, isn't it? You have to go just the perfect amount." On Day Five, Andrea teaches individual children at the writing center who need help to hold the pencil and form letters. Soon, Andrea will be asking children to add some letters to their work as they begin to write their stories. Andrea's instruction mirrors her students' strengths and needs. She builds on their strengths and supports them in time of need.

During these first weeks of school as the students are taking on the task of working independently in centers, Andrea moves about the classroom offering support as needed. She adjusts her amount of support by providing customized interactions. For example, on Day Three and Day Five Andrea offered less support (in terms of instruction and coaching) to students who were working independently and easily, and she offered more support to students still having difficulty managing tasks and sustaining engagement. Figure 2–11 illustrates this complex teaching action.

Adjusting the Amount of Support to Provide Customized Interactions	
High Progress Student	**Low Progress Student**
Day Three Student: (Looks at the workboard and heads to his next center.) Teacher: You remembered, good job.	Day Three Teacher: You're done with blocks? Student: [Nods head, yes.] Teacher: Where do you go next? Student: (No response.) Teacher: Which one is your name on, the blue, green, or red one? Student: Blue. Teacher: [Points to the blue square with the child's name on it and then points to the icon under the child's name.] So, you went to the blocks. Where do you go next? [Points to the next icon down.] So, that's where you're going to go next!
Day Five Teacher: Do you have a problem? You can check the work-board all by yourself today, can't you? Do you know where you're going? OK?	Day Five Teacher: Which color were you on? You don't remember? . . . The red one, right? You went to the writing center? Then you go to the math center. That's the math center [points]. Let's go over to the math center where the bears are. Here's the math center right here.

FIGURE 2–11
Adjusting the Amount of Support to Provide Customized Interactions

Andrea adjusts her interactions to the students' level of understanding; children's own responses provide information for fine-tuning the teaching. This process provides each student with the right amount of scaffolding to allow for success in meeting a challenge and also encourages the students to be active problem solvers moving toward independence. Figure 2–12 illustrates this idea.

FIGURE 2–12
Levels of Teacher Support in Handing over the Responsibilities of Independence to the Students

Levels of Teacher Support in Handing over the Responsibilities of Independence to the Students		
Level of Support	**Description of Support**	**Type of Support**
High	The children work in centers and move from center to center as the teacher offers support when needed. The teacher reflects on the process afterwards during sharing.	Guided practice with teacher feedback.
↕	The children work and move from center to center independently. The teacher is available to offer assistance, if asked. The teacher and children reflect on the process afterwards during sharing.	Guided practice or independence depending on need with teacher and student feedback.
Low	The children move from center to center independently. The children reflect afterwards on the process during sharing.	Independence with student feedback.

The teacher's careful planning and support provide the forward momentum the students need to get the processing going to work independently.

WHAT I LEARNED ABOUT SCAFFOLDING: CREATING A SHARED CULTURE SUPPORTS INDEPENDENT LEARNING

From the first few days of school, Andrea and her students work together to create a shared culture. The children are learning what it means to be a student in Room 103. A sense of what centertime will look like is established early on. Centertime is not incrementally implemented. Children do not rotate in a group from center to center when the bell rings. From the beginning, centertime is given a large block of time. Children rotate independently from center to center when they are finished.

The workboard becomes an external mediator that supports children's independence. The children are taught to use the workboard as a tool in their problem solving. Consistently, Andrea uses sentences like, "We have to look at the workboard," "This is the workboard and you have to follow what's on here," and "When you're done, check with me. I'll help you find where you go next." At centers as well, the children are expected to be problem solvers who keep the process going and work independently.

In Andrea's classroom, children construct the internal processing power they need to become literate. Processing is a series of actions directed towards an end. The children in Andrea's classroom are active problem solvers who notice a problem, search for a solution, and check to be sure they are right. They are learning "how to use the environment out there with its people, print, and symbols, to build processing systems that work and because they work expand and extend in speed, range, effectiveness, and complexity" (Clay 2001, 305). Success in building the internal control of a processing system for literacy depends on children's parallel development of self-management as well as a broad range of problem-solving skills. Andrea believes that children learn when they are actively engaged in self-directed problem solving, and she teaches accordingly (Lyons 2003).

From Day One, Andrea makes it easy for her young students to be problem solvers by teaching them 1) what to do and 2) how to learn. Andrea's teaching pulls her students' learning forward. Her teaching is successful because she provides scaffolds that support her children to do just a bit more than they can do alone. Her children are able to make use of her scaffolds for a variety of reasons. First of all, her language is direct and explicit so the children understand what is being asked of them. If confusion arises, Andrea provides immediate feedback that produces a quick correction. Andrea's use of problem-solving language invites her children to be active rather then passive learners. Finally, her students are able to fully participate because the tasks Andrea scaffolds offer just the right amount of challenge for them, neither too easy nor too hard. These successful scaffolds ensure that her students will be involved in the thinking process from Day One and in turn get better at what they do every time they do it.

The insights I gained from Andrea's teaching can help other teachers who want to support their students' learning. Teachers can provide scaffolds for their students' learning by

- using *explicit language* that teaches directions, prioritizes for a task, and models the activity before asking children to try it.
- giving follow-through with *feedback* that supports students to internalize expectations and become self-regulated.

- employing *problem-solving language* that supports students to work strategically.
- providing *successful challenges* with interactions that provide a forward momentum for learning because they are grounded in the known but become increasingly more complex over time as children take on the task(s).

Andrea works effectively with children. She begins the school year by building a relationship with them that helps them learn.

> The first several weeks of the school year are critical to establishing a positive working relationship with students. During this time the children and teacher begin to form their first perceptions of each other, which set the tone of the teacher-student relationship for the rest of the year. Getting off to a good start plays a major role in establishing the trust that will support and motivate children to work with (not against) the teacher. (Lyons 2003, 86)

Her ultimate goal is the same as it must be for all teachers: that their students become independent learners who get better at what they do every time they do it because they know 1) what to do and 2) how to learn.

> "Well," Andrea says, quietly, "I guess kindergarten is as simple as that. I use my tool [the workboard] and I create problem-solving contexts [learning centers]. When the children know what to do and how to learn, this internalization frees them and me, their teacher, to concentrate on content."
>
> She watches as Samantha and Zachary disappear into the busy classroom. She hears Samantha echo her words as she explains this powerful process to the new kindergartner, "And this is the workboard. This tells how we learn in kindergarten."

SCAFFOLDING QUESTIONS

1. Think of a routine that needs to be established for MIL to be successful. How would you break it down into small steps? How would you teach these steps?
2. Think of something you are good at, such as knitting, skating, or playing a musical instrument. How did you learn what you are good at? Describe one way in which your learning was scaffolded.
3. Think about motivation, engagement, and the desire to be a successful student. What motivates children? How can you scaffold motivation in your classroom?

NEXT STEPS FOR TEACHERS: SUGGESTED READINGS

Berk, L. E., and A. Winsler. 1995. *Scaffolding Children's Learning: Vygotsky and Early Childhood Education.* Washington, D.C.: National Association for the Education of Young Children.

Bodrova, E., and D. J. Leong. 1996. *Tools of the Mind: The Vygotskian Approach to Early Childhood Education.* Englewood Cliffs, NJ: Merrill.

Fountas, I. C., and G. S. Pinnell. 1996. *Guided Reading: Good First Teaching for All Children.* Portsmouth, NH: Heinemann.

Morrow, L. M. [1993] 1997. *Literacy Development in the Early Years: Helping Children Learn to Read and Write.* Boston: Allyn and Bacon.

3 | SCAFFOLDING LITERACY LEARNING FOR STUDENTS WITH MILD DISABILITIES

Troy V. Mariage
Emily C. Bouck

Scaffolding the writing of students who have mild disabilities is challenging. Part of the challenge has to do with the variety of needs and strengths in writing that exist among students with mild disabilities. For example, in the following excerpts from third- and fourth-grade students, we can see that each student has individual needs that require different emphasis for instruction. They were asked to write about something they did well, and told that their work would be published.

1. *I like to do spurs* (sports).
2. *I like to play basketball.*
3. *I like to play outside.*
4. *I like basball.*
5. *I like*
6. *I like*
7. *I like*
8. *I like*
9. *I like*
10. *I like*
11. *I like*
12. *I*

—Wes' Expert Paper

Soccer and swimming.

—Duane's Expert Paper

Win I go to Indiana I go in the wods and I go to the big pit and I go to pick bares and I go to the littol pit and I rid the 3 wilr.

(When I go to Indiana, I go in the woods and I go to the big pit and I go to pick berries and I go to the little pit and I ride the 3-wheeler.)

36

—John's Expert Paper

I now uabaut fuut ball becus I paly it. I paly safte becos I wus fast. To tacl the ball carry. And I paly runingback. A runingback will run the ball to mack a put. And I am a linmon. A linmon boc the uhr tem fum tacing runingback. My fait pven is safte

(I know about football because I play it. I play safety because I was fast to tackle the ball carrier. And I play running back. A running back will run the ball to make a point. And I am a lineman. A lineman blocks the other team from tackling the running back. My favorite position is safety)

—Carl's Expert Paper

The now ried is thye matis. it is gren and prple. it is so cool! you ned to go to cedar point will fullip you lied so you paris can ried to ok you shud promis to tack you kick to cedar point com now !!!. dw ue wit to be abot the Rater it is gren an dlack it is so COOL! Wall. Bo you wot to hve fun. Than cedar point the plas. wall By By NOW. Cam NOW!!!

(The new ride is the Mantis. It is green and purple. It is so cool! You need to go to Cedar Point—you will flip your lid. Your parents can ride, too. OK, you should promise to take your kids to Cedar Point—come now! Do we want to be about the Raptor. It is green and black. It is so cool! Well, do you want to have fun? Then Cedar Point (is) the place. Well, by by now. Come now!)

—Ernest's Expert Paper

A quick evaluation of these five writing samples might be all it takes to conclude that Carl, Ernest, Wes, John, and Duane all have a severe learning disability in written expression. If we look more closely at the sample, however, we see individual challenges that require teaching tailored to each child's needs. In this chapter we will examine five of the most common writing challenges that face students with mild disabilities, as shown in Figure 3–1.

We will provide case examples of each challenge and demonstrate ways to scaffold student learning.

RESPONDING TO STUDENTS WITH MILD DISABILITIES

Instructing students with mild disabilities and those with attention-deficit hyperactivity disorder (ADHD) in the current era of accountability represents one of education's greatest teaching challenges. Students with mild disabilities—those with language and learning disabilities (LLD), emotional behavior disorders (EBD), and mild cognitive impairments—comprise roughly 80 percent of all students in special education, and these students spend about 64 percent of their time in the general education classroom (Smith et al. 2000). Students with ADHD make up between 3 to 5 percent of the student population (Hinshaw 2000). Collectively, this group of students presents an array of language, learning, attentional, behavioral, and

Common Writing Composition Challenge	Typical Presenting Behaviors	Key Instructional Ideas and Social Supports
Metacognitve Awareness of Writing as a Process and Strategies That More Able Writers Use	• Students see writing as a single draft • Frequent resistance to editing/revising • Student does not have declarative or conditional knowledge of writing as a process involving planning, organizing, writing, editing, and revising • Student may not utilize specific strategies to make text more readable (e.g., transition words) or interesting (e.g., introduction, dialogue)	• Make visible the writing process through "thinking aloud" while using think-sheets for each phase • Frequent review of phases in writing process and key questions that each process addresses • Ask students to self-evaluate each phase of the process by using a rubric or checklist • Use examples and nonexamples to highlight why strategies are or are not effective
Difficulties in Activating Background Knowledge	• Difficulty in generating topics and details • Difficulty in brainstorming ideas • Limited text production • Difficulties in remembering steps and sequences in multistep processes like the writing process	• "Hold" idea for students by writing ideas down whenever possible (e.g., lists, categories, steps) • Utilize a focus journal prior to whole group brainstorming or discussions to give students additional processing time • Use visual scaffolds such as fact sheets, graphic organizers, outlines, notecards, pictures, cue cards • Minilessons on categorization—providing detail fact cards and category labels and having students sort details and place with appropriate category
Difficulties in Categorizing/Organizing Ideas	• No clear beginning, middle, or end of paper • Some categories may be generated, but there are few supporting details—little depth to categories • May have one category with supporting details, but lacks the breadth necessary for a complete paper • May have limited text production and write in an associative or rambling style	• Teacher think-aloud while reading lists of brainstormed ideas and using different colored markers to indicate various categories • Having students number categories in the order they anticipate writing their categories and identifying a transition word to go with category • Model and think-aloud while using a visual representation of key features of the text
Knowledge of Various Text Structures	• Students may not organize paper to address the needs and purposes of that type of paper • Student may have little idea of the needs and purposes of particular types of writing	• Model and ask students to use the language and discourse of writing that accompanies different writing genres • Embed the explicit teaching of text structures across content areas, using think-sheets as ways to organize information in reading, writing, inquiry, notetaking, etc.
Perceiving Self as an Informant	• Egocentric writing—does not acknowledge needs of external audience; may not use "You" and overuse "I" • Does not express the purpose of writing or does not interact consistently with audience throughout paper • Views writing as a "task" to get done	• Frequent sharing of writing with real audiences and for real purposes • "Publication" and "performance" are more oral concepts than written • Striving to create a community of authors where the norm is to be working on pieces of writing and collaborating with others

social skill challenges that makes access to the general education curriculum difficult.

Scaffolding Literacy **39**
Learning for Students
with Mild Disabilities

Because there are large numbers of students with mild disabilities and specific needs in classrooms, researchers have begun to support teachers by undertaking research programs that examine how teachers can support student learning within a balanced literacy approach. In the Early Literacy Project (Englert, Raphael, and Mariage 1994; Mariage, Englert, and Garmon 2000), teachers and researchers met bi-weekly over a four-year period to discuss how to provide access to students with special needs to common activities in the literacy curriculum. The results of this project on student learning in writing composition and reading were substantial, supporting the belief that with intense, explicit, strategic, and scaffolded support across the literacy program, students with learning disabilities can make significant improvements (Englert et al. 1998). Since the development of the Early Literacy Project, researchers continue to work with hundreds of teachers in course work and as participants in other teacher/researcher communities (see Englert, Berry, and Dunsmore 2001; Mariage and Garmon 2003).

In this chapter we develop and refine our understanding of what constitutes effective support and scaffolded instruction for students with disabilities. We examine how teachers can support students' literacy learning through employing a variety of scaffolds that address common characteristics of students with mild disabilities in the area of written composition. Additionally we discuss the necessary restructuring of common reading activities to maximize effectiveness in the classroom. In the first section, common written composition challenges are identified and case examples of how teachers supported students' writing are explored for each of the challenges identified. In the second section, we explore instructional scaffolds in common reading activities that are used in a balanced reading program. In each of the case examples, special attention is paid to how teachers simultaneously support literacy learning, while also providing the social and behavioral support necessary for participating in socially mediated instruction.

STRATEGIES FOR HELPING MILDLY DISABLED STUDENTS

Metacognitive Awareness of Writing as a Process and Effective Writing Strategies

The writing process, made up of recursive phases of envisioning, creating, imagining, planning, organizing, drafting, revising, and making ideas public, is difficult for the most able writers. For students with mild disabilities, this complexity makes writing among the most difficult tasks in school. Students who undertake these writing challenges often view writing as "a task to get done" rather than as a process occurring recursively over time and demanding multiple drafts. Writing is viewed as a single draft, and there is frequently aversion to editing and revision. Students often fail to employ strategies that good writers use for introducing their papers such as clear topic sentences, interesting openings to catch the reader's attention, and transitional words such as *first, next, then,* and *finally*. Students having difficulty writing may not use conventions to maintain the interest of the reader throughout the paper such as conscious attention to description, imagery, or voice.

Although advanced writers have *internalized* a process for making their writing coherent, a significant goal for challenged students is to help them *think about their thinking* so that they can consciously use strategies like outlining, organizing, writing, editing, revising, and sharing their writing. Many students can benefit, at least initially, from this metacognitive approach because it features a systematic, structured, and explicit framework that makes visible to students the invisible strategies, processes, and the internal self-talk that more able writers engage in spontaneously throughout complete cycles of the writing process. These procedures can take several forms, but they often include supports for remembering the phases of the writing process such as mnemonics or acronyms for planning, organizing, writing, editing, and revising. Other forms include graphic organizers, which provide students with a chance to offload some of their thinking onto the organizer to help more efficiently process information, or the use of language stems or "think-sheets" that remind students of the key questions or features of a particular phase of the writing process.

Fortunately, researchers have provided us with effective models for supporting students with mild impairments in their understanding and participation in the writing process (De La Paz 1999; Englert, Raphael, and Anderson 1992; Graham and Harris 1989, 1994; Troia, Graham, and Harris 1999; Troia and Graham 2002). Each of these research-validated programs has identified key ways to provide the direct and explicit support necessary to support students' access to the strategies, skills, and metacognitive awareness necessary to develop well-formed prose. To illustrate how teachers can support poor writers and address key characteristics that have been identified for mildly impaired students, we draw on a form of embedded strategy instruction that is based on Englert, Raphael, and Anderson's (1992) Cognitive Strategy Instruction in Writing.

Let's consider how a teacher can use this kind of strategy with an example from one fourth-grade teacher. Bob (a pseudonym) teaches in one of the lowest-achieving, most at-risk schools in his state. He has assessed his students by asking them to write a composition about something that they were an "expert" in. While several of his students are classified as having specific learning disabilities, it is also evident that the school's lack of a systematic writing curriculum, failure to focus on writing as a process, and lack of explicitly teaching the cognitive strategies of more able writers have left many of Bob's students deficient in strategies for writing well-formed prose. An analysis of his students' writing reveals a number of difficulties, including the fact that thirteen of fifteen students did not write more than a single paragraph.

To begin to build the writing skills of his students, Bob embeds writing strategies in exciting inquiry units drawn from core curriculum standards in social studies and science. To make the phases of the writing process more explicit to his students, he uses the acronym "POWER" to highlight each phase of the writing process, including Planning one's paper, Organizing ideas using a text structure think-sheet, Writing, Editing, and Revising (Mariage, Englert, and Garmon 2000). Bob gave each letter of the acronym a different color that corresponds to the same colored think-sheet (e.g., red for the Plan think-sheet and yellow for the Organize think-sheet). Bob gave a complete set of colored think-sheets to guide his students in their daily review of writing process phases. Each day, Bob begins by reviewing the previous day's lesson and the phases of the writing process that they had engaged in as a group. He asks his students a number of questions about writing, including requests to name the phase of the writing process and to explain the purpose of that phase, to pose specific questions that good writers ask themselves, and to list strategies that a writer might employ in that phase.

Bob's Questions for His Students

What is the writing process?	In what phase are we working now? What is the purpose of that phase?
What questions do good writers ask themselves?	What is my topic? Who is my audience? Why am I writing the paper? What do I know about this topic?
What strategies might a writer use in this phase?	During writing, I need to make sure I catch my reader's attention in the intro.

To help his students become more metacognitive of writing as a process and the specific features of a well-formed text, Bob introduced the Plan phase of the writing process by showing his students two papers written by other fourth-grade students. These papers, about baseball and ballet, are shown below.

Baseball

Because it's a good sport. Because I can win a trophy. Because I like trophy's. I could put them in my room. So my room would look nice.

Ballet

One of my favorite days of the week is Wednesday. Why? Because from 4:30 p.m.–5:30 p.m. I have Ballet! It is fun. I'll tell you about it. Here we go!

First of all, it is good exercise. It strengthens your muscles. Also, it helps your posture. And good posture is very important. In otherwords, it is like I said good exercise.

Second, it is very fun! In ballet, at least in my class anyway, we do lots of fun things like make up dances. This year we are doing one that is neat. It may be long but it is really neat to watch!

Third is my teacher. Here name is Diane Newman. She is very creative and very fun to have as a teacher.

Now don't you think you should take lessons?

After having students read and reread the two stories, Bob engaged the students in a discussion about what made the "Ballet" paper more effective than "Baseball." The students were able to identify that "Ballet" used (1) categories of information with several supporting details; (2) transition words such as *first, second,* and *third* to begin each paragraph; (3) paragraph indentation; (4) writing conventions such as exclamation and question marks or humor to make the paper interesting and grab the reader's attention; and (5) a beginning, middle, and end. Having identified these features of a well-formed informational text, Bob then wrote these down in the form of questions. These questions were later used as part of a self-evaluation checklist that the students used to edit their texts throughout the year (see Figure 3–2).

The final part of this introductory lesson to the writing process was to introduce students to a Plan and Organize think-sheet (see Figure 3–3).

These think-sheets, developed from the Cognitive Strategy Instruction in Writing Project (Englert, Raphael, and Anderson 1992), provide the students with critical language prompts for planning a paper. These prompts include

- What is my topic?
- Who am I writing for?
- Why am I writing this?
- What do I know about my topic?

After discussing how the authors of the papers might have used the Plan think-sheet, Bob then introduced the blank organization map with the word *Ballet* in the center circle. He then guided his students through a mapping of the "Ballet" story, exposing them to the inner thinking and planning that the author of the story likely went through in planning and organizing her ideas.

The phases of the writing process, the unique discourse that guides the inner thought at each phase, and specific strategies that writers can use need to be made explicit for students. Without this kind of "structuring up," the writing process will remain elusive for students with and without mild disabilities. Bob provided the students with both *content* scaffolds and *process* scaffolds or procedural facilitation that made visible the invisible thinking and procedures that effective writers have internalized as self-regulated processes. He did a great job of utilizing instruction at the point of difficulty to support student learning.

Revise

Did We:

	Yes	Sort Of	No
Make It Interesting?	Yes	Sort Of	No
Use Transition Words?	Yes	Sort Of	No
Have an Ending?	Yes	Sort Of	No
Make it Interesting?	Yes	Sort Of	No
Read Our New Draft at Least 2 Times?	Yes	Sort Of	No
Read Our Draft to at Least 2 Other People?	Yes	Sort Of	No
Publish Our Paper?	Yes	Sort Of	No
Are We Happy With Our Final Draft?	Yes	Sort Of	No
Would We Change Anything Next Time?	Yes	Sort Of	No

Edit

Remember That Good Writers:

Help their audience by **<u>organizing</u>** their paper into categories

Help their audience by **<u>sequencing</u>** their categories

Use **key words** to tell audience that there is a new category

Make their audience want to read the paper—it's **<u>interesting!</u>**

Did We:

___ Reread Our Paper at Least 2 Times?

___ Start Our Paper With an <u>Introduction Paragraph</u> That Explained the Categories We Would be Talking About?

___ Start Each Paragraph With a <u>Topic Sentence</u> That Tells the Category We Are Talking About?

___ Include at Least <u>4 Details</u> for Each Category?

___ Make Our Idea Changes by Adding New Information, New Words, or Using More Exciting Words to Replace Boring Ones?

___ Make Our Paper <u>Interesting</u> By Adding Humor, Dialogue, Questions, Exclamation Marks?

___ Make Our Spelling Changes?

___ Make Our Punctuation, <u>Capitalization</u>, and Paragraph Changes?

FIGURE 3–2 *Self-Evaluation Checklist for Assessing the Writing Process*

Plan

My Topic Is

_____

Who Am I Writing This Paper For?

_____

Why Am I Writing This Paper?

_____

What Do I Know About My Topic? (Brainstorm)

_____

_____

_____

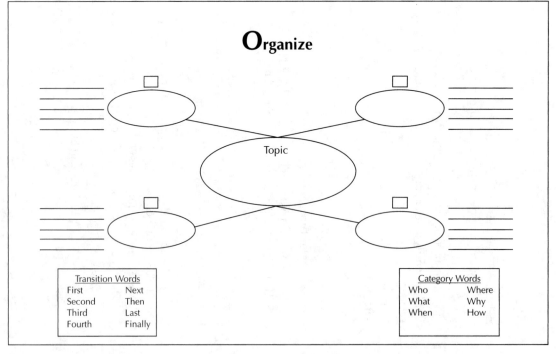

Organize

Topic

Transition Words
First   Next
Second   Then
Third   Last
Fourth   Finally

Category Words
Who   Where
What   Why
When   How

FIGURE 3–3 *Planning and Organizing Think-Sheets*

Features of Bob's Instruction to Support Learners

1. Use of the POWER acronym as a mnemonic for reducing the memory load for thinking about writing as a multistage process.
2. Color coding think-sheets that matched the colors of the POWER poster posted in Bob's classroom to help cue student attention to where they are in the process of writing.
3. Use of a rubric that makes explicit the language of editing and revision.
4. Performance of a discrimination activity where students can see both a well-formed and a less complete piece of writing by two students their age, allowing them to compare and contrast the two stories.

Over time, these writing tools, strategies, and language that are repeatedly made accessible to students through thinking aloud, modeling, and collaborative writing in class will increasingly move from direct instruction based on teacher-talk to become a part of the students' own metacognitive approach as they grow as writers.

Activating Background Knowledge

Students with mild disabilities face a second challenge in the area of writing instruction. While students have experienced many things in their lives, they find it hard to generate topics and identify supporting details. Cataloguing their experiences in readily retrievable forms and translating them into writing can be daunting. When students proclaim that they "do not have anything to write about," this is often a code for the frustration they feel in storing, accessing, and expressing information. Still other students may not see value in their experiences, may question the importance of these experiences, or may have adopted a learning stance that privileges book knowledge over their own experiences. Regardless of the cause, many students struggle to identify a topic, generate sufficient details about that topic, and then make sense of information they have generated by sequencing or organizing ideas. Difficulties in activating background knowledge often underlie what at first glance appear to be problems in organization, sequencing, and writing production. We can see examples of this by looking at features of the student writing, such as a limited number of words being written down.

One vivid example of how teachers might help support students' activation of background knowledge is through the utilization of concrete visual representations to support students' thinking throughout a writing experience. We know one elementary resource teacher (who we will call Kecia) who was told on the first day of school that her fourth-grade students with learning disabilities could "write two sentences." A quick glance at the writing curriculum for these students in the previous years indicated that the teachers teaching the students had focused on spelling, penmanship, journal free-writes, focus journals, and daily oral language. By daily oral language, we mean the editing of several sentences followed by discussion of the revisions in a small group. The Individualized Education Planning (IEP) goals related to written expression for these students were to write complete sentences and one well-formed paragraph. Few would argue that this writing curriculum has several key components, including a strong focus on practicing important writing conventions such as spelling, penmanship, grammar, and punctuation. Teachers also had provided daily opportunities to write independently. A closer analysis, though, reveals that students were not provided the type of cognitive apprenticeship in strategy instruction that might support them in the development of a more extended text. Few opportunities were made available to the students to write for authentic audiences and purposes, and there was no systematic or coherent curriculum for introducing various writing genres. Without direct and explicit instruction in how to use a variety of strategic tools to activate relevant background knowledge so that more text can be produced, students with mild disabilities may not develop into effective writers. Equally important, when students are given opportunities to see the social impact that their writing might have on others, they are encouraged to see how their writing is consequential in either communicating or failing to communicate its intended message. Over time, students develop a kind of "schema" for how much they should or should not write in school tasks.

Faced with students who had become accustomed to seeing writing as a single draft and seldom being asked to write more than a few sentences, Kecia decided to think of a creative way to provide scaffolds for the activation of background knowledge, descriptive language, and sequencing information into a comprehensible story. To accomplish this goal, Kecia drew a picture of an ocean freighter with many forms of sea life underneath the ship

FIGURE 3–4
Organizer for
Sea Life Story

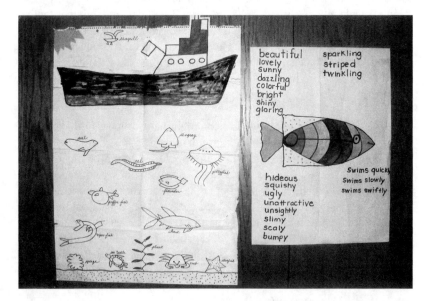

that her students were studying as part of their sea life unit. We provide this illustration in Figure 3–4.

Kecia then used a multistep process to support student learning.

Kecia's Process to Scaffold Student Writing

- Direct students in a visualization exercise, asking them to imagine they're jumping off the boat and swimming to the bottom of the ocean while passing a variety of creatures that they would study in their upcoming unit.
- Draw a second picture of a beautiful tropical fish and teach a minilesson on synonyms and antonyms using the thesaurus.
- Tell students to brainstorm descriptive words and record them on large chart paper.
- Instruct students to look up the descriptive words in the thesaurus and generate a series of synonyms and antonyms for each word.
- Direct students to copy the picture of the ship and choose ten of their own sea creatures to write on their own paper as a think-sheet to support their ideas.
- Direct students to look at the descriptive words they generated and write a word next to each of the creatures. One pair was the example "hideous octopus."
- Model, by thinking aloud and using the overhead projector, how to write an introduction to their paper.
- Model how to turn a descriptive word with the matching picture into a complete sentence. One example was the sentence "The sparkling jellyfish floated on the surface of the ocean."

One student's story follows. The text, three written pages in length, is typed exactly as it was written.

Jenny's Sea Life Unit Story

I went to the ocean and I jumped off new sparkling boat into the water. I saw a turtle and It was very slippery. Then I went all the way to the sand and I saw slimy plants and colorful seafish. It was very glorious. The sand was very sharp. Then I saw a big rock and next to it was a big blue whale. It was so big I think It was over 100 feet long. A big octopus swam right next to me. It was so cool. But the octopus looked os hideous looking. I was swimming and I saw sea horses. they were twinkling in the sum light. After that it was time to go. When I was going up I got my flipper stuck in a plant. I cut the plant and started to swim agin. Finally I got to the top. I got on the Boat and told them all about it. After that I was so tired I went right to sleep.

An uninformed reader may see few of the writing challenges that the student, Jenny, faces each day, especially given her near-perfect spelling and neat cursive writing. Jenny's text introduction catches the reader's attention, the descriptive language adds interest to each of the sea creatures, and the story is sequenced smoothly throughout. Jenny is still the same student who can write "about two sentences," but with very careful and thoughtful support, she was able to render a text that was longer, more detailed, and more interesting than she had previously written. This feature of scaffolded instruction is crucial in teaching many poor writers. Providing students with explicit scaffolds for increasing text production, quality, and voice allows students to access the academic supports used by more able writers and also to experience the social, emotional, and motivational consequences of feeling what it means to be a fluent writer. When students are afforded opportunities to read and hear their writing and to share with real audiences, writing has the opportunity to move beyond a procedural exercise and become a tool to accomplish social goals.

A close examination of this lesson reveals at least four different types of scaffolded instruction in literacy. First, the minilesson using the thesaurus to discover descriptive words and their synonyms/antonyms provided students with a *vocabulary scaffold* for descriptive language that in many cases was within students' listening comprehension, but in advance of their writing vocabulary. This opportunity to "try on" vocabulary in advance of independent functioning provides students with early language models that can later come under independent control as students develop. Second, the use of the visual icons such as "sea creatures," "boat," and "fish" provided a concrete representation that served as an *elicitation scaffold* by creating a schema for the diving adventure process that allowed students to activate background knowledge through creating details and ideas from the physical representation. The use of pictures, descriptive words, and color served as a kind of sign that helped the students generate and share ideas that formed a collective expression for the group to draw upon. Third, the reconstruction of the think-sheet by the students served to create a *sequence or process scaffold* by allowing them to focus attention on a single feature or detail. Reducing the difficulty of complex tasks by creating more comprehensible parts has been shown to be a key feature of scaffolded instruction (Stone 2002). For students like Jenny with sequential memory or organizational processing challenges, this opportunity to reduce complexity by focusing on a single detail at a time allowed her to not have to memorize the entire writing process. Finally, the act of committing words, pictures, color, and ideas to paper serves as a critical *memory scaffold* for students by allowing students with short- or long-term processing challenges to "hold" ideas. Holding ideas in writing allows teachers and students to refer back to previous work by the group and to develop a collective fund of knowledge by drawing on all students' background knowledge, which is more useful than a single student's thinking. This allows for additional prompts, which in turn elicit new ideas. Writing ideas down makes visible the group's collective thinking and provides a concrete model for how writing can become a tool for supporting learning.

Categorizing, Organizing, and Sequencing Ideas

A third area of challenge for students with mild disabilities is generating categories of information from lists of ideas, sequencing these categories, and generating a well-formed paragraph from a category and supporting details. Even when students are successful in generating background knowledge or researching ideas from multiple sources of information such as texts, the Internet, guest speakers, or video, it is often necessary for the teacher to explicitly model and think aloud while reading the lists of ideas and asking, "Do any of these ideas go together?"

Let's take the case of a teacher we will call Nichelle. Nichelle engages students in a discussion of which ideas might be linked and why, using different colored markers to circle categories of information. If details do not fit into an existing category, a new category and additional details are generated or the detail is discarded. To heighten her students' attention to the categorization process, Nichelle used large pieces of art paper to form an organizational map about their unit on giraffes. Students first gathered information from three sources, including (1) activating their own background knowledge by answering the question, "What do I know about this topic?"; (2) generating questions to ask a guest speaker who had gone on safari in Kenya; and (3) conducting targeted inquiries with a partner of expository texts to study a single category of information related to the giraffe, such as how giraffes care for their young, what they look like, and what they eat. Nichelle then took the details generated by each group and wrote them on separate eighteen-inch tagboard strips. Each of the four categories were written on the large organization map that was placed on the floor. Nichelle held up a detail card, read the card aloud (as in the phrase "grow up to sixteen feet tall"), and then gave the card to a student, who placed the card under one of the four categories (see Figure 3–5). After placing all of the detail stems under a category, the teacher and the students chorally read each list of details and carried out a discussion about why a detail should or should not have been placed in a particular category. In this way, Nichelle created a second source of practice for students who researched that category of information, while simultaneously building a collective knowledge of all the categories for each student.

After the class agreed upon the placement of all the details across the respective categories, Nichelle then introduced the students to the next phase of the writing process, moving from the categorization think-sheet to actual drafting of the text. For students with learning disabilities who often have difficulties with sequence, organization, and memory processing, the movement from think-sheet to paper or computer keyboard presents significant challenges, and students may benefit from several temporary instructional scaffolds. Writing a well-formed paragraph from a think-sheet requires turning the category label into a topic sentence, writing a sentence around each of the category details or incorporating several details into a single sentence, sequencing the details within the paragraph, and writing a concluding sentence.

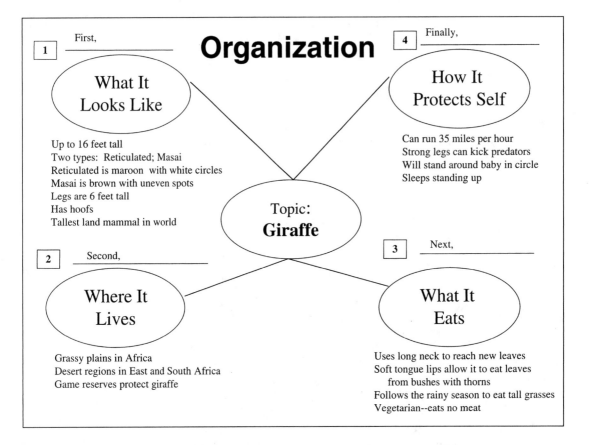

Organization

1. First, _____
   What It Looks Like
   Up to 16 feet tall
   Two types: Reticulated; Masai
   Reticulated is maroon with white circles
   Masai is brown with uneven spots
   Legs are 6 feet tall
   Has hoofs
   Tallest land mammal in world

4. Finally, _____
   How It Protects Self
   Can run 35 miles per hour
   Strong legs can kick predators
   Will stand around baby in circle
   Sleeps standing up

Topic: **Giraffe**

2. Second, _____
   Where It Lives
   Grassy plains in Africa
   Desert regions in East and South Africa
   Game reserves protect giraffe

3. Next, _____
   What It Eats
   Uses long neck to reach new leaves
   Soft tongue lips allow it to eat leaves
       from bushes with thorns
   Follows the rainy season to eat tall grasses
   Vegetarian--eats no meat

FIGURE 3–5
*Organization Map for
Giraffe Research*

One strategy for supporting this transfer was to utilize the "hamburger" metaphor (shown in Figure 3–6) of having the top half of the bun represent the physical space for writing a topic sentence, the meat of the paragraph representing the critical details that expand upon the topic, and the bottom half of the bun representing a concluding sentence. As shown in Figure 3–5, Nichelle typed the final organization map from the floor into a map that individual students could use at their desks, which eliminated the far point copying challenge of having students look at the large text map on the board. Before moving to actually writing any text, the teacher engaged the students in a discussion about what category should go first, second, and so on. To highlight the importance of organizing the sequence of one's writing, the teacher supported the students by placing numbers on the think-sheet, such as *1, 2, 3,* and *4* in small boxes above each category. Having determined the sequence in which the categories would be written, the teacher then had students look at a wall chart that contained a series of transition words. The class then chose a transition word and wrote the word directly on their individual think-sheet that they could use as a prompt when they began to write their topic sentence for that category.

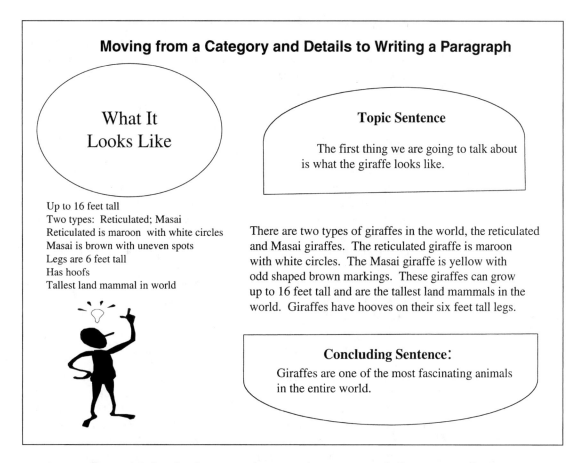

Moving from a Category and Details to Writing a Paragraph

What It
Looks Like

Topic Sentence

The first thing we are going to talk about
is what the giraffe looks like.

Up to 16 feet tall
Two types: Reticulated; Masai
Reticulated is maroon with white circles
Masai is brown with uneven spots
Legs are 6 feet tall
Has hoofs
Tallest land mammal in world

There are two types of giraffes in the world, the reticulated
and Masai giraffes. The reticulated giraffe is maroon
with white circles. The Masai giraffe is yellow with
odd shaped brown markings. These giraffes can grow
up to 16 feet tall and are the tallest land mammals in the
world. Giraffes have hooves on their six feet tall legs.

Concluding Sentence:

Giraffes are one of the most fascinating animals
in the entire world.

To actually model the development of paragraph writing, Nichelle
chose the first category, "What the giraffe looks like," and introduced the
hamburger think-sheet as an intermediary scaffold for moving from one's
organization map to the drafting of a paragraph around a category of information. The teacher introduced the hamburger strategy and then constructed the paragraph with her students, moving through each of three
parts: (1) generating a topic sentence from the category label, as in the sentence "First, I am going to talk about what the giraffe looks like"; (2) using a
single detail or combining details into sentences; and (3) writing a concluding sentence that provides closure for that category of information.

A closer look at this minilesson on teaching categorization and organization reveals several instructional scaffolds that were used to address specific challenges that some students experienced in this aspect of writing.
First, Nichelle's reading aloud the list of details and use of different colored
markers to circle ideas that fit under a category served as an *access and ori-
enting scaffold*. Reading the list aloud while pointing to each detail was essential for allowing nonconventional readers *access* to the meaning of the words
on the chart paper. The colored circles served to demarcate different ideas

FIGURE 3–6
*Support for Writing
a Paragraph from
a Category and
List of Details*

from one another and allowed students to *orient* their attention to focus on possible likenesses of ideas within the same color. In this way, the teacher could read aloud the ideas within a particular color and then ask the students to think about what superordinate category might capture the essence of the individual details.

A second set of temporary supports focused students' attention on *sequencing and categorizing* information. Placing each detail on a large paper strip and placing them next to the appropriate category, using the hamburger metaphor as a graphic organizer for the three parts of a paragraph, and numbering each category—all supported students by delimiting the complex task into more manageable chunks of activity. Some students experience difficulty in dealing with the cognitive demands of managing lots of information, or they may not have strategies for making sense and connecting that information to relevant schema. Teachers can help these students to become more metacognitive of these strategies through directly employing them as part of the writing process. As students see these same strategies, such as graphic organizers, outlines, and mnemonics, used across all content areas, the opportunities to practice, internalize, and generalize these strategies is enhanced.

Knowledge of Text Structure

One of the most important advances in writing instruction for students with disabilities is the importance of teaching students the inherent structures within different types of written texts (Englert et al. 1988). One factor to consider is the writing genre, and teachers sometimes use informational, personal narrative, comparison-contrast, or business letters in their teaching of writing. Other factors are the intended message and the perceived audience. Thus, texts may be structured in different ways. Making salient these text structures through repeated reading within different genres, using graphic organizers that make visible the key features of the genre, and using the text structure as a key site for focusing the writing discussion—all serve to focus student attention to important aspects of writing.

What is apparent in our work with students is that graphic organizers are often expected to carry the cognitive load for organizing and sequencing information. While these organizers are frequently successful in making visible key features of organizing writing, they are often insufficient to support struggling writers. For these students, it is often necessary to imbue the graphic organizers with additional supports to make them effective—to make them "think-sheets" (Englert, Raphael, and Anderson 1992). Specifically, these students should see the teacher model and think aloud while using the organizer, demonstrate how text in the organizer is translated into writing extended text, and use the organizer to reflect upon texts the students have read. A key feature of effective instruction is to ensure that there is a thoughtful transfer of control of the various aspects of using the organizer over time.

To illustrate how additional supports were built into a graphic organizer, we examine a writing sample drawn from a middle elementary classroom. In supporting graphic organizers for report writing, it became apparent that many of the common writing challenges of struggling students, coupled with a detailed knowledge of common learning and behavioral challenges, could indicate where attention may be needed. One teacher, June, identified four challenges that her students were experiencing, including (1) generating categories of information; (2) using transitional words such as *first, second, next,* and *then* to help sequence and alert the audience to a topic shift; (3) sequencing categories of information in meaningful ways; and (4) moving from the graphic organizer to actually writing the text.

To support her students in these four areas, June altered the traditional report writing organizer to include supports for each of these areas. As illustrated in Figure 3–7, June had one of her students with learning disabilities, Lance, use several strategies for supporting his writing. First, June had Lance directly write a number for each of his four categories to identify the sequence that he wanted to use in the story. She engaged the class in frequent whole-class conversations about the importance of sequencing ideas to make the text make sense to their audience, and she repeatedly asked students to think aloud about their choice of sequence. For example, June would explain that students might be talking about what something looks like at the beginning of a piece of writing first so that the audience can get a picture of what the animal looks like. Second, to encourage the development of a well-formed topic sentence for each paragraph, June had students identify a transition word (*first, second, next, then, finally*) and directly write the topic sentence next to their category. This helped to ensure that students had readily translatable text for their papers, created a momentum for paragraph writing, and helped eliminate the difficulty many students have in transferring information from the graphic organizer to their writing paper. Finally, June had Lance put a check mark next to each detail he used in the story. She had noticed that for a subset of her students with learning disabilities, they either forgot to include details they had generated or included the details several times. Students were encouraged to combine several details in more complex sentences, but for emergent writers, it was initially helpful to have students develop a single sentence using a detail on their organizer.

For some teachers, this level of support may appear to be excessive. Our experience is that many students will not require this level of support. However, for a subset of students with significant language or learning disabilities or those students who are nonconventional writers, these supports sufficiently delimit the complexity of the task to allow students to become more fluent writers and to generate far more text than they could without these supports. The fourth-grade boy, Lance, whose map is illustrated in this section, is one such example. At the beginning of the year, Lance was one of the most resistant writers in the class. He had difficulty generating topics

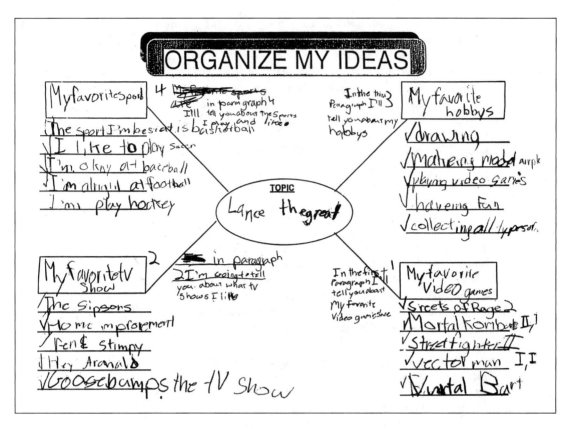

ORGANIZE MY IDEAS

My favorite sport
- The sport I'm best at is basketball
- I like to play soccer
- I'm okay at baseball
- I'm alright at football
- I'm play hockey

4 My favorite sports are in paragraph 4 I'll tell you about the sports I play, and like

In the third Paragraph I'll 3 tell you about my hobbys

My favorite hobbys
- ✓ drawing
- ✓ Matering model airple
- ✓ playing video games
- ✓ haveing Fun
- ✓ collecting all types of...

TOPIC
Lance the great

My favorite tv Show
- ✓ The Sipsons
- ✓ Home improvment
- ✓ Ren & stimpy
- ✓ Hey Aronald
- ✓ Goosebumps the TV Show

2 in paragraph 2 I'm going to tell you about what tv shows I like

In the first paragraph I tell you about my favorite video games are

My favorite video games
- ✓ Srcets of Rage 2
- ✓ Mortal Kombat II, I
- ✓ Street fighter II
- ✓ vector man I, I
- ✓ Mortal Bart

FIGURE 3–7
Lance's Organization Map

and saw himself as a poor writer. Noticing these common characteristics of many of her writers, the teacher decided to embark upon an "All About Me" unit to help ensure that students brought significant information to the writing task. For Lance, the result was a written text that was six handwritten pages, the longest text he had ever written. More important, for the first time, Lance began to see himself as an author who had something to say. It is this final characteristic, the failure to see one's self as an author and informant, that is explored in the next section.

Perceiving Self as Informant

Students with mild disabilities are often provided few opportunities to write and read for real audiences and for real purposes. The teacher is often seen as the sole audience for student work, and the nature of feedback is often corrective or evaluative in nature. The students who might most benefit from understanding the inherently social and communicative power that writing provides are often denied access to this form of instruction through extensive remedial skills training, low expectations for written expression, teachers' lack of understanding of how to structure the writing process, and in IEP goals where some school staff may stress that which is easily measurable, such as "The student will write a complete sentence" or ". . . will write a well-formed paragraph." When students are denied access to more powerful instruction, they fail to develop more complex forms of written expression in multiple genres over time. For many students with mild disabilities, some teachers use conventions such as spelling, penmanship, punctuation, and grammar as a measure of effective writing. Seldom are students encouraged to see writing as a tool to accomplish meaningful goals. From this perspective, it is not surprising that many of these students are described as being passive learners. Creating literacy events that emphasize writing as the active construction of meaning with knowledgeable others allows students to experience writing as a problem-solving activity.

MORNING MESSAGE

Over the past twelve years a group of researchers and teachers (Englert, Raphael, and Mariage 1994; Mariage 2001) have developed Morning Message, an alternative to the more simplistic literacy goals previously summarized. The thrust of Morning Message is to support teachers in utilizing an interactive writing format to make the moment-to-moment thinking of student writers come to life. This concept is based on the theory that a teacher, an author, and a student audience can co-construct meanings together. Morning Message emphasizes the importance of making the text interesting to an external parent audience who receive biweekly or monthly copies of a classroom newsletter containing the personal narratives of various student members. The parent audience, though not physically present, provides the classroom community a constant reason to assess the quality of sense making in the group. In Morning Message, the teacher chooses a student author who provides a topic for the group based upon their recent experience. The teacher serves as a scribe and facilitator to the message, stepping in to model, think aloud, and scaffold individual and group learning through the deft use of a series of discourse moves. Types of moves include instructional, involvement, literacy content, and conversational management. The primary goal of Morning Message is to turn writing into a problem-solving exercise where students are challenged to provide the necessary editing and revisions to produce the most accurate and interesting text.

In the following transcript Susan, a second- through fourth-grade special education teacher, and her class are constructing a text around a topic chosen by Lisa, a student author. In this transcript, Lisa has chosen the topic of her family. What is important to notice in the transcript is how the teacher transfers control of the meaning-making process to students and positions them to be active problem solvers who are responsible for making the text make sense.

Susan: Here we go, and the author is Lisa.

Lisa: Yeah!!

Susan: Okay Lisa, I need a topic sentence.

Heather: "My family."

Susan: "My family?" You want me to write "My family?"

Lonnie: "Lisa's family."

Lisa: No. "Lisa's family has a lot of people in it."

Juan: People or kids?

Susan: "Lisa's family has a lot of people in it." (Rereads again.)

Nathan: . . . in her family.

Susan: "Lisa's family has a lot of people in it."

Nathan: Relatives! Has a lot of . . .

Susan: Oh, "relatives." Okay, "Lisa, Lisa has"

Danny: {a lot of people . . .

Susan: {a lot of people in her

Danny: {a lot of relatives.

Nathan: Yeah, "Lisa's family

Danny: {Lisa has

Susan: {Lisa has a lot of people in her family.

Nathan: {Lisa . . .

Nathan: Lisa . . .

Danny: {relatives

Susan: Relatives in place of what?

Nathan: Family.

Danny: People, people.

Susan: People? "Lisa has a lot of relatives in her family." (Reads aloud.)

Lisa: Yeah. Like that. Yes.

Susan: Relatives?

Lisa: Yeah, because I've got a big family.

Nathan: But how about "Lisa . . ."

Susan: Put a caret there? (to add "relatives" to existing text)

Johnny: Don't "family" have to be a big "f"?

Nathan: No, "Lisa's family has a lot of relatives."

In this first minute of Morning Message, students take an active role as problem solvers who are trying to write a message that will be interesting to their parent audience. Immediately following the dictation of the topic sentence by the teacher, the student audience begins to engage in the editing and revision process. In these brief snippets of classroom conversation, several key features of scaffolding are revealed. First, the notion of instructional responsiveness, the teacher's moment-to-moment assessment of a student's (or the group's) learning zone and then making a decision to support thinking with the least amount of support possible, is important. In the transcript, the teacher's primary instructional move is to simply reread the topic sentence so the students can hear the sentence several times. Through the repetition of the topic sentence, the teacher subtly communicates that the creation of meaning rests with the students. The rereading provides the students with extra time to think about alternative meanings, while simultaneously sending a metamessage about the responsibility that students have in contributing to the message. The norms and expectations that are fostered in Morning Message and guide the group's work demand that students perceive themselves as informants who are active in their learning.

Second, the teacher creates conditions where other students' voices are heard and included in the discourse, creating opportunities for peers to serve as "knowledgeable others." For example, Danny takes up Nathan's introduction of the word *relatives* and uses this word to edit the author's original topic sentence. Scaffolding is not a one-way relationship from teacher to student. The most effective teachers are able to position their students as co-knowledgeable members and "experts," valuing and incorporating what they bring to the dialogue into the construction of the written message.

Third, the teacher provides only the support necessary and transfers control of the meaning-making process to students as soon as possible. This requires that teachers must constantly assess the student's current level of understanding and provide only the necessary support to allow them to accomplish, understanding that they would not have been able to accomplish without that support. This form of dynamic assessment is the hallmark of effective scaffolding and emphasizes a key goal of helping students to take ownership of key understandings as quickly as possible.

Morning Message allows students to participate as active constructors and problem solvers in the conventions of writing as a part of an apprenticeship with their teacher and their peers. Few literacy activities allow students to take such an active role in the dialogue while also allowing the teacher to assess the group's and individual student's thinking on a moment-to-moment basis. The goal of Morning Message, the publication of a written text that will be shared with a parent audience, creates a condition where students are empowered to see themselves as informants who are actively involved in authoring the written text.

SUPPORTING STUDENTS IN COMMON READING EVENTS

Intense early intervention in reading is necessary to improve reading performance for students who are at risk of reading failure (Lyon et al. 2001). Many students who are poor readers or who have significant difficulties in accurately hearing sounds in words are likely to benefit from direct and systematic instruction in phonological and phonemic awareness activities. Students with mild disabilities must also experience an intense, strategic, and balanced literacy curriculum that increases opportunities to hear, read, write, and listen to many forms of text (Pressley 1998; Zigmond and Baker 1994). However, simply providing balanced literacy opportunity does not easily translate into the increased intensity, attention, and opportunities to learn for students with mild disabilities. Teachers play a critical role in ensuring that students with disabilities maximize their opportunities to learn in the daily routines of independent reading, fluency building, reading one's writing, and in comprehension instruction.

Promoting Effective Reading

In this section, several common literacy events that promote effective reading in early and middle elementary classrooms are explored. These events include independent reading, choral reading, partner reading, Sharing Chair, and reading comprehension. For each literacy event, we discuss and demonstrate how teachers have modified these common routines to be more sensitive in supporting both academic and social skills for students with learning challenges.

Independent Reading

The most common instructional format for getting meaning from text is independent reading. Research supports the critical importance of increasing the amount of time spent in independent reading at one's independent reading level (Allington 2000). It would seem that independent reading would be one of the simplest and most straightforward reading activities in the reading curriculum. Our observations in tens and hundreds of classrooms suggest that this activity, if it is not structured well, presents many challenges to students with and without mild disabilities. These challenges arise in at least four areas:

1. Insufficient numbers of texts at various instructional levels are available to students.
2. Unclear parameters are made available in the amount and types of texts that students can choose to read, such as where students choose four or five different books and look at pictures but are not reading.

3. Few accountability measures ensure that reading has occurred.
4. Few or no strategies are provided for getting ideas from text and recording this information for later use in the inquiry process.

For some or all of these reasons, it is not uncommon to observe students who are actually engaged in active reading for only a small fraction of the time allotted for independent reading. For poor readers who need to increase their opportunities to read, this is time that cannot be squandered in off-task activity.

In the classrooms where we have seen highly effective inquiry or thematic units, teachers have used independent reading as an opportunity to gain information from the text. These teachers often have worked directly with the librarian well in advance to have all of the texts around a particular topic or area of study pulled off the shelf and made available to the class. Teachers often screen these texts to make sure that key facts around a particular research category are accessible to students. In other cases, the teacher actually makes copies of key pieces of text that match different students' or groups of students' categories of information. Distributing copies of the texts allows the teacher to directly model and think aloud while using monitoring strategies like searching for the main idea and identifying details by underlining key information with a highlighter. Finally, the most effective teachers often provide students with a clear goal for their reading, helping to focus attention to specific outcomes. One technique for structuring the data-gathering experience is to provide students with a simple think-sheet that has lines for recording a specific number of details about the category of information that they are researching (e.g., "What rhinos eat"). Another useful technique is to have students answer a series of literal and inferential comprehension questions by going back into the text and highlighting the sentence or sentences that provided the information.

A teacher's decision to attend to the amount and appropriateness of texts, explicit teaching of comprehension strategies for understanding the text, and providing accountability structures by having clearly stated outcomes can significantly impact the quality of independent reading. Teachers can also expect that students will share the information they have gathered with peers or the whole class, providing an additional audience for making public their work. While independent reading for getting information from text to support student inquiry will often require these forms of support to maximize their effectiveness, students will continue to need extensive opportunities to read for enjoyment.

Choral and Repeated Reading

A second literacy event that can provide students with important opportunities to build their reading fluency and support inquiry-based teaching is the thoughtful selection of poems or short pieces of text for choral reading. Research has indicated that repeated reading of text is one of the most useful ways to build reading fluency (Chard, Vaughn, and Tyler 2002). Similar to writing, students must feel what it is like to be a fluent reader. Even though the patterned and repetitive nature of poems emphasizes a memorization of words, initially the pace, intonation, and flow of reading provide students with a concrete model of fluent reading. For many young students with disabilities and for others who have experienced low levels of family literacy, there is often a lack of understanding in key concepts about print. For example, it is not uncommon to see students "reading" the poem, even though they have not yet established a concept about words and are unable to point-and-match each word as they are reciting the poem.

The most successful teachers we have worked with have provided students with mild disabilities several key instructional scaffolds and process supports. In one project, the Early Literacy Project (Englert and Mariage 1996), teachers employed a common process for introducing partner reading and then individualized supports through responsive instruction. In all of these classrooms, teachers copied poems on large chart paper and made an additional hard copy for each individual's "poem folder." A new poem, usually corresponding to the inquiry or thematic unit the students were studying, was introduced each week. To introduce a poem, the teacher first read the poem slowly, pointing to each word. She then read the poem at normal speed with proper intonation and inflection. Students then began a series of choral readings, with the teacher serving as pointer. Several students then took over the pointing role. The choral reading process was repeated each day, with different students serving as pointer throughout the week. During both independent and/or partner reading, students could choose to read the current or past poems. This was particularly important for nonreaders or early emergent readers, who often were seen with few texts that they could read. In this way, every student was seen as a reader who could participate in feeling fluent, even though the text may be partially or wholly memorized. Choral reading, more than any other literacy event, provided an initial entry point into feeling fluent as a reader.

Partner Reading

A potentially powerful alternative to independent reading is reading with a partner. Partner reading affords students the opportunity to have the support of a peer who can serve several critical functions, including

1. a more fluent model of reading who can support decoding of text,
2. a stronger comprehender of information read together,
3. a critical partner to problem-solve difficulties in text, and
4. an authentic audience for building motivation to read.

Like all instructional activities, however, learning is not contained within the activity or curriculum, but in the interaction between the text, participants, and context. Without careful attention of how to support partner reading and other literacy activities that require social interaction between peers, they may lose their intended impact. Specifically, it is not uncommon for students with mild disabilities to actively avoid partner reading if there is insufficient structure and support. We have witnessed many classrooms where students are not reading the same text, where they are reading in a parallel rather than partner fashion, where students cannot agree on a shared text to read, and where few accountability measures are employed to ensure that students are effectively engaged in the social process of reading together and are responsible for comprehending the text. Unless there are ample supports for both social and reading success, many students will not persist in the task.

To address both the content and process of partner reading, teachers have employed the use of a "T-Chart" as a tool to directly model, practice, and reinforce participation in this activity, which we depict in Figure 3–8. To introduce partner reading to her class, one teacher we observed, named April, had students generate ideas for both "what partner reading looks like" and "what it should sound like." She then undertook the following procedures with her students:

- She served as scribe and wrote student ideas down in their respective columns.
- She had two students serve as models who practiced partner reading while the remaining students observed.
- She completed the partner reading episode.
- Students evaluated the performance by reading through each of the listed ideas in the "looks like" and "sounds like" categories.
- Students commented on how the partners addressed or did not address each idea.

During the first week of partner reading, at the conclusion of each activity, April gathered her students on the floor and talked about how the partner teams had worked together. These oral discussions then gave way to a self-evaluation checklist that each group completed (also shown in Figure 3–8) on a daily basis. The self-evaluation checklist served to reinforce key word identification strategies that were modeled daily in guided reading groups such as using picture clues, sounding out unfamiliar words, skipping a word and going back, and looking for word chunks.

While the T-Chart provided the class with explicit supports for teaching the social process of reading with a partner, there continued to be a need for supporting attention to getting meaning from text to support a topic of study. In their study about Kenya, April assigned partners who were researching the same category of information. A limited selection of approximately three books was chosen for each group. To support the inquiry, each group was provided a "fact think-sheet" where they were assigned a specific number of facts about their category of study. Students engaged in partner reading with their partner wrote down at least three facts they learned from their research on their think-sheet, and then were required to share these facts with the whole group and add them to the group's large organization map.

What does it look like?	What does it sound like?
1. Two people choosing a single book to read together for Partner Reading.	1. The person holding the book is the reader.
2. Two people sitting next to one another.	2. The reader asks for help if they get stuck.
3. The person reading is holding the book.	3. The reader can ask for help from their partner.
4. Both people are looking at book while the reader is reading.	4. The partners can discuss what they read after a reader has read their section.
5. The reader passes the book to their partner when they have finished reading their section.	5. The partners discuss the book at the end of their reading and are prepared to talk about the book with the rest of the class.

Name_____

READING STRATEGIES

DURING PARTNER READING DID YOU:

1. Look at the picture for clues?   _____

2. Sound out an unfamiliar word?   _____

3. Skip a word and then go back?   _____

4. Look for a word chunk?   _____

5. Ask your partner for help with a word?   _____

Title of Book: _____

Was Your Book: EASY   HARD   JUST RIGHT?

This example illustrates the importance of supporting and directly teaching both the *what* and *how* of literacy instruction. For students with mild disabilities and many others who experience learning, behavioral, and/or attentional challenges, it is often necessary to provide explicit instruction of the social skills and processes involved in the literacy event. When teachers consciously think of the literacy, social, and communicative demands of the literacy event, they can begin to think about the types of support made available to students in each of these areas.

Sharing Chair

Sharing Chair is a literacy activity that allows students to orally share their writing or reading and then receive feedback in the form of comments or questions from a peer and teacher audience. Having the chance to share one's writing or reading with an authentic audience is a hallmark of classrooms that attempt to extend literacy instruction to include functional uses of writing and reading. Students who take the role of author receive feedback from their audience, who give them clues about the impact, clarity, and accuracy of their message through their questions and comments. Over time, many authors come to anticipate the types of questions that they need to address in a well-formed text or the type of expression needed in reading well. This form of projecting the impact of one's message to an imagined audience who will hear the story in the future is a key developmental milestone of effective writers and readers. Effective writers read, reread, and edit their text in response to the needs of this external and perceived audience.

When working with young authors and readers in the primary grades, many teachers have found it necessary to think about a range of instructional supports that match students' developmental levels from emergent to fluent writers and readers. In order to ensure that every student is a reader and author, even when they are nonconventionally literate, teachers have found that they may need to provide scaffolded support to each of four roles that are established in Sharing Chair, including scaffolds for:

1. producing written text for those students who are nonconventional or emergent writers.
2. supporting authors as they are asked to read their text to the audience members.
3. creating supports that help the audience members interact effectively with the authors' writing or reading.
4. creating interactional moves that the teacher employs to support student dialogue in the Sharing Chair.

Producing Written Text

From the earliest ages, it is important that all children, and especially those for whom writing is difficult, see the functional purpose of writing and reading as a form of communication. When students are just beginning to produce written text, it is often necessary to provide supports that might allow students to generate written or read text. For the nonconventional and preemergent reader in the early grades who has few or no sight words, several teachers have found that having students "read" wordless picture books in the Sharing Chair allows them to use their oral storytelling in advance of their ability to read conventional text. The most obvious support of written text is to allow the student to draw an illustration of the story and then dictate the story to a more able writer such as a teacher, parent helper, or peer. The pictorial rendering of the story can serve as a form of memory support that allows the student to "read" their story in the Sharing Chair. While students are encouraged to read or memorize the dictated words, the picture remains a key mediator that supports the telling of the story. Over time, the students look increasingly to the printed word for supporting their story.

A second strategy that teachers have used in this early emergent period is to have students write the initial sound of the word and then draw a line for the remainder of the word as in the example "s_____" for "snow." This initial sound prompt is often sufficient in helping the student to produce a more extended form of text. Still later, once the student has some minimum level of writing vocabulary, having the author choose a more able reader to stand behind them as they are attempting to read their own text or a dictated text has proven to be a particularly powerful way to use peers to support others' learning. For example, in one K–3 resource classroom, a young first-grade student with cognitive impairments called on a high-status third-grade student with great pride, turning to him throughout his reading and having this older partner whisper the words into his ear. Using peers to support one another in Sharing Chair creates new roles for students as leaders and teachers and can have a dramatic impact on the nature of the classroom as an inclusive learning community.

A final support for the emergent writer that has been used with lots of success has been the use of word banks. One important goal of the writing curriculum is to increase the writing vocabulary of students over time, and we depict this in Figure 3–9. While the students may not initially be able to read the words, a picture cue next to the word is often sufficient to support the use of that word in their writing. For example, during a unit on Thanksgiving, one teacher included the words *corn, Mayflower, turkey, Pilgrim, Indian, tepee, family, fire, potato, carrot, acorn,* and *pumpkin pie* on a large poster board. From this single support, students were able to include several of these words into their stories and write more elaborate texts. As we noted earlier in the chapter, the increased quality of the papers often had an impact on the excitement that students felt as authors who shared these enriched texts, creating a positive cycle of interaction and reinforcement. Later, as students matriculated from the primary to middle elementary grades, this same teacher began introducing action words and characterization words as additional word bank scaffolds to support students' writing and response to fictional text.

"Thanksgiving" Word Bank	Action Words		Characterization Words	
corn	pinch	turn	happy	brave
	wink	tickle	handsome	jealous
fire	smile	point	ugly	colorful
Mayflower	dance	scratch	angry	lazy
family	throw	stare	excited	intelligent
turkey	blink	push	unhappy	playful
potato	frown	catch	furious	quiet
Pilgrim	hop	eat	graceful	well-behaved
carrot	pull	stamp	clumsy	jumpy
Indian	hum	sing	obedient	beautiful
acorn	clap	wave	afraid	silly
tepee	twist	run	fearless	sly
pumpkin pie	talk	wiggle	friendly	young
	laugh	yawn	eager	honorable
	whistle	swallow	moody	joyful
	skip	bark	famous	envious
	spin	cry	enthusiastic	sad
	stretch	jump	honest	organized
		nod		hardworking

FIGURE 3–9 *A Teacher's Series of Word Banks to Support Writers from Emergent to More Fluent Levels*

Supporting Authors

A second set of supports are useful for supporting audience members to more effectively interact and engage with the author. When studying primary age students' participation in Sharing Chair, it was evident that some students with language, reading, cognitive, and/or attentional challenges may experience difficulty (Mariage 2000). To support the language demands of responding appropriately to text as audience members, three types of supports, varying in specificity, have been used. At the broadest level, one teacher we observed created a specific set of classroom rules for the writing community. The teacher used a station model of collaborative teaching and saw three different groups of writers each morning from two other classrooms. Recognizing that students would occasionally berate or tease others when they attempted to share their reading, she established a set of simple rules that we provide in Figure 3–10, including

1. everyone is a writer,
2. use nice words,
3. don't give up, and
4. respect your friends.

Though not formally meeting an interactive definition of the scaffolding that occurs on a moment-to-moment basis, this kind of foreshadowing of the expectations expected in the writing community served as a visual reference that was frequently referred back to each lesson as the teacher was establishing the learning community.

A second level of support for students was to create a mobile in the classroom that included all of the "question words," including *who, what, when, where, why,* and *how*. Hanging from the ceiling, these words served as a constant facilitator of question generation in a wide range of activities. In Sharing Chair, students with significant language difficulties often experienced difficulty in asking questions of authors, opting instead to make a statement such as "I like your story." When audience members had difficulty generating questions or were nervous about entering the discourse, the teacher pointed to the question words and thought aloud:

> I am wondering if one of the question words might help us. I am thinking that we haven't asked a "who" question yet, so one question might be "Who went with you to the movie?" Can you think of another "who" question or use one of the other question words to ask the author?

The question mobile provides teachers with a reminder to think about the quality and complexity of question generation by individual members of the class, serves as a way to link the teacher's modeling of increasingly complex question asking in the group over time, and allows the teacher to use the question words as a way to assess whether the author has received a sufficiently complete number of questions to explore their written story. Over

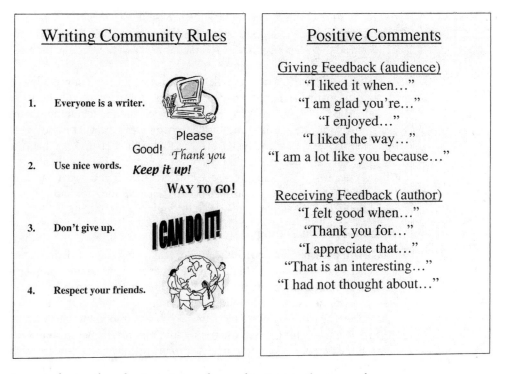

Writing Community Rules	Positive Comments
1. Everyone is a writer.	**Giving Feedback (audience)**
	"I liked it when…"
	"I am glad you're…"
	"I enjoyed…"
Please	"I liked the way…"
Good! *Thank you*	"I am a lot like you because…"
2. Use nice words. **Keep it up!**	
WAY TO GO!	**Receiving Feedback (author)**
	"I felt good when…"
	"Thank you for…"
3. Don't give up. **I CAN DO IT!**	"I appreciate that…"
	"That is an interesting…"
4. Respect your friends.	"I had not thought about…"

time, student authors begin to internalize and anticipate the types of questions that audience members ask, helping them to improve the clarity of their own writing as they address the questions. The social scaffolding of question-asking in the Sharing Chair is internalized by individual authors and can come to impact the quality of future writing attempts.

FIGURE 3–10
Writing Community Rules and Language Stems

A final and more detailed set of instructional supports was the creation of a set of language stems for audience members to give feedback to the author, such as:

- I liked it when . . .
- I am glad you're . . .

Stems for the author to respond to the audience member include:

- Thank you for . . .
- That is an interesting . . .

These language stems, posted on the wall near the Sharing Chair, were first developed as a whole-class activity, then modeled, and finally referred to and reviewed when there was a breakdown in the quality of conversation or when new students entered the classroom.

Supporting Audience Members

A third category of supports may be helpful to ensure that students can accurately and fluently read their writing. For students with reading disabilities, the ability to read aloud to a public audience is one of the most challenging activities in school. To support students' reading, the teacher can have students reread their papers to one or several partners as a prerequisite for reading in Sharing Chair. For example, in one classroom, the teacher had her students read to two partners and then to her before the student was allowed to read in Sharing Chair. This type of extensive previewing of the story accomplished at least three literacy goals in the classroom, including significantly increasing the opportunities students had to read, providing additional opportunities for students to make revisions to their written text, and increasing chances that students would be more successful readers in the Sharing Chair. A second type of support for the emergent reader and writer has been the opportunity to call on a more able peer to stand behind the Sharing Chair and provide reading support only when the author asks for help.

Teacher-Student Dialogue

A final and particularly important source of scaffolding student performance is teacher-student discourse. Initially, the teacher serves as an important language apprentice for students while modeling more complex question asking, as in the example, "Would you recommend to others that they see that movie? Why or why not?" Teachers also play an important role in working in students' learning zones, calibrating support on a moment-to-moment basis. For example, in one resource classroom, a third-grade student with cognitive impairments and significant language delay was having difficulty communicating his story to the peer audience. To support this student's attempt, the teacher asked a series of questions that moved from more open-ended questions to increasingly narrow and specific questions.

Like every reading activity discussed in this section, what appears to be a fairly straightforward and simple activity is complicated for many students with and without disabilities. One challenge for students with disabilities is having and coordinating the language and social skills required for providing meaningful and appropriate feedback to their peers. To temper challenges and provide the concurrent academic and social support for participating in reading one's writing, teachers have employed and adjusted scaffolds in the ways we described.

Reading Comprehension

One of the most significant risks for young students with reading disabilities is a narrowing of curriculum to develop basic reading skills in lieu of higher-order comprehension. It is important that students have the opportunity to participate in the rich discussions that their general education peers routinely experience. In this section, we introduce a comprehension framework called POSSE (Englert and Mariage 1991; Mariage 1995) that provides teachers with one way to introduce key reading strategies prior to, during, and after reading. To illustrate the level of explicitness that may be necessary for some students with mild disabilities, we draw on a single minilesson of how a teacher taught the "search and summarize" part of POSSE.

Students who struggle with constructing meaning from text often experience difficulty in utilizing effective reading strategies before, during, and following reading. These students often fail to generate a meaning or purpose for reading, struggle to bring their own prior knowledge to bear on the meaning of the text such as activating and connecting background knowledge, may not employ a number of monitoring or "fix-up" strategies while reading, and may not interpret or evaluate the text at the conclusion of reading (Pressley et al. 2002). In order to support students' ability to comprehend text meaning, teachers must engage students in extensive explanation and modeling of comprehension strategies, must encourage the use of the strategies in multiple content areas across the school day, and must encourage students to demonstrate their ability to use strategies flexibly in multiple contexts.

POSSE is a framework that highlights comprehension strategies for understanding informational text. It was developed by Englert and Mariage (1991) and uses Predicting, Organizing, Searching, Summarizing, and Evaluating. POSSE encompasses critical strategies such as activating background knowledge, questioning, and predicting categories of information that might occur in the text before reading. The framework itemizes searching for the main points in the text, summarizing main ideas and identifying specific details, and questioning the meaning of the section of text during reading. Last, clarifying unclear vocabulary or ideas in the text, comparing the text's information to prior knowledge, and predicting what might come next in the text after reading a section of text is noted in POSSE. In the POSSE framework that we provide in Figure 3–11, four instructional supports are used, including

1. a POSSE think-sheet to visually represent the collective knowledge and work of the group in writing;
2. a number of sentence stems that provide an initial model for apprenticing students into a language of comprehension, such as "I predict that . . ." and "I think the main idea is . . .";
3. the use of a reciprocal teaching format where students take the role of discussion leader by initiating the use of during- and after-reading strategies; and
4. a summary of the role of the teacher as a model, facilitator, and apprentice to guide the comprehension process, while gradually transferring increasing control to students over time.

An overarching challenge for many poor comprehenders is developing and then becoming metacognitive of strategies for getting meaning from texts. Teachers can help their students by highlighting strategies that "good readers" use. Through frequent modeling, thinking aloud, and demonstrating strategy usage, teachers provide students with explicit examples of *what* strategies to use, *when* to use them, and *why* they are useful. Over time, as students become more comfortable in using reading strategies, teachers can ask students to begin to demonstrate their own self-regulated use of the

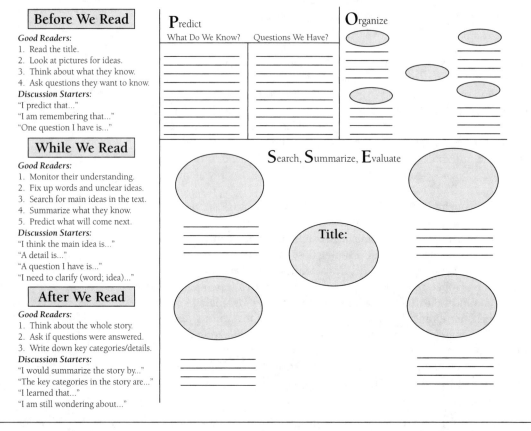

Before We Read

Good Readers:
1. Read the title.
2. Look at pictures for ideas.
3. Think about what they know.
4. Ask questions they want to know.

Discussion Starters:
"I predict that..."
"I am remembering that..."
"One question I have is..."

While We Read

Good Readers:
1. Monitor their understanding.
2. Fix up words and unclear ideas.
3. Search for main ideas in the text.
4. Summarize what they know.
5. Predict what will come next.

Discussion Starters:
"I think the main idea is..."
"A detail is..."
"A question I have is..."
"I need to clarify (word; idea)..."

After We Read

Good Readers:
1. Think about the whole story.
2. Ask if questions were answered.
3. Write down key categories/details.

Discussion Starters:
"I would summarize the story by..."
"The key categories in the story are..."
"I learned that..."
"I am still wondering about..."

Predict

What Do We Know?   Questions We Have?

Organize

Search, **S**ummarize, **E**valuate

Title:

FIGURE 3–11
POSSE Strategy Framework for Supporting Reading Comprehension Dialogues

strategies through having them think aloud and make visible their thinking as they experience comprehension challenges.

To illustrate the level of explicitness that may be necessary for supporting some learners, it is helpful to draw upon a typical minilesson where teachers are introducing one of the most difficult comprehension strategies: searching for a main idea through the identification of supporting details when the idea and the details are buried in a piece of text. Let's look at a minilesson taught by Becky, a teacher who chose a well-written informational paragraph that has a clear but not explicitly stated main idea with several supporting details. We provide this sample in Figure 3–12. Becky retypes the paragraph, makes handouts for each student, and creates an overhead transparency of the paragraph so that she can read the passage aloud while facing the students. She then reads the passage and rereads it, beginning to think out loud:

Becky: "As I read the paragraph, I am trying to think about what this paragraph is about—what is the main point or main idea of this part. Sometimes the main idea is clearly stated in a topic sentence or a concluding sentence. But sometimes, I have to look at each of the details in the paragraph and ask myself whether those details are part of a category. I think that is what I have to do in this case. Let's look at our paragraph and take our highlighter markers and see if we can find some of the details. The details are the key facts in the paragraph."

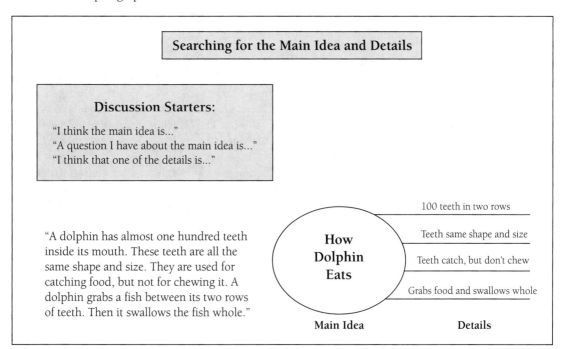

After students searched for details, Becky focused her students' attention on sentence stems such as, "I think the main idea is . . . ," "A question I have about the main idea is . . . ," and "I think that one of the details is . . . ," reviewing them with her students. Becky then called on students and mapped the details on the accompanying graphic organizer. She then continued to think aloud, reading each of the details in succession and asking her students, "What are all of these ideas about?" When students were unable to come up with the main idea, Becky reread the details and again stated,

FIGURE 3–12
Organizer for Minilesson on Teaching Summarization

> I am wondering what these are talking about . . . the paragraph says that the dolphin has one hundred teeth, it tosses its food in the air to swallow it whole, and it can't chew its food. I am wondering if this paragraph talks about "how the dolphin . . ." yes, that's right. This paragraph talks about how the dolphin eats. So what is my main idea? How dolphins eat. So I am going to write that in the main idea circle.

In this short minilesson on teaching students to find main ideas in a chunk of text, Becky supported her students both directly and indirectly.

The first consideration was the thoughtful selection of a single paragraph that delimited the complexity of the text. For the purposes of initial teaching, the teacher wanted to have students begin their practice on a passage that contained a clear main idea, but stretched the group just slightly by not having the main idea explicitly stated in the paragraph. The teacher then provided the students with their own passage and highlighters, allowing them to have access to the text and become active participants in the lesson. Reading the text aloud twice allowed low and nonconventional readers in the group to have access to the text, even though it was beyond their instructional reading levels. Modeling and thinking aloud gave all students access to the inner thinking of a more able reader, but students were asked to contribute to the thinking through a series of open questions such as "I wonder how these ideas go together?" The language stems provided students with an explicit scaffold for the teacher to help students jump-start their discussions. The graphic organizer provided students with an explicit way to understand the complex relationships between a series of details and the main idea that it represented. Using a different colored marker to identify the main idea and details also served to clue students to the difference between supporting details and the superordinate category of which they are a part. Finally, the group's thinking was written down, providing the group with a memory scaffold that represented the collective thinking of the group.

CONCLUSION

This chapter has examined how teachers can support and scaffold written composition and reading instruction for students with mild disabilities. While the heart of effective scaffolding will continue to be the moment-to-moment responsiveness of teachers working reciprocally within students' zones of proximal development, we have attempted in this chapter to demonstrate how a deep knowledge of the common literacy challenges that face many struggling readers and writers can also preempt and forestall difficulties before they begin. In this sense, scaffolding may be most effective when it serves to ameliorate well-known cognitive and social challenges before they are allowed to become negative trajectories of learning. The notion of scaffolding instruction as a form of preempting poor literacy learning is an important addition to the more common and narrower definition of scaffolding between teachers and students or students and students. In reality, coordinating preemptive and moment-to-moment scaffolding has the greatest chance to promote academic and social competence.

The orchestration necessary to support students with mild disabilities in writing and reading is extensive. We end this chapter with several key considerations to help teachers think about scaffolded instruction. Drawing on common characteristics of students with mild disabilities, content-specific challenges in writing and reading, and principles of effective instruction (Englert, Tarrant, and Mariage 1992), this list highlights the broad potential for extending the scaffolding metaphor. Scaffolding from this perspective has elements that are developmental, relational, and preemptive in nature. There are also elements of cognitive apprenticeship, including extensive modeling of the discourse unique to writing and reading; thinking aloud; utilizing the tools of a discipline such as graphic organizers, pencils, and keyboards; and gradually transferring increasing control of learning from more knowledgeable to less knowledgeable members of the classroom community (Englert and Mariage 2003).

Scaffolding does not occur in a content vacuum, and teachers must consider the cognitive, social, and behavioral profiles that each student brings to the classroom. Students with mild disabilities often have difficulty with basic language and literacy skills, and these often have an impact on social skills and behavior. Teachers must understand scaffolding as existing in the context of students' cognitive, communicative, social, motivational, and behavioral profiles.

Many academic and behavioral challenges that are exhibited in classrooms have their root in instruction that does not support students' language, literacy, social skills, and learning strengths. The very strengths of a more empowering and purposeful literacy program for students with and without disabilities occur when the inherently social aspects of literacy are brought forward—sharing, discussing, listening, and inquiring with others in collective activity. Making literacy more meaningful, authentic, and purposeful will require very careful attention from teachers to help ensure that the functional needs of students are being addressed. The intensely linguistic and social nature of schools places a constant press on students' academic and social competence, creating a challenging environment for students who struggle with precisely these cognitive and social skills.

Scaffolding exposes new zones of possibilities for both teachers and students. When students with mild disabilities are supported and provided scaffolded instruction that encompasses academic, social, and behavioral supports, they can create new trajectories of possibility. Social identities are at least partially created in situated activity settings. When students with mild disabilities are given the necessary supports to access core content and given instruction into the social processes demanded in socially mediated learning, teachers can create new zones of expectation, performance, reinforcement, and persistence. It is not a stretch to suggest that effective scaffolding can be a key to helping thousands of students to reconnect with schools. Hopefully, the following points will be helpful to teachers in realizing these new zones of possibility.

Key Ideas in Scaffolding Literacy Learning for Students with Mild Disabilities

- Understanding common academic and social characteristics of students with disabilities can give teachers a head start in understanding potential challenges in their classrooms and prevent academic and social difficulties through the preparation of academic and social supports.

- Mild disabilities do not just impact academic skills, but also social and behavioral participation. Effective scaffolding must often include employing best practices in teaching the social and behavioral demands of the event.
- Scaffolds appear at multiple levels: (1) moment-to-moment as a teacher responds to a student's ideas; (2) choosing the type of activities that children participate in; (3) choosing the mediational tools that students have access to in the activity; (4) organizing "knowledgeable others" (e.g., peers, partners, adults) in the environment; (5) determining the participant structure for the activity, including rights, roles, and responsibilities of participants; (6) understanding that apprenticeship into a discipline of study requires that students participate in the ways of thinking, talking, acting, behaving, and valuing used in that domain (e.g., inquiring in science, constructing written text as an author). This apprenticeship into higher-order thinking demands an overtime perspective where students are asked to take on increasing responsibility for participation with appropriate support.
- Scaffolding is not and cannot be limited to academic content alone. Literacy and becoming literate in disciplinary fields of study are inherently social, relational, and communicative. Students with mild disabilities, who often have social and/or behavioral challenges, require teachers that are sensitive to and have strategies for scaffolding the sociobehavioral environment.
- Scaffolding is inherently bidirectional and relational. Being a good "kid watcher" is the most fundamental skill of effective teachers.
- Scaffolding is seldom only valuable for students with disabilities.
- Over time, teachers can begin to internalize and develop a set of perspectives that considers the necessary scaffolds needed for successful performance.
- By definition, scaffolds should provide only enough support to allow children to do what they would not be able to do alone. Transferring and ceding control of the meaning-making process to students as soon as they are capable is necessary for learning and internalization to occur.
- Scaffolding complex processes like written expression and reading comprehension require disciplinary apprenticeships that have no clear endpoints and require years of participation.
- Collaborating with special educators, parents, and other ancillary personnel (e.g., school psychologist, social worker, counselor) can provide practitioners with a wealth of ideas for supporting students with mild disabilities in the inclusive setting.

4 | SUPPORTING TEACHER AND STUDENT LEARNING FOR BETTER PHONICS INSTRUCTION

Gay Su Pinnell
Irene C. Fountas

Imagine walking down the halls of an elementary school you might be visiting. As you pass each doorway, you could eavesdrop one by one on the hundreds of conversations taking place in the building. The effect would be a little like playing with the tuning knob on a car radio.

As you pass one open door, you overhear some children chanting:

"If you know *make,* it helps you know *lake.*"

"If you know *but,* it helps you know *bit.*"

You move on to the next open door and overhear the teacher:

"Today we are going to think about how it helps us to find the parts in a word that we know."

We move on, entering the teachers' workroom where we overhear a group of teachers engaged in a lunchtime professional book study to help them grapple with issues related to teaching phonics. One reads aloud: "Although children need to be taught the consonant and vowel letter-sound relationships, they also need ample reading and writing activities that allow them to practice this knowledge."

As literacy educators, we find ourselves challenged along several dimensions, some to do with the nature of teaching children and others to do with preparing teachers for this demanding role. In this chapter, we explore the dual responsibility of teaching children about the nature of written language while simultaneously supporting our teacher colleagues in refining and increasing the effectiveness of their instruction. In both arenas, support systems are essential. First, we briefly outline contextual factors confronting educators today; then we describe a multifaceted approach to phonics instruction followed by suggested ways to provide professional support for teachers.

In literacy education for the last few years, it would be hard to find a hotter topic than phonics. A major report that is guiding current federal policy strongly supports both *phonemic awareness instruction,* which helps students become aware of and able to manipulate the specific sounds in words, and *phonics instruction,* which is designed to help children learn about and use the relationship between sounds in oral language and the graphic symbols (letters) in written language (Armbruster, Lehr, and Osborn 2001; National Institute of Child Health and Human Development [NICHD] 2001a, 2001b). While claiming that systematic and explicit instruction is better than nonsystematic or no instruction, the report (NICHD 2001a) and two other documents derived from it (Armbruster, Lehr, and Osborn 2001; NICHD 2001b) also states that "there are many ways to teach PA effectively. In implementing PA instruction, teachers need to evaluate the methods they use against measured success in their own students" (NICHD 2001b, 8).

The report has received criticism both on the nature of studies included in the research base and in the conclusions and interpretations (Allington 2002; Bracey 2003; Garan 2002; Yatvin 2002). There is general agreement that children need to learn about letters and sounds as well as how words "work," that is, the general principles of how oral and written language are related. Educators disagree, however, about just when, how, and how much direct phonics instruction is required to make competent readers. There should not be disagreement about why! The report states that

> Programs should acknowledge that systematic phonics instruction is a means to an end. Some phonics programs focus primarily on teaching children a large number of letter-sound relationships. These programs often do not allot enough instructional time to help children learn how to put this knowledge to use in reading actual words, sentences, and texts. Although children need to be taught the major consonant and vowel letter-sound relationships, they also need ample reading and writing activities that allow them to practice this knowledge. (Armbruster, Lehr, and Osborn 2001)

And we note that while the report emphasizes phonics, it warns that

> Phonics instruction should not become the dominant component in a reading program, neither in the amount of time devoted to it nor in the significance attached. (NICHD 2001b, 2–97)

Stating that good teaching is essential for "leaving no child behind" in reading, the same report states the following:

> Few if any studies have investigated the contribution of motivation to the effectiveness of phonics programs, not only the learner's

motivation to learn but also the teacher's motivation to teach. The lack of attention to motivational factors by researchers in the design of phonics programs is potentially very serious. . . . Future research should be . . . designed to determine which approaches teachers prefer to use and are most likely to use effectively in their classroom instruction. (NICHD 2001b, 2–97)

The above recommendation was not highlighted in the two derivative documents (Armbruster, Lehr, and Osborn 2001; NICHD 2001b) and will be easy to ignore as educators seek structured and easy-to-implement programs in phonics; however, we have long known that engagement is a critical factor in learning and that teachers' passion, enthusiasm, and creativity make ideas come alive in and stay in children's minds.

Combining the National Reading Panel's broader conclusions with general knowledge about good practice, the evidence indicates that the dimensions of good phonics teaching should include:

- direct and explicit instruction that is systematic and well-designed
- many opportunities to use phonics knowledge within meaningful and extended reading and writing of continuous text
- activities that promote interest in words and how they work so that children become interested in language

The relationships between oral and written language are so complex that it would be impossible to teach everything children need to know directly. Luckily, competent readers and writers learn a great deal from their continuous use of literacy; but to do so means that they must become *inquirers*. They learn to search for and recognize patterns and to test and apply them; this inquiry process becomes automatic as they increase their proficiency and extend their reading and writing powers.

TEACHER EDUCATION

In phonics instruction, as with any other area of learning, teachers' expertise is generally considered the critical factor. Here too, controversy is evident. A major report published by the federal government (U.S. Secretary of Education 2002) represented a major attack on teacher education programs in the United States. This report actively argues for dismantling teacher education programs and for severely limiting preparation for teaching.

Agreeing that teacher quality is essential and that some teachers are more effective than others, Darling-Hammond and Youngs (2002) provide a rebuttal to the report, stating that

The report suggests that its recommendations are based on "solid research." However, none of these arguments has strong empirical support, and the report does not cite the scientific literature that addresses them: Only one reference among the reports' 44 footnotes is to a study that was eventually published in a peer-reviewed journal, and the study's findings are misrepresented in the report. Most references are to newspaper articles or to documents published by advocacy organizations; some of these are known for their vigorous opposition to teacher education. (13)

Organizations such as the National Council for Accreditation of Teacher Education, the Interstate New Teacher Assessment and Support Consortium, and the National Board for Professional Teaching Standards affirm the role of teacher preparation, although working for a stronger model that "sets the stage" for lifelong learning (for a recent description, see Holm and Horn 2003). There is general support for a continuum of professional growth from preservice to novice to experienced teacher.

In our experience and research, we have found that teacher education is complex. Preservice education can give a novice a good foundation, but ongoing learning is required to give teachers the skills they need. The literature supports and our own experiences and research (see Lyons and Pinnell 2001) have indicated that novice teachers can profit from

- decision-making tools
- demonstration, coaching, and reflection
- a supportive network of professionals

TEACHING PHONICS WITHIN A COMPREHENSIVE LITERACY PROGRAM

Effective phonics is nested within a broader approach to literacy instruction that includes not only direct lessons but "echoes" of that instruction across reading and writing tasks. First, we present an example of clear teaching.

A First-Grade Lesson

Children need to learn letter-sound relationships and word patterns to solve words. Word solving is assisted when children know how to use their current knowledge in a strategic way. In this lesson, Alice taught her students Alan, Brenda, and Cheyenne to use known words to help them solve new words. She begins with very easy examples.

Alice: Today we are going to think about how it helps us to find the parts in a word that we know. This says, "If you know." [She points to the top of her first column of words on the whiteboard.] That means that when you are looking at a word, you think about what you know. You know this word. [She places *is* on the board in magnetic letters.]

Children: Is!

Alice: Since you know the word *is* so well, you can also read another word. [She places *his* in the second column of the whiteboard, explaining that at the top, the words say, "It helps you know."]

[Alice asks her class to describe the new word.] I have made another word. How is it like *is?*

Alan: *His.*

Brenda: The last part is the same.

Alice: The last part is the same: *is his.* What is different?

Brenda: *His* starts with *h.*

Cheyenne: You added an *h* at the beginning.

Alice: There is an *h* at the beginning. So *his* is like *is* except for the *h.* If I know *is* and I know the *h* sound at the beginning, I know this word is *his.*

As the lesson continued, children noticed that you can substitute a letter to make a new word (*hat, bat*) and that you can delete a letter to make a word (*pin, in*). After the lesson, Alice directed the children to engage in an application activity that encourages children to take words they know and add, substitute, or take away letters to make new words. Children worked in partners to select words they knew and made known words. They created a miniature version of the chart Alice used in the lesson and then took turns reading: "If you know ____, it helps you know ____." Alice prompted them to think about words they knew how to read or write, words that were on the word wall, or words in their word card collections. Children selected their own known words and derivations. As a culminating activity, each selected a known word to write on a small card, writing the derived word on the other side.

This explicit lesson didn't take much time but it represented a key principle that children needed and were ready to learn.

A Decision-Making Tool

To decide when to teach specific topics, Alice uses a decision-making tool—a continuum of understandings relative to phonics and word study that is organized from easier to harder concepts. She uses both formal and informal assessment to determine her students' current knowledge within an area of learning and refers to the continuum, which provides a range of principles in nine categories related to learning about sounds, letters, and words. These areas represent a comprehensive picture of what children need to learn about the relationships between spoken and written language and an organizational framework for instruction in phonics/word study (see Figure 4–1).

FIGURE 4–1
*Letters, Sounds, and
Words: Nine Areas of
Learning*

Letters, Sounds, and Words: Nine Areas of Learning

1. Early Literacy Concepts
2. Phonological Awareness
3. Letter Knowledge
4. Letter-Sound Knowledge
5. Spelling Patterns
6. High-Frequency Words
7. Word Meaning
8. Word Structure
9. Word-Solving Actions

We will briefly describe each.

1. Early Literacy Concepts

Children need to develop basic concepts (such as "letter" and "word," as well as the way print "works"). Most early literacy concepts are developed within the context of authentic and enjoyable reading and writing, but teachers also do some explicit teaching for concepts such as "first" and "last" as they apply to print. To develop early literacy concepts, extensive use is made of the children's own names. For example, kindergarten and first-grade teachers use name charts and name puzzles. As children learn more about words, they can make connections between their names and other words, including the names of their classmates. Early literacy concepts are generally established by mid-year or at least end-of-year kindergarten; if not, children need intensive lessons in this area.

2. Phonological Awareness

Phonological awareness includes the ability to identify and make rhymes, hear syllables in words, hear the parts of words (onsets and rimes), and hear individual sounds in words. Phonological awareness is a broad term that includes phonemic awareness, which refers to the ability to identify, isolate, and manipulate the individual sounds ("phonemes") in words.

The National Reading Panel's examination of selected research indicated that short instructional programs

> that spent between 5 and 18 hours teaching phonemic awareness yielded very large effects on the acquisition of phonemic awareness. Studies that spent longer or less time than this also yielded significant effect sizes, but effects were moderate and only half as large. Transfer to reading was greatest for studies lasting less than 20 hours. In fact effect sizes were more than twice as large for shorter programs than for the longest-lasting program. (NICHD 2001a, 2–42)

Given that phonemic awareness can be established easily (for most children) and in very little time, lessons are recommended in kindergarten and may continue at the beginning of Grade 1. Children who have difficulty hearing and identifying sounds in words by the end of kindergarten may need one-to-one assistance for a time.

3. Letter Knowledge

Letter knowledge refers to what children need to learn about the graphic characters that represent the sounds of language. A finite set of twenty-six letters, two forms of each, are related to all of the sounds of the language (forty-four phonemes). The NRP analysis shows that one of the characteristics of effective phonemic awareness training was "explicitly and systematically teaching children to manipulate phonemes with letters" (NICHD 2001b, 8). In fact, the report states that "the Panel concludes that teaching PA with letters is more effective in helping nondisabled readers acquire phonemic awareness than teaching PA without letters" (NICHD 2001a, 2–21).

Knowing letters does not guarantee proficient literacy, but not knowing letters will severely limit literacy learning. Specific lessons and a great deal of practice in noticing letters both in isolation and embedded in print are recommended during kindergarten and at the beginning of Grade 1.

4. Letter-Sound Knowledge

Prior to Alice's lesson, her students had many opportunities to notice letter-sound relationships and to develop phonics skills (the ability to use sound-to-letter relationships to solve words). Learning the connections between letters and sounds, as well as letter clusters and sounds, is basic to understanding written language. Lessons on letter-sound information begin in kindergarten with simple and basic concepts and continue through second and third grade as children learn how larger word patterns are related to sounds.

5. Spelling Patterns

Efficient word solving involves knowing word patterns, which include phonograms and consonant-vowel-consonant patterns. Recognizing and using these patterns helps children notice and use larger parts of words, thus making word solving faster and more efficient. Patterns also help children to write parts of words quickly rather than laboriously working with individual sounds and letters. Alice's students have become "pattern seekers" in that they know to look for connections between words in ways that go beyond individual letters and sounds.

6. High-Frequency Words

As young children experience print through shared reading and interactive writing, they will notice words that appear frequently and begin to learn them. These known words are powerful examples that help them develop the concept that a word is always written the same way. They can use known high-frequency words to check on the accuracy of their reading and can also use them as resources for solving other words. Kindergarten, first-, and second-grade teachers not only provide specific lessons on high-frequency words but also give children many opportunities to encounter new words through daily independent reading.

7. Word Meaning

Comprehension depends on the reader's ability to orchestrate visual information from print and language information including syntax, larger text meanings, and the meaning of individual words. It is important for language instruction to include both implicit and explicit meaning. Children must know the meaning of most of the words they are expected to read; and in addition, meaning is deeply related to spelling. An effective phonics program will include both lessons on word meanings and expansion of vocabulary through extensive reading aloud and independent reading.

8. Word Structure

Word structure refers to the way words "work." Words are structured into syllables, have beginnings and endings, and take different forms for plural forms and different tenses. Words may have affixes (prefixes and suffixes) that change meaning. Good readers and writers understand that they can look for how words are related to each other; they can change words by adding letters, letter clusters, and larger parts of words; they can break down words into smaller units that are easier to analyze. Learning about word structure begins with simple lessons on syllables in kindergarten, but continues to expand in sophistication across the elementary school years.

9. Word-Solving Actions

Word-solving actions are the strategic moves readers and writers make when they use their knowledge of the language system to solve words. These "in the head" strategies incorporate all areas of phonics knowledge and represent children's ability to use the principles they have learned.

At the beginning of this chapter, we presented one example of a teacher's ability to help children use known words to solve unfamiliar words. The children probably knew most of the first examples ("if you know") and the new words ("it helps you know"). As children engaged in the application activity, they began to move to other examples, and during sharing time, they made some comments like these:

> "If you know *make,* it helps you know *lake.*"
> "If you know *but,* it helps you know *bit.*"
> "If you know *Polly,* it helps you know *Molly.*"

Lessons on word-solving actions begin in kindergarten and continue throughout elementary school, demonstrating to children how they can put into action the knowledge they have gained through studying letters, sounds, and words.

Organizing Word Study Lessons

In this first-grade classroom, phonics lessons do not occupy the center stage of literacy instruction, but they are systematic and daily. Alice uses the following structure (see Figure 4–2).

Structure for Word Study

Lesson
Application
Sharing
Linking Across the Curriculum
Expanding the Learning
Connecting with Home

FIGURE 4–2
Structure for Word Study

Lesson

Each explicit lesson is related to one of the principles in the word study continuum. The word study continuum suggests clear language for each principle that "rings in students' heads." Talking too much or stating principles in many different ways can confuse children. Alice tries to state the principle in one (at most two) sentences that children can understand; she also uses visual displays such as charts.

Application

To apply and get hands-on practice using the principle, children engage in an application activity that promotes inquiry. They actively explore words and have a chance to discover more. This application activity is multilevel in that more advanced students usually can go beyond the specific demands of the task; teachers may work with small groups of children who have difficulty working independently with the activity.

Sharing

A group meeting at the end of the time period (or later in the day) provides the opportunity to reinforce and restate the principle. Children usually have the responsibility to share their discoveries and, in so doing, play a very active role.

Linking Across the Curriculum

It is important to make strong connections between the word study lessons and other reading and writing contexts. In guided reading, writing workshop, and other settings, teachers keep the principle in mind and take opportunities to remind students of examples. As students become accustomed to the structure of word study, their awareness is aroused; they notice more examples of the principle and also remember to use it.

Expanding the Learning

This lesson may be repeated with different and/or more complex examples to help children truly internalize the principle and develop the habit of using connections to solve new words. Alice may decide to repeat this lesson with more challenging word patterns.

Connecting with Home

There are also opportunities to extend language learning into the home. In the case of this lesson, Alice had children take home an "if you know" sheet and letter cards and asked them to make three word pairs with family members. These do not represent homework assignments; rather, they are a way to provide simultaneously the opportunity for families to participate in children's learning and to let them know what children are learning about letters, sounds, and words.

A Balance of Word Study

We have described how Alice provides direct teaching of phonics in a highly systematic way. She also integrates teaching about letters, sounds, and words across many instructional contexts and extends learning into students' homes. The program that she and her colleagues provide to students includes the opportunity to explore word properties for themselves. From the students' point of view, all aspects of the instructional program fit smoothly together, and they are becoming "noticers" of words.

MEETING THE DUAL CHALLENGES OF LITERACY EDUCATION: NEXT STEPS TO SUPPORT EFFECTIVE TEACHING

We have discussed how Alice as a teacher supports student learning. Now let's think about what teachers can do to enhance their teaching by understanding children's literacy learning.

Meeting today's challenges requires attention to development at several levels. In this chapter, we have explored phonics teaching, a complex area of instruction that requires explicit and structured teaching and at the same time motivates active exploration of language. The key to providing this explicit instruction is teachers' ability to ascertain children's needs, select critical principles to teach, plan effective lessons, structure active learning, and connect learning across many literacy learning contexts. This complex sequence of teaching skills must be applied over and over to instruction across a range of critical areas of knowledge, including early literacy strategies, phonological awareness, letter knowledge, letter-sound knowledge, high-frequency words, word meanings, spelling patterns, and word structure. The goal of instruction is to help children put their understandings to work through the word-solving actions that make them continuous problem solvers who learn from every experience in reading, writing, and word study.

Now that we know the activities and procedures through which children might be led to support literacy, let us consider what other teachers in Alice's school might do. After all, Alice is an experienced teacher. But in her same school, there are novices, either newcomers to teaching or to word study as an area of study. They have been supported in their work by the use of decision-making tools such as the phonics continuum and prototype lessons, by demonstration, by coaching and reflection, and by the supportive network of professionals that includes not only the colleagues in her own school but across schools. In this section, we describe the teacher training that helps teachers provide effective phonics instruction in this school.

Next Steps: Tools

Word study lessons must be carefully selected to work on the edge of children's learning; they are crafted to be clear and efficient; and principles are powerfully connected to reading and writing activities and to children's homes. We have described the nine areas of learning organized on the word study continuum (Pinnell and Fountas 2003a, 2003b, and 2003c). The continuum helps teachers to select principles and to express them in clear language as they work with children.

An additional decision-making tool is a yearly map that helps them look across areas of learning from "early" to "late." For example, the lesson "Using What You Know about Words" (Making New Words) would typically be appropriate early in Grade 1 (although depending on children's current levels of learning, a teacher might make a decision to use it later). Around the same time, teachers might be helping children learn about vowels in words, beginning and ending consonant letter-sound relationships, efficient ways to form (write) letters, simple phonograms, syllables, and high-frequency words. The yearly map helps teachers work across areas and also serves as a way of keeping a record of systematic instruction because they can check lessons used, lessons added, and lessons that children do not need because they already exhibit (as determined by assessment) the competency required. A month-by-month guide provides very specific suggestions as to routines to teach, lessons, and behaviors to notice and support across the year.

Prototype lessons provide additional support for teachers to whom phonics teaching is new. Lessons follow the structure described for Alice's lesson, with specific suggestions and language for components. Lesson prototypes include suggestions for assessing children and selecting and adjusting lessons, working with English language learners, implementing the lessons, applying knowledge, linking across the curriculum, expanding the lesson in different ways, and connecting with homes.

It may seem that these structured written documents would be a sufficient support for teachers in providing effective phonics instruction, but that is not the case with any materials. A multifaceted approach is needed.

Next Steps: Demonstration, Coaching, and Reflection

In Alice's school, a staff developer is on site to provide the support that teachers need to take on new instructional practices. The staff developer may demonstrate effective lessons, often using prototype lessons so that teachers can not only read about but see the teaching, including the clear use of language, examples, visual displays, and application activities.

Demonstration is only a small part of the staff developer's role. The greatest emphasis is placed on coaching and reflection. The staff developer regularly observes and coaches teachers as they implement prototype lessons as well as those they design themselves to meet the particular needs of their students. Coaching provides the constructive feedback that helps them refine their teaching and, even more important, to reflect on it in a self-evaluative way. They think about questions like:

- Was my lesson efficient and well managed?
- Did I make the best use of time?
- Were children engaged throughout the lesson?
- Was my application activity appropriate, well demonstrated and explained?
- Did I provide for multilevel learning?
- Did the principle I selected meet children's current needs?
- Was the principle explained in clear language that children could understand?
- Did children demonstrate (during the lesson, the application activity, and sharing) that they understood the principle and could apply it?
- What should I teach these children next?

The final question, always, is: "What can I do to improve my lessons?" Coaching is a collegial activity. It does not involve one person evaluating another; rather, the coaching conversation resembles a discussion among friends. Both individuals express opinions and observations; the focus is on children's behavior and what it indicates. Teachers are invited to reflect on their own teaching; self-evaluation is the goal and the key to better instruction.

Next Steps: A Supportive Network

Professional development is an integral part of Alice's role as a teacher. A learning community has been created in her school; colleagues help each other to reflect on their practice and develop their skills. The premise here is that if we are to "leave no child behind," everyone in the school must provide expert education. Vulnerable children need more than one year of good instruction; truthfully, six will be needed; and that means that teachers must help each other. The teachers in Alice's school meet regularly to discuss their vision and learn more about instruction. That internal network is important, but they need the support of a larger community.

Teachers in this school have made a commitment to a project that gives them access to a larger network of colleagues, one committed to improvement in literacy education. In these changing times, it is very difficult for isolated schools to have access to the research and professional development that will help them move forward. Larger networks can provide not only training for teachers and in-the-school professional developers but also give them access to research-based practice, which must change as we learn more. Teachers in Alice's school can connect with colleagues at their grade levels across urban and suburban school communities; they can learn about the current state of knowledge. They also adhere to a well-articulated set of standards that describe excellent education. This larger commitment is essential for helping the staff developer and leaders in the school chart direction.

The broader network provides support for teachers as they work toward meeting the standards they have adopted. In addition, the network helps them constantly update their practice in response to current research. Finally, the network represents a vision that teachers across many settings share. (To read more about the professional development program described in this chapter, see Lyons and Pinnell 2001. We have also written about professional development in Rodgers and Pinnell 2002.) All of these factors work together to support the important work of teachers in the school (see Figure 4–3).

Next Steps: Supporting Professional Development

Tools
Demonstration, coaching, reflection
Network

Tools; demonstration, coaching, and reflection; and a supportive network of colleagues form the three supports to make ongoing learning possible.

CONCLUSION

Professional development of a very specific nature helps teachers to implement instruction effectively. Teachers use helpful tools to make decisions about instruction; in addition, they require support in ongoing learning through demonstration, coaching, and reflection. Finally, a professional network of colleagues keeps learning alive and ongoing. Literacy education, even in an area such as phonics instruction that (purportedly) can be implemented through directive materials, is best delivered through a broad-based teacher support system that includes not only materials but demonstration, coaching, and self-reflection as well.

FIGURE 4–3
Next Steps: Support Professional Development

5 | RECIPROCAL MAPPING
Scaffolding Students' Literacy to Higher Levels[1]

JOYCE C. FINE

Maria, a second-grade teacher, sits with her class on the floor. Today she has chosen to share the story *Red Riding Hood* by James Marshall (1987). Maria waits for a little quiet and then holds up the cover, asking "How many of you know this story?" "I do, I do," most of the youngsters respond, leaning forward to get a better look at the cover. "Well today, we have to do a little detective work," Maria says. "This book is a little tricky, because it is different than some other books. We will need to read very carefully and see how things might be different than the story that we all know." Maria begins to read: "A long time ago . . ."

The above scenario focuses on Maria beginning a lesson in which she is seeking to use a model of authentic literature to scaffold her students' writing. In an era of high accountability, teachers often face pressure to teach reading and writing by using prescriptive, formulaic structures and materials. One teacher decided to require all of her students to write the same first three sentences every time they wrote in response to a prompt. It consisted of this formula:

1. *("Exclamation!")*
2. *(About the prompt because.)*
3. Now why don't you sit back on your plush purple pillow while I bend your ear and tell you why *(prompt)*.

One of her students wrote:

Holy Moley! My school is so special because I said so. Now why don't you sit back on your plush purple pillow while I bend your ear and tell you why my school is so special.

---

[1]Note: Special thanks to Mrs. Judith Baker and her class at Park Trails Elementary School in Broward County, Florida, and Mrs. Analexis Kennedy and Mrs. Tina Cash and their classes at Key Largo K–8 School in Monroe County, Florida.

The teacher's intent was to *train* students with a conditioned response for the purpose of scoring points on the state standardized writing exam. Ruben, the uninspired fourth grader who filled in the blanks in the previous example, finally rebelled by refusing to write anything, saying he hated writing! Such misguided practice results in student frustration, de-skilling teachers, and not only failing to teach students to write, but inadvertently producing detrimental, negative feelings toward writing. Instead of short-changing students with a lack of quality instruction designed to trump standardized assessment, this chapter describes how teachers explore a strategy to allow students to appreciate the authentic ways authors write. Reciprocal mapping, an integrated reading/writing strategy, uses visual representation to make concrete the process of examining author's craft. By appreciating and paralleling the techniques authors use, students indirectly experience an author's apprenticeship. The strategy is designed to be a leading activity—one that takes students to a higher level of cognition.

WHAT WE KNOW ABOUT MAKING SENSE OF TEXT

From cave drawings or pictograms in prehistoric times, to hieroglyphs from ancient Egypt, to stained glass images of medieval times, to computer graphics in today's technological society, the use of visual images has been critical in the development of communication skills. Their use has advanced human communication by providing a means for sharing and preserving ideas on a continuum between oral language and written language.

Theories About Text

Modern theory and research supports the idea that visuals are important in students' literacy development. Jerome Bruner's (1975) theory of cognitive growth explains that children go through three stages: the enactive stage, in which they must interact with their environment; an iconic stage, in which information is carried by images; followed by the symbolic stage, in which children mediate learning with language. Combining this theory with Vygotsky's (1986) zone of proximal development suggests that using iconic models such as visual representations can help students reorganize their brains for higher cognitive function.

Before children learn to read, they begin taking meaning from visual cues (Moats 1998). Visuals serve as intermediary links to literacy development (Armstrong 2003). Rudolph Arnheim (1991), speaking on the importance of imagery for concept development, says that "language is no mental realm of its own: it has no substance other than the meanings of the images to which the words refer" (16). Indeed, differences in language processing and reading comprehension may be attributed to differences in the ability to store and retrieve visual images (Gambrell and Bales 1986).

Vygotsky (1986) also explains that in a child's development, "imitation and instruction play a major role. They bring out the specifically human qualities of the mind and lead to new developmental levels. In learning to speak, as in learning in school subjects, imitation is indispensable" (188). The use of visuals to support language development may be a needed step for children whose learning style is more visual than linguistic (Gardiner 1983). Some English-speaking struggling readers found it easier to learn to read visually based Chinese than phonologically based English (Rozin, Poritsky, and Sotsky 1971). Just as we have learned that phonemic awareness training is needed by many children, so this visual progression seems a necessary bridge to mediate learning.

Graphically interpreting an author's story offers a scaffold to mediate comprehension. Siegel (1994) calls the process of using one sign system (visual representation) to understand another sign system (written text) *transmediation*. Marzano and Arredondo (1986) have described deep processing concept development as including linguistic information, mental pictures, physical sensations, and emotions. From this theoretical base, I have researched the development of story elements using explicit instruction and found that second-grade students included story elements in their writing when they had been taught these concepts with deep processing (Fine 1991). Students drew characters in settings, identified a problem or goal, and drew the response and outcomes. After drawing, they wrote sentences that went with each picture. Then with discussion, they attached emotions and physical sensations to characters in each part. When the students wrote using their deep processing prewriting plan, they incorporated more story elements.

Visuals can be used to scaffold writing as well as reading, two processes that are reciprocal in nature. Smith (1983) said the amount of specialized knowledge needed to write must come from reading like a writer. Portalupi (1999) suggests that students need to study literature with a "writer's eye." Instruction in writing is needed. Tierney and Leys (1984) found that there was only a modest correlation between reading and writing achievement scores, with not all good readers being good writers, or vice versa. They also found that process-oriented writing influences students to read like a writer, using the structure of text to help comprehend the author's message. They suggest that if teachers provide children with the opportunity to think of themselves as writers, they will pay attention to the conventions writers use. Wittrock (1983) reminds us that even though both reading and writing are generative, readers and writers use different thought processes and behaviors. These processes can be paralleled and explored visually. As Pressley (1998) points out, readers develop strategies as they engage in processing continuous text. Readers need time, some challenging text, and most important, explicit and supportive instruction.

Procedures Others Have Used

Judith Langer (1995, 9) speaks of "envisionment building," a process for constructing meaning of text. She identifies four stances or relationships of readers to text. First is *being out and stepping in.* When students are first introduced to a story, they are outside and getting ready to step in. In the previous scenario, the teacher used a fairy tale with which the students had some familiarity to link from what the students know to what is new. Next, *being in and stepping through,* the students engaged by listening intently to see how it compared to the story version they remembered. Third, when they compared it to what they remembered, they were *being in and stepping out.* Finally, *stepping out and objectifying the experience* is the process of reflecting on the author's craft. The reciprocal mapping strategy, in which students draw the story parts, helps students make verbal and nonverbal connections quickly and efficiently. The term *envisionment* has the word *vision* as part of its structure. By drawing the boxes and using text or drawing pictures of the ideas for the parts of text, the linguistic elements connect to other related images and help the student generate related words. This visual literacy activity simulates what proficient readers do automatically and what learning disabled students may not do (Swanson 1989).

An example of writing instruction that uses these ideas is the work of Tompkins and McGee (1989) with kindergarten and first-grade students. They recommended using the predictable nature of stories to help children write parallel ideas and then to write stories. As the students progress through the grades, they can learn more complicated ideas from closely mapping more complex stories. Teachers can help children progress from their current level of functioning by scaffolding their growth with such opportunities (Palincsar 1986). This builds on Vygotsky's concept of the zone of proximal development (1986, 187), the area within which a student can function when supported by a more knowledgeable adult. With explicit instruction, the student is able to grasp the conventions that the author uses. From the neo-Vygotskyian approach (Karpov 2003), there need to be leading activities for learning content and process that contribute with other factors, such as maturation, to assist the learner in moving from one stage of development to another. By using touchstone texts (Calkins 1994), texts that can teach about literature, students learn from their favorite authors as mentors (Moss and Fenster 2002). As students gain control of writers' skills, they are able to absorb more and more complex writing techniques, progressing to the next level of development.

Researching Reciprocal Mapping

As a university professor, I have been working with graduate students who have been encouraged to use reciprocal mapping with their students. The teachers have shared their work with me, and some have even allowed me to observe and participate with them and their students. I have also taught the strategy along with a colleague in a reader's club as part of an afterschool program. This action research has provided qualitative evidence from multiple classrooms leading to insights into how the strategy is able to scaffold children's development by building on their prior knowledge and experiences and in giving them the models to imitate along with instruction to produce original work on a theme. Over time, I have been able to discuss the process and outcomes with numerous teachers and will share the findings in this chapter.

HOW MARIA USED RECIPROCAL MAPPING

Now that I have explained how I collected my data, let me describe a couple of days that I spent with Maria's Grade 2 class. Maria's class is a gifted class in which the range of reading is from about second grade through fourth grade. The students have had writing instruction that emphasized ideas such as using vivid vocabulary and several writing techniques. The chart on display in their classroom suggests using writing targets such as color words, vivid words, "big fat juicy words," concrete nouns, similes, statistics, onomatopoeia, alliteration, and passion. Some of the students were able to give examples for the devices. These examples showed that the class had been introduced to these concepts, although it was not obvious if they would be able to incorporate them in their writing.

To begin the scaffolding process in this lesson, Maria introduces mapping with an analogy to using a geographic map, a concept with which the students are already familiar. In beginning with a concrete item with which students have experience, the teacher builds on their schema from their experiences for what a map is. In order to get the students actively involved, she holds up a local map of the area and asks, "What does this help us do?" The students offer different answers, including that it helps us find places, know where we are, or that it helps us go where we want to go. The map provides a concrete analogy from the students' prior experiences for the concept of mapping or representing a charted course of action.

Maria is also able to help her students understand that the author is a person who is thinking about the writing he or she is doing. She explains that authors have a plan or map of their stories before they write. This type of scaffolding is helping the students appreciate that the writer is a real person who is thinking about communicating to them, the readers. Maria also explains that since the students had been talking about the beginnings, middles, and ends of stories, they would be able to map a story and describe what was in the beginning, middle, and end. Here she briefly reviews familiar concepts and expands them to introduce the new terms, constantly linking background knowledge to accommodate the new cognitive information, much as Piaget described this phenomenon (Singer and Revenson 1996).

As Maria reads the story, she speaks her thoughts aloud, demonstrating a reception scaffold, one that helps students take meaning from text. The students learn how to read the text carefully to find information. Then she provides a transformation scaffold by explaining how she thinks about the information and puts the ideas into pictures or her own words. When she writes the information or draws pictures on the graphic, she is demonstrating a production scaffold. The process is transmediating information between two coding systems (Pavio 1986). This approach scaffolds students at all levels of ability, especially those who are reluctant readers or have low ability by modeling a way to process information. For more capable students, the transmediation of information from one system to another adds a method of gaining depth of understanding.

Drawing a Map

Maria draws an oval in the middle of a large sheet of paper. The students are able to help the teacher label the title and author just above the oval. Then they draw a similar oval on their papers and label the title and author. The students are allowed to create their own map even though it may not be as neat or as perfect looking as it would have been if the teacher had made the map. Maria believes the physical involvement in the drawing activity supports those students who are kinesthetic learners. Here it is possible to see that some of the students are not able to reproduce the placement of the shapes exactly where directed. She simply adds sheets by taping them together so that the students have more space to draw. The maps are later hung up around the room as works in progress to remind students that writing is a process. By having the maps displayed in the room, each child is able to quickly find his or her own map. Because some of the students have trouble keeping track of their own materials over an extended period of time, this helps scaffold their development of organizational skills. Students can work in groups beside their maps around the room. Their discussions, using the maps as cues, help to build depth in students' comprehension (Hibbing and Rankin-Erickson 2003).

Following this, Maria links their prior knowledge once again with the new terms, telling them that the beginning has the characters and setting, the middle has the problem and action related to the problem, and the end has the solution. This is visually represented on the top half of the reciprocal map. Students may use words or pictures in the blocks. Instead of drawing the form freehand, a graphic form may be produced as an alternative (see Figure 5–1).

Maria draws a box above the oval to the left, labels it "Characters," and connects the box with a line to the oval. She writes the names in the box that the children are able to supply: Mother, Grandmother, RRH, Wolf, and Hunter. Then the same is done with the setting, which the children say is RRH's house, the woods, and Grandmother's house. Even little points such as the abbreviation of Red Riding Hood to RRH become a scaffold because most of the students take too long to write out Red Riding Hood. The students learned that it was okay to use just the initials. The teacher then draws another box and labels it "Problem" and explains that the middle of the story starts with a problem and continues with the action taken in response to the problem. The students have some discussion and decide that the problem is that Grandmother is sick and RRH must go through the deep, dark, scary woods to take her a basket of food.

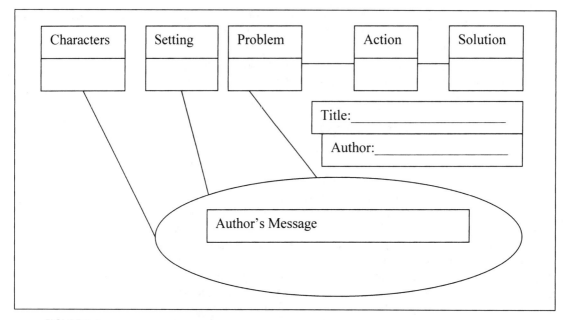

FIGURE 5–1
*Top of Reciprocal Map
Depicts the Story Map
from the Commercially
Published Story*

"What does RRH's mother tell her?" asks Maria. To go straight to Granny's and not to talk to strangers, the students all agree. They continue making boxes attached to the problem box to show the actions. Some of them are busy taping a page next to their page to have the extra room to draw and fill in the number of boxes they need. When the hunter comes, Granny and RRH are set free. RRH says she will never talk to strangers again. Everyone labels their last box with the word *solution* as they all note that the solution is the end of the story. Maria then asks the students what they think the author is trying to tell them. They all say: "Do not talk to strangers." They write this in the oval on their papers. Maria and her students each label the oval on their copy as the author's message. This scaffolds the students to think of theme as the author's critical literacy message. As Galda, Rayburn, and Stanzi (2000) suggest, it is important to emphasize that readers look for themes by asking such questions as, "What did this teach us about life?"

Maria reiterates that the story map is the way the author planned the story to tell his message. As readers, we can read, think, and backtrack if necessary to find ideas in the text and place them on the map.

They also remember that the author used humor to tell the story. They point out that Granny saying that it was so dark inside the wolf that she could not read was an example of this. The last illustration in the book, which has an alligator that is not in any other version, is another example of the author's humor. The teacher explains that that is how this version of *Red Riding Hood* is different from others. The author adds his own style to the story. This careful look at the author's use of humor scaffolds their understanding of the author's style as adding to his unique way of telling his message.

Here, Maria scaffolds children beyond the text by talking about the outside world. In considering the issue about not talking to strangers, Maria links to lessons the students' need to remember personal safety. This is a text-to-world connection that demonstrates to the students that comprehending authors' messages teaches meaningful lessons about life that provide patterns for living.

Constituting a New Story

Continuing on with explicit instruction, Maria provides students a cognitive cue or concrete mental image for the concept of theme, saying that she could have a folder with the message on the outside and lots of different stories on the inside that have the same message. Someone suggests an amusement park for the setting, and they all agree that this is an appropriate place for a story on this theme because it is an example of a place where they have been told not to talk to strangers. They then are given freedom to create the characters. The group decides there should be a little princess person (LPP), a robber who is the evil one, and a Mr. Mashed Potato, who, like the hunter, saves LPP. They draw the boxes for the parallel story parts below each part that is being reflected from the story. The new story uses some of the features of author's craft, which allow the young writers to "stand on the toes" of the favorite author. The new story involves a passage through a tunnel, instead of going through the woods, and a stolen crown instead of the wolf eating the main character. There is enough change to show that they are making the story their own. Yet, with the teacher guiding them, they carefully examine the way the author crafted the original prototype (see Figure 5–2).

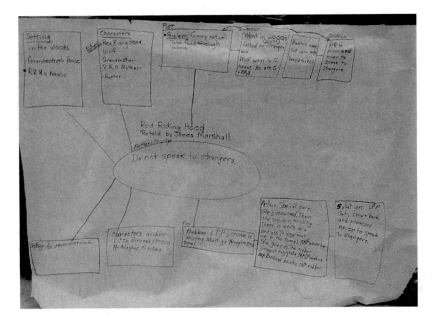

FIGURE 5–2
Group-Created Reciprocal Map.
The reciprocal map, created with a group of students on the back of leftover wrapping paper, hangs from a counter in the classroom.

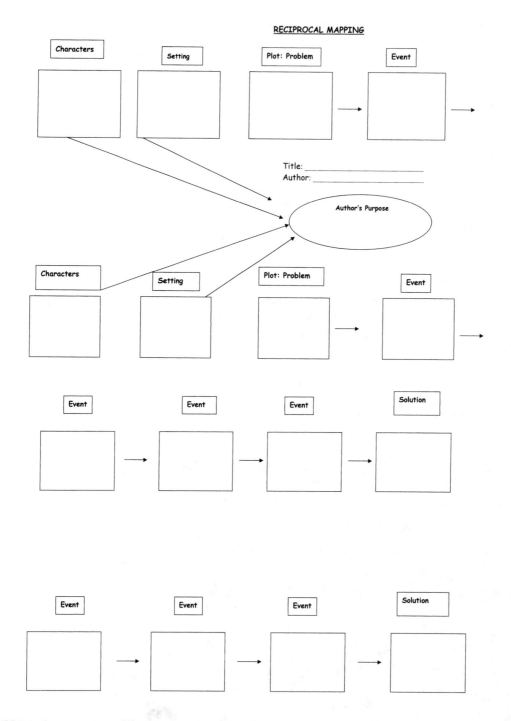

RECIPROCAL MAPPING

FIGURE 5–3 *Computer-Generated Map Forms. Students may need to use computer-generated forms to support their ability to fill in the ideas with words or pictures. They often need to continue onto additional sheets of paper that are taped together, one after another.*

The teacher reminds them that the author has a plan in which the problem is related to the content of the story, the action is related to the story problem, and the outcome is related to the problem. This helps the students see that there is a relationship among the parts (see Figure 5–3).

The Next Day

The next day one group uses the literature book that they have been reading, *The Year of the Panda* by Miriam Schlein (2000), to see if they can also map that story. Other reading groups, reading other books, also map their group's book in small groups and are now ready to begin to map their individual stories. All three groups are reading books on the same theme. They start by stating the characters and describing the setting. They identify the theme or author's message: "Take good care of animals." They map their story parts with discussion and support from the teacher.

They look closely at the map of their group's literature stories and then compare what they have on the author's map to what they want to write in planning their own stories. This backtracking to the text in the book to look for details is to draw lessons from authors.

Once they have made sure that they have identified the parts, they each begin to write a map for their own story. The students then map a personal story, parallel in structure, below the map of the published story. While reading and writing may begin with simple exposure to stories, a teacher's mediation is needed to scaffold students to be able to write as Langer (1995) described for the stepping-out stage. Students manipulate text not to just imitate, but to understand how to construct text to mean what they want. With this strategy, students transfer their thinking in comprehending and communicating with their own text. From the authors' stories, the teacher is able to mediate the children to think on higher levels (see Figure 5–4).

FIGURE 5–4
Students are engaged in mapping their original stories following the map of their different group's literature book. They look closely at the map of their group's literature story and then compare what is there to what they want to create in planning their own story.

In creating the map in Figure 5–5, the student followed the lead of E. B. White in *Charlotte's Web* (1952). It is an example of the student's thinking through of the story elements and a carefully planned story on the same theme.

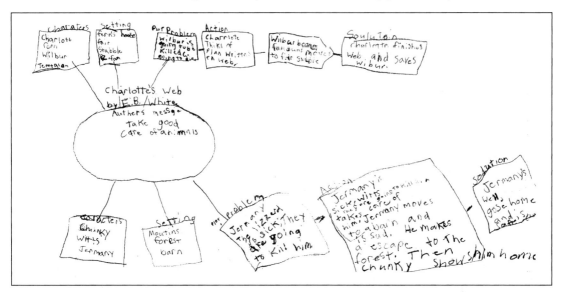

FIGURE 5–5
Reciprocal map showing an original story plan following the work of E. B. White in Charlotte's Web *(1952).*

Students transform the semantic information into a graphic organizer that visually helps them to remember all of the essential parts of the story. The kinesthetic involvement builds engagement and motivation.

To scaffold the students as they move to individual story planning, it may be necessary for some students to work in groups to support each other until they are ready to work independently. The students may draw the map freehand or use technology such as Inspiration (see Figure 5–6), Kidspiration, or a teacher-created template (as shown in Figure 5–3) in a word processing program such as Microsoft Word. When creating the maps, pictures help build the alinguistic information bridges to the semantic content needed for comprehension (Bransford and McCarrell 1974). The strategy scaffolds not only Exceptional Student Education (ESE) students, but all students.

The students are told that sometimes writers change their minds about the number of characters, details about the setting, or any of the other parts. If they decide to change, all they have to do is put a line through the parts that they have changed and add the changes in the right place. This is another scaffold because it lets the students know that authors also go through a process in writing. They can change their minds about characters, settings, and many other details.

Sharing Stories

Now the teacher must scaffold the students to be able to use the map as a guide. Before beginning these conferences, the students must be taught the

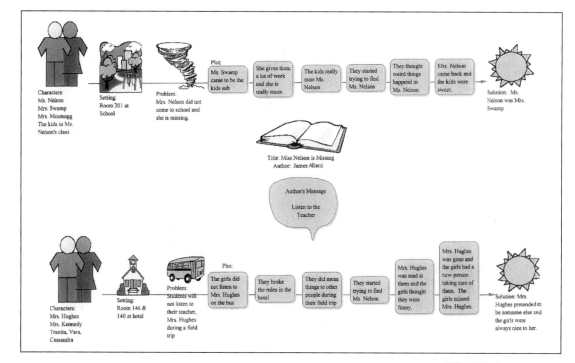

Characters:
Ms. Nelson
Mrs. Swamp
Mrs. Mesmogg
The kids in Ms. Nelson's class

Setting:
Room 201 at School

Problem:
Mrs. Nelson did not come to school and she is missing.

Plot:
Ms. Swamp came to be the kids sub

She gives them a lot of work and she is really mean.

The kids really miss Ms. Nelson

They started trying to find Ms. Nelson

They thought weird things happend to Ms. Nelson

Mrs. Nelson came back and the kids were sweet.

Solution: Ms. Nelson was Mrs. Swamp

Title: Miss Nelson is Missing
Author: James Allard

Author's Message

Listen to the Teacher

Characters:
Mrs. Hughes
Mrs. Kennedy
Tranita, Vera, Cassandra

Setting:
Room 146 & 140 at hotel

Problem:
Students will not listen to their teacher, Mrs. Hughes during a field trip

Plot:
The girls did not listen to Mrs. Hughes on the bus

They broke the rules in the hotel

They did mean things to other people during their field trip

They started trying to find Ms. Nelson

Mrs. Hughes was mad at them and the girls thought they were funny.

Mrs. Hughes was gone and the girls had a new person taking care of them. The girls missed Mrs. Hughes.

Solution: Mrs. Hughes pretended to be someone else and the girls were always nice to her.

procedures for participating in a group conference. If they are in the author's chair, they read their stories and tell what they like about their story first. Then they wait for a response from someone in the audience. The audience will be playing TAG, in which they tell something positive, ask questions, and give advice to the author. This teaches the students that they are to be respectful and supportive to each other. With step-by-step guidance in small groups, the students practice this process. All the while, they get extra practice in identifying the story elements and the relationships between them. Each time a student listens and states feedback orally to another student, the metacognitive aspects of the relationships between the elements of the story are being solidified in their minds.

Students are asked to label and highlight the story elements in different colors on their rough draft. Who are the characters? Why are they chosen for this story? Where is the setting? Is that an appropriate place for the story with the particular author's message to take place? Do the characters fit the setting? What is the problem? Is the problem directly related to the author's message? Where is the problem stated? Is the action in response to the problem? Is the solution one that fits the problem? As classmates listen, each student identifies the elements of the story, making sure that the stated elements relate to the author's message. These checks showed that the student had the main concept of creating a story following the author's intended plan to tell a message. Once a student had related the problem to the message and checked that the action was related to the problem,

FIGURE 5–6
A sample of a reciprocal map produced using Inspiration *software, a program that provided the motivation for students creating reciprocal maps for* Miss Nelson Is Missing! *by Harry Allard (1977). Access to technology may support students to be able to work faster and to produce more. The students then created books using a word processing program with the Inspiration icons as illustrations for their stories. The teacher used digital photography to illustrate the students' progress in creating the book.*

considering whether the solution actually was a solution to the problem became the next point to check.

During the conference, students take turns reading their stories aloud and playing TAG. While checking to see if they have identified the parts and have related those parts to the author's message, some students realize that even though they have spent time and effort in writing, they may not have included all of the parts. Sometimes, the realization that they did not include parts makes the children feel uncomfortable. They have produced a product that they had thought was ready to be turned in to the teacher, only to find that it does not meet their standards. This is an example of Piaget's concept of disequilibrium (Singer and Revenson 1996, 18). The child may have thought she included the parts, but her peers say they are not all there. This is a key point for the teacher to scaffold the students beyond the text aimed at improving their affective disposition toward learning with the additional benefit of improving their writing. Students need to learn that the purpose of the instruction, sharing with an audience and listening to constructive criticism, is to help them become better writers and that revising is a way of learning and improving. Students may not have previously used criteria for critically judging their writing, or any of their work, for that matter. This moves the students to a higher level of cognitive thinking through instruction, including peer and self-evaluation as a means for learning and improving skills.

One student, who had been told that she did not have all the parts correct, cried and had to be consoled. After Maria spoke with her individually in class and with her mother in the evening, the student returned to school the next day saying she understood this is how she can learn. This is where good communication between home and school supported a student's growth.

With the feedback, the students began to edit and to revise. The students used rainbow writing, in which they edit and rewrite the paper on different colored sheets of paper, making revisions and editing along the way. When they were ready, the students typed their stories. These were pasted on larger sheets with room for illustrations on both sides of the story and posted on a display board in the hallway for all to read and enjoy.

PRACTICAL SUGGESTIONS FOR TEACHERS

Reciprocal mapping is a strategy that provides a procedure for scaffolding student writing. Here are some practical suggestions:

- Scaffolding is beneficial to both general education and special education students. Some of the classrooms that have used reciprocal mapping have been inclusive rooms with general education, special education, and gifted students. All became very involved with the process. They needed close supervision in the beginning, but soon were able to create maps independently. Capturing the picture icons with the technology in the computer program provided an approved diversionary aspect that motivated these easily distracted students. Such scaffolds are designed to consider behavioral aspects for better classroom management. Teachers may want to consider the strategy with a class that has a range of abilities.

- Scaffolding can be done as a total group even when the students are on different reading levels. When using reciprocal mapping for guided reading with an entire class, groups may be reading books that have the same theme but are on different levels. The stories can be compared in a language chart (Roser, Hoffman, Farest, and Labbo 1992). Two other books used in the classroom of the scenario described were *Charlotte's Web* by E. B. White (1952) and *Joshua Poole and Sunrise* by David Collins (2000). These books had the same general theme: taking care of animals. With reciprocal mapping, even though the students were reading on different levels, a second-grade teacher was able to see that the same concepts could be taught. She felt that this gave a message to the students that they were learning the same content. They usually are quite aware that the groups are being taught different lessons. She was able to hold a total group discussion in which the students filled in the maps and compared story elements across the texts. Such text-to-text discussion motivated students to read the other groups' books (see Figure 5–7).

FIGURE 5–7
Literature chart for reciprocal mapping making text-to-text comparisons.

Title	Joshua Poole and Sunrise	The Year of the Panda	Charlotte's Web	Student's Title:
Author	David R. Collins	Miriam Schlein	E. B. White	Student's Name
Characters	Joshua, Uncle Ben, Sunrise, Emma	Lu Yi, Daxiong Mao, Su Lin, Parents	Fern Arable, Mr. & Mrs. Arable, Wilbur, Uncle, Charlotte	
Setting	Glenbrook Riding Stables	Mountains, China Rescue Center	Farm, Country Fair	
Problem	Sunrise will be sold	Family moving Pandas dying	Wilbur will be killed	
Action	Joshua's plan to enter show	Lu Yi's plan to save Su Lin	Charlotte's plan to make Wilbur special	
Solution	Sunrise stays	Su Lin lives	Wilbur lives	
Author's Message	Take good care of animals.	Take good care of animals.	Take good care of animals.	Take good care of animals.

- Reciprocal mapping can be combined with other strategies and methods to scaffold students in different areas. One of the classes that used Inspiration software was able to create links to the Internet for their settings.

The students were able to read the information about the settings to create rich descriptions. The teacher also wants to adapt the story structure reciprocal mapping activity to apply it to her expository reading and writing. For example, for persuasive writing she will have a topic and author and then list the points in the boxes with the most important decision-making factors.

- This strategy mediates between linguistic thought and visual processing to scaffold students as they extract and construct meaning. It allows students to use their preferred modalities as a reception scaffold to construct meaning, as a transformation scaffold from text to visuals and then back to text, and as a production scaffold as they create their own stories.

ADDITIONAL STRATEGIES THAT WORK WITH RECIPROCAL MAPPING

In the *Red Riding Hood* vignette, Maria began a close reading of a story to help her students learn about author's craft and apply those lessons to their own prewriting and writing. This stage of comprehension development linked to writing comes after the teacher has gradually scaffolded the students' understanding by first using other strategies such as the use of dramatizing, visualizing, learning about story elements, and story mapping. Strategy raising, going from more simple comprehension strategy use to more complex strategy use with the goal of building students' knowledge of strategic thinking for comprehension, spirals the process knowledge needed for reading in much the same way as content knowledge needs to be built.

Strategy raising allows the teacher to build understanding of story elements gradually by using more and more complex strategies that focus on the same target area of reading comprehension. For example, the class had already had experiences beginning with dramatizing stories in which they listened and then acted out the actions of stories, going from oral language to concrete actions. Next, they used visual thinking strategies (Housen and Yenuwine 2000), in which they discussed what they saw happening in pictures, using images to bridge to oral language as they told what was happening in a picture. They also illustrated the meanings of vocabulary and idioms, first the literal and then the figurative interpretation. Students were able to develop their "sense of story" (Applebee 1978) or sense of narrative structure, by practicing retelling (Brown and Cambourne 1987) either what was read or heard. This transformation from text to oral or written language allows teachers to determine if the student has understood the meaning from literal or more inferential levels of text. The retelling activity has a spillover effect of building oral language and, specifically, vocabulary that comes from the story. This activity is especially important for second language learners as they seem to "absorb" the language of the text (Fine and Moreyra 1997). Following this, they experienced the group mapping activity (Davidson 1982), in which students represented the relationships of characters and actions of a story with geometric shapes in drawings, going from text to abstract representations. When teaching the group mapping activity, the teacher explains that the maps may all look different, but they may all be correct in telling the story.

The students had also learned story elements with deep processing (Fine 1991), incorporating concept development of story grammar (Stein and Glenn 1979). Then Maria introduced story mapping including story elements (Idol and Croll 1987), which has been shown to help improve reading comprehension for both regular and learning disabled students. At this point, they were ready to look very closely at the author's craft in order to learn techniques from writing well enough to build their own stories upon it. The teacher had shared *Drawing Lessons from a Bear* by David McPhail (2000) and discussed how the bear had practiced his skills over time and especially how he had looked at masters' works to improve his own. As the bear explains in McPhail's story:

> I love going to the museum. Seeing all those wonderfully drawn pictures inspires me. It made me want to draw even more. As I copied, I discovered things that made my own drawings even better.

Just as Bear drew lessons from the masters in the museum, the teacher facilitates the situation for students to draw lessons from authors. She gradually raised the level of complexity of the strategies, building more and more depth of understanding for the process of improving students' skills.

RECIPROCAL MAPPING: TIPS FOR SUCCESS

There are lessons that can be drawn from the work on reciprocal mapping to scaffold literacy learning in similar ways. These include:

- building on students' prior knowledge and experiences. A basic for all teaching, this involves teaching developmentally appropriate skills and materials.
- using methods that allow the students to transform information from one symbolic communication system to another. Visuals seem to be a critical mediating step. Other forms appeal to students with different learning styles or preferences.
- using strategy rising. Whatever strategy a teacher wants to use should be evaluated with a task analysis to identify the skills needed to be successful. Are there more simple strategies that could be used first that will allow the student to build one upon another as described earlier?
- providing students the opportunity to learn from studying the models provided by quality children's literature authors along with instruction by knowledgeable teachers. The appeal of these authors has much to motivate and inspire, making teaching more interesting to all.

- creating a learning community by establishing rules for respect and responsibility. Allow time for discussion and critical interaction between students under the guidance of the teacher. Students often learn and teach each other more than we can ever imagine. Peer conferences with TAG, for instance, allow students to gain feedback from others so that they begin to take responsibility for their own performance.
- teaching as an opportunity to focus on the high-minded, caring goal of supporting the total student's learning in everything you do. Select books with quality themes that relate to life, so that the students realize that you are encouraging them to connect with their life and the world, building essential life lessons, not just meaningless test-taking strategies designed to satisfy a standardized test.
- celebrating successes. This means we must display even the work in progress. Each day's accomplishments are important. It gives the encouragement to keep working toward higher goals.

NEXT STEPS FOR TEACHERS: SUGGESTED READINGS

Armstrong, T. 2003. *The Multiple Intelligences of Reading and Writing: Making the Words Come Alive*. Alexandria, VA: Association for Supervision and Curriculum Development.

Fletcher, R., and J. Portalupi. 1998. *Craft Lessons: Teaching Writing K–8*. York, ME: Stenhouse.

Galda, L., S. Rayburn, and L. C. Stanzi. 2000. *Looking Through the Faraway End: Creating a Literature-Based Reading Curriculum with Second Graders*. Newark, DE: International Reading Association.

Mantione, R. D., and S. Smead. 2003. *Weaving Through Words: Using the Arts to Teach Reading Comprehension Strategies*. Newark, DE: International Reading Association.

Moss, J. F., and M. F. Fenster. 2002. *From Literature to Literacy: Bridging Learning in the Library and the Primary Grade Classroom*. Newark, DE: International Reading Association.

NEXT STEPS FOR TEACHERS: CHILDREN'S BOOKS TO USE

Allard, H. 1977. *Miss Nelson Is Missing!* Boston: Houghton Mifflin.

Collins, D. R. 2000. *Joshua Poole and Sunrise*. Barrington, IL: Rigby.

Marshall, J. 1987. *Red Riding Hood*. New York: Dial Books.

McPhail, D. 2000. *Drawing Lessons from a Bear*. Boston: Little, Brown & Co.

Schlein, M. 2000. *The Year of the Panda*. New York: Scholastic.

White, E. B. 1952. *Charlotte's Web*. New York: HarperCollins.

6 | SCAFFOLDING WORD SOLVING

Sharan A. Gibson

Picture a busy, literature-rich kindergarten classroom one morning in November. One group of students quietly chants the rhyme of *Fuzzy Wuzzy*[1] as they paste shapes onto a design at their center table. As they reach the end of the story, they enthusiastically shout together, "Wasn't fuzzy, was he?" Nearby, three other students use a long pointer to read a chart of *The Itsy Bitsy Spider* together. As they finish reading, Sarah says, "Hey look! The letter's like my name!" Marissa adds her own comment: "I got a mistake, but I fixed it up!" Wilson is sitting by himself at a table with a book. He says quietly to himself, "I'm gonna practice." After he finishes two consecutive independent readings of his book he says, "I read the whole story! That's a easy book!" As he makes this statement, his teacher, Mary, walks by: "Great! How'd you do? You're a reader!" Mary is on her way to the reading table, where she will work with a group of five students. Here's a snippet of their conversation, after they read a book together:

Mary: The only word that was tricky for your group was *and*. Does that sound familiar?

Mander: Yeah! A-N-D!

Mary: [Writing the word *Mander* and the word *and* on a card in front of the group] Did you see what he was doing to help you?

Sarah: E-R!

---

[1]The titles named within the opening vignette for this chapter are KEEP BOOKS™, emergent reader books produced on a not-for-profit basis by The Ohio State University literacy projects.

Mander: Sar. . .ah!

Kevin: E-R. Mander.

Mander: E-R at the end. And look, *and!* They always use my name! Because for all, it's got E-R and in the middle a *and.* All the time we use it!

As these students start applying removable tape to their individual books, locating and highlighting all occurrences of the word *and* in their text, Mary leans behind her to Jen and Billy, who are reading together at a nearby table. Billy has made an error on the word *finger,* substituting *arm* instead:

Mary: Nice try. But this word starts with an *F.* Look at the picture. What starts with *F?*

Billy: [reading] Look at my finger.

Mary: Did that look right and make sense?

In answer, Billy simply smiles proudly and broadly to himself!

Children learn. Every day, every classroom, minute by minute, and month by month, children are learning. What children learn and the ways in which this learning transforms their current understandings, however, are largely dependent on the specific classroom contexts that we create. In classroom contexts like Mary's kindergarten room, individual children learn that they can take ownership over their own literacy learning and, with effort, experience success on a task-by-task basis.

In this chapter, I describe instructional conversations, like the two just described between Mary and her students during text reading. These instructional conversations serve as scaffolds, in the way described by Gallimore and Tharp (1990) and Goldenberg (1991), in that they allow teachers to support and extend their students' application of strategies for word solving. The term *strategies* is used here in the sense of "knowing how to work on words, sentences and texts to extract the messages they convey" (Clay 2001, 127).

Within this chapter I share understandings about scaffolding gained from observations of reading lessons and interviews with kindergarten and first-grade teachers (Gibson 2002; Scharer, Gibson, and Van Order 2001). I will draw from case studies of two teachers in particular, Mary and David, to provide an analysis of teacher decision making during text reading. The excerpts that I will share are included for the purposes of learning more about scaffolding, rather than as positive or negative exemplars. None of the excerpts presented here is either perfectly correct or entirely wrong.

SMALL GROUP READING INSTRUCTION

The teachers that you will hear from in this chapter use small group reading instruction to provide these opportunities for learning. I will not go into detail about how to teach reading in small groups because that is not the focus of this chapter, but I will briefly describe the format of lessons and the importance of teacher prompts to scaffold learning.

The purpose of small group reading lessons, as opposed to classroom word study and spelling instruction, is to teach students how to use all sources of information more and more effectively when reading new texts. Teachers work to help students understand how to notice and utilize such meaning- and language-based sources of information as background knowledge, the text's plot, concepts, vocabulary, and language structures. Teachers also, across time, help children to use such text-based, visual information as the phonological identity of letters, digraphs, clusters, syllables, and affixes.

It is usually not necessary to spend a lot of time on either rereading familiar texts or teaching lessons on phonetic elements. These activities are certainly important but can typically be implemented quite well at other times throughout the school day. Instead, small group reading time is better conceptualized as an opportunity to provide strong teacher scaffolding in support of students' text-reading decisions within the reading of a new text.

The scaffolding is provided through the teacher's language or prompts to help support the student's word solving at difficulty. In the following example, Mary uses such prompting language as "What can you do?" and "Would *walk* fit there?"

Mary: Why did you stop?

Student: I'm stuck on that [pointing to the word *walk* in the text].

Mary: You're stuck on that? Okay, what can you do?

Student: I, go back.

Mary: Go back and then do what?

Student: /w/ /w/ [looks at the picture] /w/

Mary: Would *walk* fit there? Try that.

Student: [reading] We walk home.

Of course the challenge is to be able to utilize these general types of prompts effectively in order to scaffold student problem solving. In the next section I will describe the nature of effective scaffolding and then give some specific suggestions for fine-tuning prompts during text reading.

ANALYZING THE NATURE OF SCAFFOLDING

Learning occurs in a context of social interactions leading to understanding. Learners are active risk takers who accept challenges and understand how and why to learn. They are given opportunities to restructure information in ways that make sense to them (Roehler and Cantlon 1997, 8).

There are several key aspects of effective scaffolding during text reading to think about:

- Although accurate reading itself is important, the focus should generally be on supporting the student's growing understanding of what actions can be taken in order to figure out words and how, why, and when these strategies are useful.
- The language used by the teacher for prompting during students' reading should be consistent and precise, but must also be modified in interaction with each student's growing level of understanding.
- Effective scaffolding during reading requires a great deal of knowledge about students' current knowledge base as well as expert teacher decision making.

Scaffolding cannot be said to have occurred simply because a teacher has discussed a difficult word in text with the learner. Scaffolding refers specifically to the ways in which a more expert person assists a learner for a particular task, resulting in the learner's internalization of ways of conceptualizing and acting for that task.

It is important then to understand effective scaffolding during text reading as something much more important than simply getting a student to say the correct word. Working from the perspective of scaffolding requires teachers to consider how they can help children to extend their reach, rather than to test whether or not they can operate on the task independently. Given targeted assistance, what word solving can be accomplished by the reader so that more powerful ways of working for reading will be internalized? Scaffolding should be targeted at helping children transform the ways they work on solving challenging words. Scaffolding thus requires a degree of intersubjectivity or shared understanding of the task between teachers and students (Roehler and Cantlon 1997, 9). Teachers are responsible for establishing this shared understanding.

When analyzing scaffolding in classroom contexts across a three-year study, Roehler and Cantlon (1997) identified a number of specific types of scaffolding:

- offering explanations
- inviting student participation
- verifying and clarifying student understandings
- modeling desired behaviors
- inviting students to contribute clues

A similar set of teaching moves can be identified for teachers' scaffolding of students' problem solving of unknown words during text reading. Several of these categories are listed in Figure 6–1.

In the dialogue of Figure 6–1, the teacher is engaging in an instructional conversation aimed at scaffolding the student's attempt to problem-solve the difficult-to-her word *kitchen*. Taking a careful, analytic look at the teaching

An Analysis of Categories of Teaching Moves Made During Teacher-Student Interaction for Text Reading	
Teacher-Student Instructional Conversation	**Type of Teaching Move**
T: [reads a line of the text, stopping just before the word *kitchen*]	
S: That says *kitchen*!	
T: And how did you know that said *kitchen*?	Requesting student thinking
S: Because that's, it has a *K*.	
T: Remember yesterday when we talked about when you're reading and you come to a place where you're not sure? What did you do to figure that word out?	Requesting student thinking
S: Look at that first letter.	
T: Right. And what is that first letter?	Confirming student response, interrogating the student
S: *K*.	
T: So it goes /k/ /k/.	Drawing attention to a critical feature
S: Kitchen.	
T: So you have to think, now let's see, *table* doesn't say /k/ /k/. What would *table* start with?	Teacher demonstration, interrogating the student
S: *T*.	
T: Yeah, and it doesn't have a *T*. Good job.	Teacher demonstration, confirming student response.

moves made during this teacher-student interaction should help to clarify and refine teachers' abilities to engage effectively in this type of scaffolding.

The teacher has (1) called for the student to think about his or her understanding of the task at hand; (2) asked known-answer, direct questions; (3) called the student's attention to critical features of the text; (4) talked explicitly about strategic action that readers can utilize; and (5) confirmed the student's responses. In addition to the teaching moves listed in Figure 6–1, we should frequently remind students to take specific action (e.g., "Read it again") or provide a label for the student's actions and thinking (e.g., "That makes sense"):

Mary: You said *coloring* [a substitution error for the word *drawing*] and that makes sense, doesn't it? But what letter does *coloring* start with?

Student: *C?*

Mary: *C.* And what does this word start with?

Student: D.

Mary: And what else?

Student: R.

Mary: Okay. Check it. Read it again and start that word.

Student: I am drawing.

Mary: It's *drawing*. What does that *D-R* say?

Student: Dr . . . drawing.

Mary: I am drawing. Does that make sense and sound right to you?

Some of the teaching moves can also be thought of as either feedforward or feedback (see Figure 6–2), with feed forward providing an orientation to the task and feedback some knowledge of results (Bruner 1974).

FIGURE 6–2
Feedforward and Feedback, and Teachers' Scaffolding Decisions

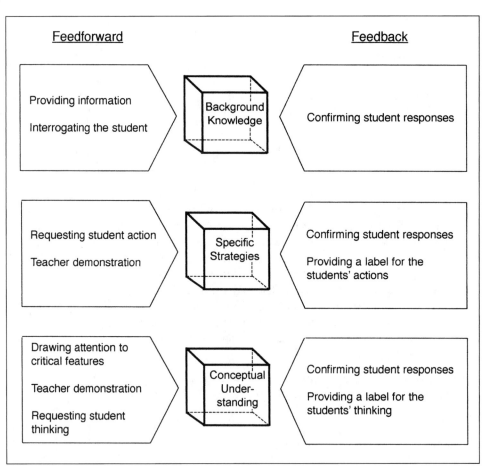

Requesting student thinking about how a difficult word might be solved (or was solved) can serve as feedforward for the ways in which readers work on words in order to extract messages from text, as in, "Why did you stop?" It is important to notice here that a teacher's request for student thinking to occur does not necessarily require a verbal response (especially for young children).

Similarly, the teacher's labeling in strategic terms of the work a student carried out to assist herself can serve to provide feedback to the student: "You reread that part and thought about what would sound right." The student may have, in fact, carried out those strategies and actions without being consciously or verbally aware of having done so.

Many students not only need to be scaffolded in their work to discover *what* actions to take (such as rereading a portion of the text when a difficulty is encountered) but how, when, and why such actions are likely to be useful. Declarative knowledge (Paris, Lipson, and Wixson 1994) includes knowing that there is a set of useful ways for thinking and acting about word solving; readers need to monitor meaning while they are reading and reread and self-correct words when necessary. Procedural knowledge includes knowing how each of these actions can be carried out during text reading. Can the reader recognize a word choice that does not make sense, either in general or in light of the plot and information of a particular text? Does the reader know how far back to go within the text when rereading? Conditional knowledge includes knowing when and why it could be appropriate to read a word, a sentence, or a page again or to look for part of a word that the reader already knows.

Teaching prompts can be conceptualized as existing along a rough scale of difficulty, from high amounts of teacher support provided to minimal teacher support. Prompts that request a specific action from the reader (e.g., "Say the ending part") or directly identify a critical feature that the reader should notice (e.g., "What would the character say next?") typically comprise high teacher support. Prompts that ask for a more general response from the student (e.g., "Try that again") comprise lower levels of teacher support.

As teachers work to scaffold their students' text reading, they are helping students to develop the background knowledge, specific strategies, and conceptual understanding needed in order to learn how to solve words more and more independently during text reading. It is the specific aspects of scaffolding along several dimensions that will be likely to transform prompting during text reading into a true dialogue about reading strategies between teachers and students.

In addition, then, to having a set of useful prompts memorized, teachers need to work to develop a sense of the use of these prompts for (1) teacher demonstration, requests for students' thinking and acting, and teacher labeling; (2) feedforward or feedback; (3) the development of declarative, procedural, and conditional knowledge about strategies; and (4) adjustment relative to the degree of teacher support currently needed by the students.

Reflection along these lines described will lead to a useful analytic stance; evaluating if, when, and what kind of teacher assistance would be useful to the students' growth in knowledge, strategies, and conceptual understanding. Are you seeing appropriate change in students' thinking and performance as a result of scaffolding during text reading? Learning how to scaffold students' text reading effectively typically develops over time in response to teachers' (1) experience in small group reading lessons, (2) careful observation of students' responses and progress, and (3) conversations with other teachers and instructional coaches. One of the ways you can evaluate your own scaffolding of students' text reading is by asking whether the prompting language you are using has altered over time in response to your students' understandings and strategic actions as well as to your own deeper levels of expertise.

FINE-TUNING SCAFFOLDING INTERACTIONS DURING TEXT READING

There are five general ways to fine-tune scaffolding when prompting students during text reading, and they are shown in Figure 6–3.

FIGURE 6–3
Fine-Tuning Scaffolding

Fine-Tuning Scaffolding
1. Know when you're telling
2. Avoid word inducing
3. Remember to prompt to visual information
4. Don't forget meaning
5. Prompt for structure, too

Know When You're Telling

Be wary of falling into a recurring conversational pattern where you provide a prompt or two and eventually tell the student the word in question. In the following excerpt, the teacher is attempting to get her student to notice the substitution error of *laying* for *resting*, and then to problem-solve the correct word *resting:*

Teacher: Okay. He's laying and he could be sleeping. What does the first letter begin with?

Student: *R.*

Teacher: When you don't know it, this is what I want you to do. I want you to say, "I am. . . ." and then I want you to make that first sound. What is he doing?

Student: He's laying.

Teacher: He's laying down, but that doesn't start with /r/. He's resting.

Student: I am resting.

In this interaction, even though the student was eventually able to read the word, it's doubtful that his use of strategies was scaffolded. It's easy to overlook the fact that the student was able to read the word because the teacher said it, not through any problem solving.

While reading the next text excerpt, take the child's perspective and ask yourself what the child has learned about problem solving that can be used the next time a difficult word is encountered.

Teacher: What's he cleaning?

Student: A house.

Teacher: Not a house. It's a *W.*

Student: Wall.

Teacher: It's a window. So dad is a window cl . . . cleaner. I like the way you went back and started all over again. Dad . . .

Student: [reading] Dad is a [long pause].

Teacher: Window.

Student: Window [long pause].

Teacher: Window cleaner.

Just like the previous interaction, even though the student is eventually able to read the difficult word, it's questionable whether the student's word problem solving was scaffolded. Instead of engaging in problem solving, the student is simply repeating the word that the teacher told twice.

The teacher in the following excerpt acknowledges how easy it is to tell a student a word and then mistakenly attribute the solving to the student.

> I need to have them learn to be independent in their problem solving. And I find myself, I'm saying, "sh . . . out." And then I'll say, "Oh good. He got it." But no, he didn't, I did. And I think that I [need to] pull back and let them solve the problems, but still teach along the way. It's difficult to know how much support to give.

So one way to fine-tune scaffolding is to be aware of how the problem solving came about. Was it because you told the student the word or because you prompted the student to take some problem-solving action that can be used again?

Scaffolding has occurred where teachers' decisions for their prompting of students can focus on helping students to transform the ways they think about reading tasks and the actions they take to assist themselves. Where teachers tailor their conversation with students such that they are responding to what the students are trying to do, scaffolding is more likely to occur.

In this last example, the teacher prompts the student several times in order to solve *window*, but notice how she doesn't simply tell the student the word:

Teacher: What's he cleaning?

Student: A house.

Teacher: Not a house. It's a W. [pointing to the letter w in window]

Student: Wall.

Teacher: Yes, *wall* starts with a W and might make sense. But does that look like *wall?*

In this third interaction, the teacher is prompting the student to think about meaning ("What's he cleaning?"), visual information ("It's a W") and then supporting the student to weigh up both meaning and visual information together ("*wall* starts with a W and might make sense, but does that look like a wall?"). In this example, the teacher is scaffolding the student's ways of knowing and acting during problem solving—ways that the student can apply to the next encounter with a difficult word.

Avoid Word Inducing

As we saw in the previous section, not all prompting scaffolds problem solving. While these interactions may result in the student accurately reading the word, the student's thinking and acting may not have been transformed because it was the teacher who solved the word. A second kind of prompting to fine-tune is the kind of assistance that amounts to inducing a word. In the example that follows, the student problem-solves the word but likely hasn't learned anything that will help with the next unfamiliar word.

Teacher: It rhymes with *awake*. What could you do if you were awakened by a noise and you thought it was a monster? It made me . . . [the teacher shakes his body, acting out the phrase *shake with fear*]

Teacher: It has to start with an *S-H*. Shake.

Student: [reading] Shake with fear.

It is important to ask whether the ways of thinking and acting that are being demonstrated and prompted for by the teacher for word solving in that example are going to be helpful to the child in future word solving. It's unlikely. The hints or prompts that the teacher used do not equip the child to use sources of information differently the next time. In fact, the ways of thinking and acting that the teacher is demonstrating are available only to the teacher and only because he already knows what the text says.

Remember to Prompt to Visual Information

A third way to fine-tune your scaffolding is to remember to prompt to visual information rather than avoiding it or doing so only in limited ways. A first-grade teacher was exactly right when she commented that

Some words you just can't figure out by looking at the picture. And if they know those other strategies that deal with visual information I think that they would have a better shot at figuring them out without my help.

In the previous transcript, the teacher referred primarily to initial letters as a critical feature for the purposes of word solving. Although initial letters can be a good "way in" for beginning readers who are not yet decoding in more sophisticated ways, it is also essential that beginning readers show consistent growth in their ability to use many kinds of phonetic or visual cues. Even for beginning readers, for example, the teacher can demonstrate how to clap a word, hear the parts within the word, and then locate those parts within the text:

Teacher: Yes, that word is *window*. Clap *window*. Clap it again and hear the parts, *win-dow*. Let's see what those parts look like in the book.

The teacher's demonstrations showing children a variety of ways to tell whether a word looks right or not should evolve over time, so that they are requesting such thinking and acting from students where it is appropriate and students are transforming their ways of working on print as a result. In the following interaction, the teacher is showing the student a useful way to solve the word *better*:

Teacher: Go back and reread it if you need to. Start that word.

Teacher: [writing the word *get* on a Post-it note] Do you know that word?

Student: Get.

Teacher: It's like that word. Find the parts that you know.

Student: Et. Bet. Better.

Teacher: How did you know?

Student: Because I saw the *E-R* too.

Should beginning readers be taught to regularly and laboriously sound out word after word, letter by letter while they are reading text? Should beginning readers be taught to simply guess at what a particular word in text might be? Beginning readers should over time be able to decode phonetically regular words letter by letter, but should not need to do so on a regular basis. Beginning readers in fact need to learn how to utilize all sources of information in a more and more complex and sophisticated manner over time. This is not only a matter of knowledge of phonetic elements, but of learning how to locate and use these items within text:

Faced with the challenges of beginning reading the child develops a scanning sequence that is appropriate for printed text, and practices this scanning pattern until it becomes habitual. While he engages in the formation of this scanning process, he simultaneously learns more and more about the detailed patterns in print. (Clay 1991, 263)

Given the nature of strategies and of scaffolding, we can speculate that students' learning of a variety of strategies that they can use to access the phonetic information within words in text will not only provide opportunities for the application of their current phonetic knowledge but of an extension of that knowledge as well. Having understood that it is helpful to look for known orthographic patterns within difficult words (e.g., *et* as in *get*), students are also likely to listen and look for these patterns within other words learned and solved. We might conceptualize strategies, then, as skills under construction.

Don't Forget Meaning

A fourth way to fine-tune scaffolding is to remember the role of meaning- or language-based sources of information. Beginning readers should learn to maintain a consistent focus on the meaning of the texts they are reading, with meaning as both the product and process of reading (Clay 1991). The meaning of texts (i.e., information, plots, characterization, and concepts) should be comprehended and used by the reader for assistance with any necessary problem solving of difficult words. When David, a first-grade teacher, began to understand the importance of prompting students to pay attention to meaning-based information when reading text, he primarily used the prompt "Look at the picture":

Student: [sounding out the word *broccoli* letter by letter] b . . . rrr . . . o . . . c . . .

Teacher: [pointing to the picture in the text] What vegetable does that look like?

Student: Broccoli.

Teacher: [nods his head yes]

David commented initially that one of his strengths as a reading teacher was "pushing" students by choosing harder texts for them to read:

> I feel like one of the good things I do is I push them. Even if they don't get through it perfectly . . . I would rather try a harder book and know that they feel confident that they got through it.

Although the pictures in very early emergent reader texts do in fact tell a great deal of the story and can be used as a source of information, it is thinking about background knowledge, the plot, and language of the story that will best serve readers' purposes. After some further experience with reading group instruction and reflection on the responses of his students, David began to prompt to the plot of texts rather than just to the pictures:

Teacher: They're telling us the sequence of events. First they planted the seeds, then they watered the seeds, soon they saw the plants growing. Think about what would make sense here.

Student: The yellow flowers.

Teacher: So, start that word and see what would make sense.

Student: [reading] Ne . . . next we saw little yellow flowers on the plants.

Teacher: Did that make sense and look right?

Student: Yeah, because it's got *X* like *fox* and then a *T*.

As David's prompting of his students during text reading became more complex and more interactive, he continued to emphasize that it is important to push students but to do so through scaffolding rather than just giving students harder text to read. David said

> I think it's working well . . . I've noticed, I was really worried about getting the kids to [understand]. But ever since I've started doing this, I'm pushing, pushing, pushing, and it's getting better. . . . The more they work with those [prompts] and they think about what I've told them, the better it's getting.

David also began to scaffold students' use of both meaning and phonetic information in a more integrated fashion:

Teacher: [As the student has become stuck on the word *brand* in *brand-new bike*] Is there a word you know in here?

Student: [shakes head no]

Teacher: *A-N-D.*

Student: And.

Teacher: Now, what kind of bike is this? It's a . . .

Student: [reading] And, br . . . and, brand-new bike.

At this point in his own learning, David observed that his students appeared to be internalizing his demonstrations and prompts for student action that he had been utilizing within his prompting:

> I've seen progress, I think so. A lot more than I was before the [prompting]. Because I wasn't giving them enough to think about, enough information about what to do, in their heads. So that they could come back and say, "Okay I need to look at the picture, and then reread the sentence. What would make sense?" For them to start thinking it themselves [and] internalizing it.

The concept of the learner's internalization of ways of thinking and acting is an important one from the perspective of scaffolding. Both over time and for each particular strategy or concept, students take over responsibility for understanding and acting. They are then able to solve words with less teacher support than was needed in the preceding lessons.

Prompt for Structure, Too

Beginning readers are language learners. Although primary grade children typically use and understand a large vocabulary set and many different language structures, they have much more to learn in this vital area. Helping students to develop strategies and ways of thinking using their existing language knowledge as a source of information for their problem solving of difficult words can be very powerful. An earlier example showing the teacher's scaffolding for the difficult word *brand* could be improved by a reminder to the student that language is a helpful source of information.

Teacher: [As the student has become stuck on the word *brand* in *brand-new bike*] Is there a word you know in here?

Student: [shakes head no]

Teacher: *A-N-D.*

Student: And.

Teacher: Now, what kind of bike is this? *Think about what word would sound right in this sentence.* It's a . . .

Student: [reading] And, br . . . and, brand-new bike.

Additionally, be prepared to simply and directly teach new language structures where needed:

Student: [reading] Peter was first asleep. [rereading and self-correcting] Peter was f . . . fast asleep.

Teacher: You did a great job. You know what? You got here and it didn't make any sense. Have you ever heard anyone say that?

Student: [rereading] Peter was fast asleep.

Teacher: Peter was fast asleep. It's like sound asleep. And it was a good thing, wasn't it? What if dad didn't like hot cocoa?

Student: He didn't drink his own.

Teacher: That's right. He didn't stay awake. Dad had to just drink it. Hopefully he likes [cocoa], huh?

SUMMARY

Given the nature of scaffolding, it is helpful to conceive of your role during students' text reading as one of an interaction between (1) your own knowledge of how, when, and why beginning readers need to think and act in specific, strategic ways; and (2) the changing competencies of the individual children you are working with. This perspective requires a view of scaffolding as a complex set of interactions between teachers and students rather than a linear and prescriptive phenomenon (Many 2002).

This chapter has focused on the ways in which teachers can effectively scaffold the word problem solving of individual children. It is, of course, important to state that such scaffolding does not necessarily occur between one teacher and one student, but between a teacher and one or more students and from student to student as well. Learning how to effectively scaffold students' word problem solving during text reading encompasses a set of skills and conceptual understanding that are useful within almost any type of reading program or classroom organization for instruction. This area of learning is complex and challenging. The teachers in the two case studies reported here were actively seeking assistance from their own analyses of students' responses and from colleagues and other experts. Although the types of scaffolding that have been analyzed for this chapter are typically utilized intensively during small group reading instruction, the results of such instructional conversations should be well supported by and pervasive within a variety of other classroom contexts:

> Nearby, three other students use a long pointer to read a chart of *The Itsy Bitsy Spider* together. As they finish reading, Sarah says, "Hey look! The letter's like my name!" Marissa adds her own comment: "I got a mistake, but I fixed it up!"

NEXT STEPS FOR TEACHERS: SUGGESTED READINGS

Reading Instruction

Fountas, I. C., and G. S. Pinnell. 1996. *Guided Reading. Good First Teaching for All Children.* Portsmouth, NH: Heinemann.

———. 1999. *Matching Books to Readers. Using Leveled Books in Guided Reading, K–3.* Portsmouth, NH: Heinemann.

Pressley, M. 2002. *Reading Instruction That Works.* 2d ed. New York: Guilford Press.

Language Development and Classroom Instruction

Clay, M. M., M. Gill, T. Glynn, T. McNaughton, and K. Salmon. 1983. *Record of Oral Language and Biks and Gutches.* Auckland, NZ: Heinemann.

Wells, G. 1986. *The Meaning Makers. Children Learning Language and Using Language to Learn.* Portsmouth, NH: Heinemann.

Wood, D. 1999. *How Children Think and Learn.* 2d ed. Malden, MA: Blackwell.

AUTHOR ACKNOWLEDGMENTS

The author thanks the Martha Holden Jennings Foundation for their generous funding of one of the research studies from which material was drawn for this chapter.

The author gratefully acknowledges the expert assistance of the following mentors: Professors Gay Su Pinnell, Caroline T. Clark, Karin L. Dahl, Ian A. G. Wilkinson, and Patricia L. Scharer. The author is also deeply indebted to the talented and courageous teachers who participated in these studies.

7 | USING PEER PARTNERSHIPS TO SCAFFOLD READING

MARY LEE PRESCOTT-GRIFFIN

Nestled in one of several classroom reading nooks, Bobby and Pete sit side by side in a cocoon of pillows. Bobby holds a copy of *Big Egg* (Coxe 1997), a story that tells of a very large egg which lands in a hen's nest. This inspires both the characters in the story and the readers of the story to speculate as to the kind of creature that will hatch from *the big egg*. Pete rests his head on Bobby's shoulder, his eyes following along as Bobby reads, beginning on page 22.

Bobby	Pete
(looks at Pete, smiles) It's my egg! He just takes it. *The small eggs* (pauses on *crack*)	
	(Leans forward, studying the pictures.) Think it's a monster?
(shrugs) *The small eggs . . . crack.* (Bobby turns to page 23.) *P-p—peep! Peep*	
	(laughs) Peep, peep, peep, peep!
Peep! Peep! . . . say the small chicks. (Bobby turns to page 24.) (pauses, studying the word *squawk*) *Squ—squ—* *SQUAWK!*	

SQUAWK!

SQUAWK! (adds) squawk,
squawk, squawk . . . *says
the big*

chick.

duck (for *chick*)

ch-ch-chicken.

That's not a chicken or a goose or an ostrich.

Note: *Italics* = text read; regular print = children's conversational remarks

* * *

Peers, as young as first graders, can and do scaffold one another's reading if they are given the context to do so, and the guidance to understand their roles.

MacGillivray writes that "classroom communities construct their own view of what it means to read through daily interactions with each other, the world around them, and print" (1997, 145). As Bobby and Pete make their way through *Big Egg* (Coxe 1997), they construct a mutually defined view of reading that suits them as peer partners. In tandem, they discuss, play, and read their way through this tale of a very large egg that lands in a hen's nest, inspiring a great deal of speculation as to the sort of creature that might be inside the big egg.

Peer partnerships differ from "buddy reading" (Samway, Whang, and Pippitt 1995) and cross-age or cross-ability paired reading (Muldowney 1995; Nes 1997; Topping and Lindsay 1992). Unlike these models, where an experienced child or adult is paired with a younger reader, peer partnerships involve beginning readers of approximately equal expertise. When partners are at approximately the same level, they are able to construct text collaboratively, without a stronger, more experienced reader usurping the task from the less experienced or struggling reader. In peer partnerships, each reader brings expertise to the task, drawing from a unique background and set of skills.

Peer partners often converse, creating and maintaining shared contexts supportive of their reading development. Most talk, rather than distracting readers or pulling them off-task, serves to organize the activity setting and keep partners involved and interested in text. Bobby and Pete are immersed in a continual process of text construction and meaning making as they move fluently through each page of *Big Egg*. Their focus repeatedly shifts from print to pictures as they make predictions, conjectures, and comments concerning the narrative, reading and playing with the story's simple, repetitive language. Their interaction demonstrates the scaffolding, as defined by Wood, Bruner, and Ross (1976), that readers give each other as they collaboratively and individually move toward independence as readers.

My excitement about the learning potential of peer partnerships, especially children's scaffolding and assistance of one another, led me to study these relationships more closely in my own first-grade classroom. I had often asked my first graders to "pair up" and read together for twenty to thirty minutes when they arrived in the morning. The structure was simple. Children would greet me, take care of their morning jobs, find their reading buddy (usually a person suggested or assigned by me), gather books, and sit down to read. As I moved among reading pairs, pausing to listen, offer encouragement, or lend support, I observed many instances of collaboration, scaffolding, teaching, conferring, questioning, and suggesting. The examples of partner talk that follow illustrate the kinds of assistance or scaffolding that I overheard my students providing to one another as they read:

"Why don't you use your finger?"
"Try that again."
"If we read it fast it might sound better."
"What if we saw the monster?"
"This [word] starts with the same sound as your name."
"I'm the jet. Watch me fly!"
"Just cover the last part and do this part first."

Heads together, fingers pressed to the page, they processed the text in tandem, each supplying a word or phrase as they were able, constructing text, sometimes word by word, together.

Fascinated by the informal data I was gathering, I began to research the literature. While I found many resources on learning collaborations and a number on cross-ability paired reading, where a more capable peer or adult pairs with a younger reader to scaffold reading, there were only a few resources devoted to beginning readers' peer partner interactions (MacGillivray 1997; MacGillivray and Hawes 1994). Wanting to learn more, I conducted my study of peer partnerships with my students over one full school year. This chapter describes the findings of that initial study where I observed my students in daily collaboration over new and familiar texts.

THE SOCIAL NATURE OF LEARNING

Watson, Burke, and Harste (1989) state that "when we cooperate we work towards some mutual goal, but when we collaborate we expect to go out changed in the end, to become a different person" (65). This statement speaks to why we should create peer partnerships for our youngest readers. The key to learning, according to Vygotsky (1978), does not lie in the child's innate ability, but in the social support received from adults or peers. Social support, embodied in young children's verbal and nonverbal behaviors when reading as peer partners, provides both a context and rationale for using this strategy during independent reading time. As emergent readers of approximately equal expertise pool their resources in task-related endeavor, shared motivation develops (Tharp and Gallimore 1988). Through collaborative interaction with peers, students develop cognitive capacities as they are helped toward greater independence as readers, arguably an important goal of any literacy program.

Approximately equal expertise does not mean the *same* expertise. Collaborators compensate "for each other's blind spots" (Olby 1970, 963) When young children read, there are many blind spots—unknown words, confusing language, and misinterpretations of text. Even the structure of books may be blinding, unfamiliar territory for the beginning reader. Emergent peer partners bring different capacities and strengths to the shared task of reading, capabilities and strengths that allow them to read longer with less struggle, and more enjoyment. "Collaboration operates through a process in which the successful intellectual achievements of one person arouse the intellectual passions and enthusiasms of others, and through the fact that what was first expressed only by one individual becomes a common intellectual possession instead of fading away into isolation" (Olby 1970, 963). This is a beautiful description of how first graders work, arousing the passions and interests of one another, sharing a thought, an idea, a book, or a project, their common intellectual ownership becoming an integral part of their learning.

CONDUCTING THE STUDY

Since I sought to expand my understanding about beginning reading in a social context, I studied Vygotsky's (1978) theory of the zone of proximal development. He defines it as "the distance between the actual developmental level as determined by independent problem solving and the level of potential development as determined through problem solving under adult guidance or in collaboration with more capable peers" (86). In observing emergent readers of approximately equal expertise, I wondered if the role of capable peer, rather than being fixed, might instead involve continual shifts from learner to learner as children scaffold each other's text. I also wondered what I, as the teacher, might do to encourage partners' scaffolding, assistance, and collaboration with each other.

The central question guiding all phases of my research was, How do emergent[1] first-grade readers of approximately equal expertise influence one another when reading as partners? In exploring readers' behaviors, the influences of the social context on partner behaviors emerged as a parallel focus. The questions that guided my study and their relation to my analysis are outlined in Figure 7–1.

---

[1]The definition of "emergent readers" used in this study was taken from Fountas and Pinnell (1996). According to Fountas and Pinnell, emergent readers are "just beginning to control early behavior such as directionality and word-by-word matching. They use pictures to support meaning and rely on language as a strong cueing system" (177).

Phases of Data Collection and Analysis

Phase	Research Questions	Data Collection and Analysis
1	1. How do emergent readers influence one another when reading as partners? 2. How should students be paired in order to maximize assistance? 3. How do the following student behaviors relate to collaboration in reading events: word-by-word switching, verbal play, off-text remarks and nonverbal gestures. 4. What were students' perspectives about reading with a partner? 5. What kinds of books enhanced or hindered collaboration?	• Assessed students' reading in order to pair them • Made changes in pairings as needed • Maintained a research log and transcribed field notes • Selected and focused on certain behaviors *and* readers through use of two cameras during final weeks • Viewed all videotapes, collecting verbal and nonverbal behaviors • Conducted student interviews • Collected and examined texts readers choose
2	6. How should data be transcribed in order to capture students' interactional behaviors?	• Sent interview tapes to be transcribed by an independent transcriber • Transcribed all videotaped sessions • Noted all miscues, additions, deletions, etc. in transcriptions • Focused coding on interactional behaviors and sequences • Retained 22 videotaped sessions for analysis
3	7. What is the influence of readers' behaviors on each other? 8. What is the influence of social context on readers? 9. What is the influence of readers on social context? 10. What kinds of behavior signal reader involvement? 11. What effect do teacher-facilitated strategy sessions have on reading pairs?	• Focused on interactional behaviors in making coding decisions • Created summaries of all partner interactions • Triangulated and compared specific behaviors to influences of classroom context, strategy sessions, and teacher modeling
4	12. What is the structure of reading events? 13. What behaviors enhance/inhibit collaboration and assistance? 14. What behaviors enhance/inhibit understanding? 15. What behaviors display reader confidence? 16. What is the structure and function of word-by-word switching, verbal play, and off-text conversation? 17. What do negative sequences reveal about reading in partnership? 18. How does turn-taking structure influence tone of reading events?	• Collected and reexamined all behaviors, particularly word-by-word switching, verbal play, and oral language use • Mapped word-by-word switching sequences • Collected and analyzed behaviors related to control, turn-taking and organizational structures • Classified tone of each session • Examined negative aspects of paired reading • Compared turn-taking strategies and tone of interactions
5	19. How do teacher and student define reading in social context? 20. Does where partners read influence their behaviors? 21. How do successful and less successful collaborators define reading in partnership? 22. How does classroom context (teacher, curriculum, and classroom rules) influence reading partners' behavior?	• Compared and reexamined all data sources • Compared tone of the interaction and location for reading • Compared data reviewers' observations with those of the researcher and those of the students, focusing on definitions of reading • Examined leadership in paired reading events and its presence or absence in relation to overall tone and turn-taking strategies (Griffin 2000)

FIGURE 7–1 *Phases of Data Collection and Analysis*

The nature of this study dictated that I would need to collect data in the fall of first grade when most students were still at an emergent reading level. In early fall, I established classroom routines for independent reading. I used an informal reading inventory, the *Bader Reading and Language Inventory* (Bader 1983), as well as running records (Clay 2002) and daily observations to determine children's reading levels. Using the data from these informal assessments and taking social relationships into account, I paired readers of approximately equal expertise and began collecting data.

In qualitative research, collecting data from multiple sources enhances the validity of finding. I collected data on paired readings in my classroom in several ways. I

- kept a research log of my observations,
- audio- and videotaped their readings and transcribed events, and
- interviewed the students about their perspectives on shared reading.

As a teacher in this setting, I brought an insider's view to interpreting the data because of my closeness to the setting and students.

SCAFFOLDS TO LEARNING IN PEER-PARTNERED READING

The vignette at the beginning of this chapter illustrates two students' scaffolding one another's reading in a peer-partnered setting. In the remainder of this chapter, I will describe how peer partnering provides opportunities for scaffolding reading, and then I will describe how a classroom can be organized for peer-partnered reading.

SCAFFOLDING IN PEER-PARTNERED READING

Readers scaffolded one another in verbal and nonverbal ways. They offered hints and words of encouragement or gave brief instructions. They also supported one another's reading in nonverbal ways, the most frequently used being pointing. In the next two sections, I'll describe each of these scaffolds in more detail.

Pointing

Just as readers cue each other verbally with their talk by offering hints, words of encouragement, and brief instructions, they also scaffold and assist one another's learning through pointing.

In various forms, pointing provided scaffolding and assistance in several ways as partners worked together. I observed children pointing to track and match word-by-word, to assist one another with left-to-right decoding, to indicate turn taking, and to direct or refocus their partner's attention. The most frequent instances of pointing as scaffolding occurred when readers struggled with unfamiliar words, indicating that peers were using pointing in a strategic, helpful way, not haphazardly. At such times, a partner might point to assist with focus, point while telling the word, or point to give an orthographic cue (usually the initial sound).

The readers in my classroom usually pointed with their index finger, occasionally using an open hand with all fingers under a line of text. They also pointed with a closed fist or, in one case, a paper tube. Early in my analysis, I observed that pointing was used as a tool to scaffold or help oneself reading in tracking print.

It is interesting that partner-assisted pointing often evolved after instances of self-assisted pointing (pointing to assist self). When readers struggled with unfamiliar words, partners introduced pointing as a tool to scaffold decoding either by providing extra focus on the word or as an aid in left-right processing. In the latter form, a partner might either run a finger slowly under the word or cover part of the word, focusing the partner's attention on one syllable at a time.

Pointing was also used to indicate turn taking at the start of a new page of text. When used in this way, pointing is often accompanied by eye contact or a verbal cue such as, "Your turn . . . you read . . . okay." Other nonverbal ways partners indicated a switch in turn taking were eye signals, nudging, poking, tapping, flapping the book up and down, or waving the book in the partner's face.

Word-by-Word Switching

Often during peer-partnered reading, students used word-by-word switching to scaffold each other. I defined word-by-word switching as occasions when partners continually shifted the role of reader. This switching often contained multiple instances of scaffolding and seemed to be especially indicative of collaboration and joint construction of text (Griffin 2000). As I analyzed data, I found that word-by-word switching facilitates smooth and efficient reading. In the word-by-word switching sequences found in nine out of twenty-two paired reading events, readers appeared to be constructing text together, often word by word. The following example illustrates two readers, Bobby and Pete, word-by-word switching as they move through the book *The Tiny Woman's Coat* (Cowley 1987g, 9), pooling their expertise in order to successfully process text.

Bobby	Pete
	The tiny
woman put on her	*woman put on her*
coat	
and went out in the	*and went out in the*
	snow (for storm)
	(skips a line of text)
(points and redirects Pete's gaze)	

	Oh! (points to the line above)
	She (pauses on stayed)
stayed	*stayed*
as	
snug	*as*
bug in a rug	
in a rug	
	with with
a coat	*a coat*
to keep	
	to keep
her warm.	*her warm.*

Note: *Italics* = text read; regular print = children's conversational remarks

*   *   *

Embedded in this sequence of word-by-word switching are six instances of choral reading, when Bobby and Pete read words and larger segments of text together. In fact, I found choral reading to be present in all but one sequence of word-by-word switching. Both choral reading and word-by-word switching indicate active reader-to-reader scaffolding as partners pool expertise and share competence. Much more than simply who supplies a word at any given moment, word-by-word switching constitutes a meeting of the minds as young readers scaffold one another's thinking about structure, context, and visual cues in the text.

In terms of its boundaries and structure, word-by-word switching sometimes begins when one reader struggles and the partner steps in to assist. At other times, when reading challenging text chorally, readers may begin shifting responsibility for the reading of unfamiliar words from one reader to the other. Responsibility in these instances fall upon whomever possesses the necessary expertise, supplying a word or phrase at any given moment. This flexibility suggests that the role of capable peer shifts many times within these mutually defined, meaning-making interactions.

In another example, Bobby and Pete again share responsibility, word-by-word switching as they construct text of *Ira Sleeps Over* (Waber 1972).

Bobby (reading from page 20)	**Pete**
(points)	
in a	*in a*
	big hurry to

go

          someplace

suh (for see) *see you*

          tonight

tonight, he

said. See you   *said. See you*

I said

(Bobby turns to page 21)   *I said*

I (pauses on decided) *buh*

Teacher intervenes and tells the word, *decided.*

Note: *Italics* = text read

*   *   *

For most young children, books like *Ira Sleeps Over* are quite difficult, with their challenging vocabulary, smaller print, and more limited "white space" than books they chose to read independently. I deliberately chose more challenging texts because I wanted to provide opportunities for students to engage in problem solving while reading with a partner.

Before I began closely observing my students' interactions during reading, I would not have thought that peers could scaffold one another's reading. I thought that scaffolding occurred when partners of varying reading abilities were grouped (e.g., older students reading with younger students or more proficient readers reading with less proficient ones). My close observation of students in my first-grade class lends support to the notion that students of equal ability can also scaffold one another. I saw evidence of their scaffolding in their strategies of pointing to help their partner figure out a word and in their word-by-word switching as they read.

As every teacher knows, collaboration such as peer-partnered reading requires careful planning in order for the organization to be successful. Students need teacher guidance in order to learn how to work together. In the next section, I'll describe how to select books and organize the classroom for peer-partnered reading.

Selecting Books for Peer-Partnered Reading

Books provide literate building blocks for peer partners. They zip through patterned, predictable text with joyous familiarity (Martin and Brogan 1972).

They often use predictable, patterned texts to stretch their reading muscles before tackling more challenging text. With warm-up books such as *The Long Long Tail* or *Snap!* (Cowley 1987a, 1987e), children's familiarity with the book allows for silliness—funny voices, singsong delivery, and off-text remarks. Rather than detracting from the reading experience, however, the silliness seems to enhance collaboration, drawing readers together in shared conspiratorial fun.

The spirit of buoyant confidence developed through reading the warm-up books often carries over into greater ease and fluency with more difficult text.

Noise by Joy Cowley (1987c), for example, draws the listening partner into active collaboration. In this case, the "noise" words "yukka-dukka, yukka-dukka, ya, ya, ya" calls back partners whose attention may have wandered, retaining their focus and involvement for the remainder of the book. In one instance in my research, the listener then offered support with unfamiliar words as the reader continued through the text, the listener spontaneously joining in on the remaining choruses of "yukka-dukkas." This interaction occurred within a negotiated context where readers had previously decided to take turns reading a whole book to each other. The listener's role in this case appeared to be as audience and supporter. Several other reading partnerships demonstrated similar behaviors when reading *Noise*, such as joining in on the chorus of "yukka dukkas." These behaviors were evident when children alternated page reading or read chorally.

Spider Spider, also by Joy Cowley (1987f), is another example of a predictable text with repetitive language. It draws readers (and listeners) in, provoking a variety of behaviors—rereading for fun, echoing partner's reading of a page, off-text remarks (about the pictures, science concepts), and listener's finger-pointing to aid reader's focus. These behaviors serve to involve readers more deeply in the process rather than drawing them away.

Mr. Grump by Joy Cowley (1987b), a popular choice for many reading pairs, proved to be a text that encouraged collaboration and off-text remarks, bringing readers together in shared enjoyment. I observed four reading pairs engage in word-by-word switching while reading this book, often with spontaneous choral reading of the chorus "Mr. Grump, Mr. Grump, Mr. Grump, grump, grump" in all cases except one. One reader extended this chorus by adding many extra "grumps," to the delight of his partner. His partner, playing off of his lead, created an innovation—a chorus of "Mr. Happy, Mr. Happy, Mr. Happy, happy, happy," echoing the linguistic patterning while foreshadowing the story's happy conclusion. *Ratty Tatty* (Cowley 1987d), another popular choice, elicited similar behaviors.

Picture books such as *Five Little Ducks* (Aruego and Dewey 1986) contain words from familiar children's songs, presenting yet another type of predictable text. This singable text elicited unique behaviors not observed in other types of predictable texts. As one would expect, readers often sang the story, their singing enhancing fluency, confidence, and fun. Singing kept motivation high as they negotiated their way through the more difficult passages where the text patterns changed. For example, the spirited singing of two boys as they read/sang *Down by the Bay* (Westcott 1988) carried over into their subsequent reading of other books as they attempted to sing new books to the tune of *Down by the Bay*. Several pages into the new text, singing tapered off, evolving into a drawl that readers continued through the reading of several more books. Drawling served to maintain rhythm, sustain interest, and boost readers' confidence.

In addition to predictable texts and picture books, peer partners occasionally chose to read decodable texts. Decodable texts focus the readers' attention on print by using words with particular rimes or vowels repeated throughout, with meaning of secondary concern. As such, they reinforced children's growing awareness of the alphabetic nature of language. While a basket of short, decodable texts was always available to my students, independent readers or peer partners selected only a few with regularity. Three decodable texts that partners read during observations for this study were *The Jet* (Makar 1980b), *Meg* (Makar 1980c), and *Cop Cat* (Makar 1980a).

Children often do surprising things with decodable text. *The Jet* provoked active, thoughtful joint construction with sustained sequences of word-by-word switching and spontaneous, choral reading. In all twelve observations of peer partners reading decodable text, partners alternated page reading. In none of the twelve interactions did one partner become so carried away by the story that he or she read on, forgetting to give the partner a turn (a common occurrence when reading predictable, repetitive text). Peer partners' reading in decodable text tends to be slow and plodding, with children often using a finger to keep place or focus their partner's attention. While illustrations in most little books create important scaffolds for beginning readers (Hiebert 1999, 559), this type of scaffolding was limited in the decodable texts available in my classroom. The simple line drawings failed to capture the listening partner's attention as effectively as did the colorful illustrations in other books. This often precipitated a breakdown in collaboration, as the listening partner disengaged, no longer providing assistance, support, and audience for the reading partner.

Organizing the Classroom Environment for Peer-Partnered Reading

The classroom's routines and literacy practices must be given special attention when organizing for peer-partnered reading.

Frequently during the first half of the year, children would read with peer partners during independent reading time. Independent reading began the first day of school when I helped students to select "just right books" and encouraged them to explore and read them for fifteen to twenty minutes. This independent reading time increased as the year progressed from thirty to sixty minutes and children took over my role of selecting books. Ordinarily they did this first thing in the morning by organizing their day's books in their reading baskets.

Pairing Students

I paired children of approximately equal expertise, taking into account their social and emotional needs as well as reader interests. I then provided guidelines for children that included making good book choices and choosing books so that partner reading time would be spent reading. Usually, children selected books independently or with their partners first thing in the morning and placed them on the side of their desks or in their individual "book baskets" until partner reading began.

During partner reading time, I circulated around the room, providing guidance and encouragement to partners as well as drawing attention to responsible collaborative behaviors.

Teaching Strategies for Peer-Partnered Reading

During writing workshop, Calkins (1986) uses minilessons as a kind of scaffolding process, grounded in modeling theory, direct instruction, and developmental theory (Bruner and Ratner 1978; Cazden 1988; Graves 1984). Drawing on Calkins' work, I considered the scaffolding potential inherent in reading minilessons and brainstorming sessions devoted to strategies for partner reading. If, as Fosnot (1996) argues, these sessions perturb the learner, contradicting what he or she thinks is good reading behavior, do children return to reading with new, evaluative perspectives with which to examine their own behaviors? While an examination of the data found no direct connections between a particular session and subsequent changes in reading partners' behaviors, the opportunity to share strategies would seem, at the very least, to increase readers' meta-awareness of their own behavior. The minilessons described below focus both on general reading strategies and on strategies and ideas specific to peer partnerships.

Reading minilessons began the first week of school and covered a variety of topics, such as

- reading from left to right
- reading a book in different ways (pictures, text, etc.)
- deciding what to do when encountering an unfamiliar word
- choosing appropriate books
- using classroom libraries, book bins, and bookmarks (line markers)
- pointing to keep your place
- matching print word by word
- using the word wall
- reading within your space (using a quiet reading voice)
- asking for help
- using semantic clues to help decoding efforts

All of the above lessons as well as a number of others were covered in the first few months of school. Such strategies were then revisited with the whole class and individually by reminders before or during reading or by discussions after reading about strategies students had used.

Reading minilessons began in early October and continued throughout the year. While the lessons were teacher-facilitated, they often took the form of brainstorming sessions[2] where the children's ideas were solicited and

---

[2]By early October, these students were already experienced "brainstormers." Their ideas and suggestions had been solicited in establishing class and playground rules, planning science and social study units, deciding how to spend afternoon activity periods, and selecting projects they would enjoy during free time (arts and crafts activities, holiday events, science museums, etc.).

written on chart paper and posted on the wall (see Figure 7–2). During one session, I asked for volunteers to model a reading-partner behavior. Another session was initiated by two readers who volunteered to model choral reading for the class. These strategy sessions typically lasted for about five minutes, after which the children would pair up and begin reading. In addition to these whole class strategy sessions, other strategies and skills were suggested and reinforced as the teacher conferred with individual reading pairs.

During one minilesson I announced changes in partnerships and the children added to the strategies wall chart (see Figure 7–2). Another session (11-9-98) featured students modeling how to read side by side using quiet voices. Two partners volunteered to sit in front of the circle with the book *Ratty Tatty* (Cowley 1987d) between them. They read most of the book by taking turns reading each page. This alternating page-reading strategy was their own decision, made without teacher input. After they read, the group discussed what they had observed. The class then paired up to begin reading.

During the fifth minilesson devoted to partner reading (11-23-98), the children again added to the reading strategies wall chart, and we discussed what was working well. At a December session, two students demonstrated another paired-reading strategy, volunteering to model "reading at the same time" (their description of choral reading). They read three pages of *Mr. Grump* (Cowley 1987b) to the class. A short discussion followed, giving the other children a chance to share what they had observed.

Another session (1-5-99) had us gathered in front of the reading tools wall[3] where we read through the "strategies for pairs" wall chart, reviewing all ideas about strategies to help partners. The final strategy session that occurred during the study period was held on January 12, 1999. At this time, the children added to the partner strategies wall chart (see Figure 7–2).

Teaching Children to Take Turns

In analyzing data, I discovered a relationship between turn-taking structures and motivational homogeneity, or mutual situational definition of the task of reading. When my students took turns alternating page reading, they provided greater assistance and scaffolding to one another and engaged in collaborative behaviors such as word-by-word switching, choral reading, verbal play, and text-related discussion with much greater frequency. These behaviors then contributed to the overall positive tone of an interaction. When partners chose to read chorally, they also engaged in collaborative behaviors, literally building text in tandem. On the other hand, when readers took turns reading an entire book to one another, they engaged in little or no collaborative behavior, and their interactions were sometimes punctuated with unfriendly talk and behaviors.

---

[3]Reading tools consist of phonetic elements with pictures and mnemonic cues. Tools are posted as needed by the group.

Wall Chart of Student-Suggested Paired Reading Strategies				
SESSIONS	Session 2: Oct. 19, 1998	Session 3: Oct. 28, 1998	Session 5: Nov. 23, 1998	Session 8: Jan. 12, 1999
During each of these sessions, students were asked to contribute answers to the questions: (1) What can I do when my partner doesn't know a word? or more generally, (2) what can I do to help my partner? I then recorded answers on chart paper. Each session's responses were added to the existing wall chart. I often referred to the chart to remind students of ways to assist each other.	Students' suggestions were: • Tell the letter it starts with. • Say, "that starts like my name." • Give a hint. • Give a rhyming word. • Help sound it out. • Help break it up. • Ask your partner. • Ask a grown-up (teacher or other classroom helper).* *Note: I specified that this strategy must go last.	Students added the following suggestions: • Sound it out. • Look at the word wall. • Look at the reading tools. • Read the whole sentence.	Students added the following suggestions: • Tell your partner to skip the word and read ahead to see what makes sense. • Give a clue. • Tell your partner half of the word. • Say, "try to cut the word." • Say, "look at the pictures." • If the word is *horse*, say, "it lives on a farm."	Students added the following suggestions: • Think. • Look for the little words in the big word. • Try different letter sounds (e.g., short vowel e, or long vowel e). (Griffin 2000)

FIGURE 7–2
Wall Chart of Student-Suggested Paired Reading Strategies

While all students were acquainted with my expectations during partner reading—to share reading, to assist one's partner, and to spend reading time reading—my analysis of their interactions suggests that turn-taking structures impact heavily on children's ability to conform and honor classroom and teacher expectations. During brainstorming sessions, the children and I discussed and modeled several turn-taking frameworks (choral reading and alternating page reading); however, partners were free to use whatever organizational framework they wished. This may be too much freedom, and teachers may want to specify that partners either alternate pages or choral read during this time. When readers had no role in choosing a book and no apparent responsibility for reading it, they were not invested. Often, in such instances, while one person read the "whole book," the listener looked around the room or flipped through another book, while awaiting a turn.

WHAT I LEARNED ABOUT SCAFFOLDING

The notion of enhanced capacity when working with a peer suggests that there are resources available to learners over which they have explicit control only in collaborative contexts (Karmiloff-Smith 1979). Within the structural support provided by this classroom, peer partners demonstrated that they are well able to design and maintain collaborative, assisting systems accessing resources to enhance the reading process and scaffold one another's learning. When emergent readers work with the peers closest to them in development, they interact with readers whose imaginative and heuristic uses of language most closely match their own, readers in close relationship to their task (Tharp and Gallimore 1988). As Joan, a first-grade colleague and data reviewer, remarked, "their interaction provided instructional scaffolding. The children know instinctively when to mediate and when not to."

During brainstorming sessions, children shared strategies for assisting partners. In structuring and organizing reading events, they established shared definitions of reading that kept both readers focused and involved. Clearly, children's literacy development is not solely linked to teacher-student relationships or teacher-student scaffolding. When emergent readers are allowed to organize, plan, and structure their shared interactions, they work productively and collaboratively in processing texts of varying levels of difficulty, scaffolding each other's literacy development in substantive ways. My students displayed a complex and varied range of verbal and nonverbal behaviors, with gestures such as pointing serving multiple interactional functions. Organizational structures adopted by partners often determined the presence or absence of collaboration during reading events. Children used language to organize, structure, and negotiate decisions during reading events. Through language play, peer partners created supportive, interpersonal relationships that enhanced reader involvement and task persistence.

While my research into peer partnerships uncovered many aspects of these complex relationships, the following findings may assist teachers in planning and implementing peer partnerships in classrooms of beginning readers. Findings described include teacher and student roles and definitions of peer partner reading; the function of talk in peer partnerships; the concept of joint construction, or word-by-word switching; readers' relationships with books; and the organizational implications of readers' turn-taking decisions. Finally, I conclude with some suggestions for teachers interested in planning and structuring peer partnerships for beginning readers.

Teacher and Students' Roles and Definitions of Reading in Partnership

In this setting, my role as teacher was multifaceted and included all of the following: structuring, instructing, modeling, coaching, and conferring. I grouped students, then provided assistance as needed, constantly viewing and evaluating the effectiveness of reading partnerships. This dual role as viewer and evaluator helped me to support and encourage children's scaffolding of one another's reading. Sometimes, behaviors and strategies originally suggested by me during instructional times were volunteered by readers during strategy sessions. Also, my teaching behaviors such as pointing or cueing were often mirrored in student behaviors during reading events.

My analysis suggests that my definition of partner reading differed in form and function from student definitions. From my perspective, reading in partnership was defined as a process of *reader construction*, the listening partner providing assistance as needed while allowing the reader to retain ownership of the task. The goal in this view was *instruction* and the building and strengthening of *individual* readers' skills. Students, when allowed to control their activity settings, defined the task of partner reading somewhat differently.

For peer partners, the goal of reading was success for the *partnership,* and success was defined as smooth, fluent reading. While peer partners internalized, and indeed articulated, the importance of assistance and scaffolding, they often stepped in to usurp the task when the reader struggled, providing the kind of scaffolding that would maintain fluency and flow of the story. This is illustrated by the fact that the most frequently used cue, "telling the whole word," was also the most expedient. My analysis suggests that the process of gradual hinting was too slow for partners reluctant to pause in their mutually defined, meaning-making process. In comparing data sources, I also wonder if readers' expedience might be linked to the notion of shifting expertise since behaviors such as word-by-word switching involve frequent shifts in ownership of task.

Through talk and gesture, successful peer partners created structures to support and maintain reading effectiveness. They pointed to help partners keep their place. They corrected, they hinted, they held the book, turned the pages, nudged, and cajoled in order to help peers and themselves stay on task. They employed many strategies that proved highly effective in sustaining and redirecting partners' attentions. They sang, drawled, chanted, and spoke in high or screechy voices. They reinvented text, using familiar patterns and repetitive choruses to amuse and draw their partner into reading. Less successful peer partners did not define paired reading as a mutual activity. Instead, they assumed an isolationist stance to text that involved little interaction, collaboration, or assistance. This necessitated my invention in the form of conferencing and/or changing partnerships.

Partner Talk

If "successful scaffolding involves the construction of shared situation" (Stone 1993, 178), then children's language played a critical role in creating such situations for scaffolding. My research into the contexts of peer partnerships suggests a critical role for oral language in young children's literacy learning, suggesting that classrooms must foster and provide many opportunities for *peer talk* throughout the school day. Children's talk contributed to their involvement and shared motivation and, by extension, helped to create and support the "shared situations" necessary for scaffolding or assistance. Verbal and nonverbal scaffolding behaviors often follow or are embedded in sequences of verbal play or sequences of children's organizational or explanatory talk. As Melinda, another data reviewer, observed, "there was happiness, of relief and ownership, in their talk."

Peer partners' talk served a variety of functions—questioning, responding, affirming, clarifying, confirming, and conjecturing—as they worked at making meaning from the printed pages in front of them. Partners used language to predict ("I bet it's a goose egg") and to express likes and dislikes, as in Pete's comments about his partner's book selection ("Oh, I like that one"). Sometimes readers were distracted by other readers or the teacher, precipitating bursts of talk and accompanying actions as they redirected and returned to their task.

Gallimore and Tharp (1990) write that "the intersubjectivities of activity settings are created through the use of words in discourse, these signs and symbols taking on new and shared meanings as they are hallowed in discourse by use during joint activity" (193). My analysis of data found many instances of new and shared meanings, as children played with the language of text creating an intersubjectivity in activity settings that enhanced effectiveness of collaboration and increased success with the task of reading. Cazden (1992) argues for keeping play alive in social settings for its critical benefits in developing children's language and metacognitive awareness and competence. Verbal play emerged as having a crucial role in sustaining involvement and in creating supportive, interpersonal relationships, helping children to work collaboratively in processing text. While children's language play was supported and encouraged by teacher behavior and modeling, many of children's imaginative, playful transactions with text were uniquely their own.

Partners' Relationships with Text

Through their actions, my students demonstrated again and again that books are not static, one-dimensional entities foisted upon them by others, but doorways into possible worlds (Bruner 1986) in which they can *act,* forming dialectical relationships with text. Like the work of others, my research into peer partnerships contradicts the theory of reading as a simple transmission of knowledge or information from text to reader. Peer partners *constructed* challenging text word by word. They played with text, they experimented with it, changed it, chanted it, and sang it, bringing their backgrounds and experiences into creative, fanciful interpretations. They argued about the meaning of print and illustrations, they disagreed about what was said. They spoke directly to characters and responded to text questions as if they stood, not outside in a first-grade classroom, but inside the book as a character. To observe these readers was to observe the reading process as an alive, multifaceted, interactive process. Reading, according to Rosenblatt (1978), involves a transaction between reader and text that changes both in the process. The transactional nature of reading was revealed many times in the course of this study as readers interacted with the printed page.

One further observation about partners and books relates to who holds the text when children read together. When I compared my students' partner interactions, I found that when readers hold their own copy of the reading book, scaffolding and collaboration are more frequent. In the sessions where I could make such comparisons, reader assistance and scaffolding occurred with greater frequency when readers held their own copy of a book as opposed to sharing one book.

Joint Construction or Word-by-Word Switching

In relation to Vygotsky's (1978) theory of zones of proximal development, my research suggests that, as teachers, we should pay attention to the processes of peer-partner interactions for what they tell us about the *shifting nature of competence and collaboration* (Tudge 1990). I found many instances of students' verbal and nonverbal behaviors that mediated reading effectiveness, with continual shifts in the role of capable peer as readers moved through text. When participants engaged in the joint constructing behavior designated as word-by-word switching, the role of capable peer underwent many shifts, with learners contributing expertise as they were able. This intersubjectivity, focused on the task of reading, enabled children to read even challenging text, pooling expertise often word by word. Successful collaborators used word-by-word switching and choral reading to move fluently through text. While word-by-word switching, they pointed, they gave cues, they discussed possible strategies.

CONCLUSIONS

Ashton-Warner (1963) writes of her young Maori students, "between them all the time is togetherness, so that learning is so mixed up with relationship that it becomes part of it" (103–4). In peer partnerships, learning is indeed mixed up and central to these relationships as first graders take active roles in creating, organizing, and maintaining reading partnerships. In activity settings they create, emergent peer partners influence one another's learning in myriad ways. Partners provide scaffolds, enabling readers to continue their text construction. Partners listen, appreciating the readers' work by their presence and collaborative support. Partners talk, helping to organize and structure activity settings for themselves and their partners. They predict, question, conjecture, respond, confirm, and affirm, engaging in text-related talk that enhances and develops shared motivation. Partners laugh together, increasing one another's enjoyment of reading and text. They also develop child-centered strategies (see Figure 7–2) that serve as scaffolds for peers' text construction.

When they work *together,* readers pool their resources, each contributing to the task as they are able. Not all interactions are positive. Certain children have great difficulty sharing and collaborating, particularly at the start of the school year. When negative interactions are viewed as elements of process over time, however, it has been my experience that even recalcitrant collaborators slowly begin to engage and support one another, taking the first tentative steps toward assisting or accepting assistance from peers.

If the task of school and teachers is creating assisting systems, then nurturing and supporting instructional conversations within them, we must, according to Tharp and Gallimore (1988), resolve the paradox between two concepts that seem contrary to one another: instruction and conversation, the first implying authority and planning, the second implying equality and responsiveness. In observing peer partners, I have found many instances of both instruction and its accompanying constructs of authority and planning as well as many instances of equality and reader responsiveness. Peer partners plan and, in many cases, exert their authority over one another. They also respond to each other in genuine, thoughtful ways. Children's responsiveness to one another is revealed not only in their language play and organizational talk, but also in their expressions of frustration with and intolerance of one another's behavior and in their willingness to step aside, making a place for partners to act, learn, and grow. That they converse is not in doubt. That their conversation is instructional is illustrated by the many instances of verbal scaffolding and assistance I observed and recorded. Students' talk, whether in fun or frustration, continually contributes to the intersubjective whole created within social relationships focused on the task of reading.

Mehan (1982) states that "if we are interested in understanding, and possibly changing the structure of education in society, then knowledge about organizing principles is crucial" (60). Describing children's organizing structures for reading in the context of this classroom is a major focus of my investigations of peer partnerships. Children do not collaborate all of the time, just as organizational structures differ in form and effectiveness. Children's language use, as well as their willingness to share their expertise with others, contributes to the creation and maintenance of organizational structures. These structures, in turn, provide the contexts within which participants discover and develop their expertise and competencies as they construct text together.

While my classroom program was literature rich, providing many opportunities for students to hear, read, and interact with all genres of books, children's own reinventing of text and the creative, playful diversions their imagination brought forth during twenty-two paired reading events are uniquely their own. My first graders demonstrated through their actions and behaviors that effective teaching did not require adult authority but was sometimes displayed more creatively and effectively in its absence. Through the structures they created, their behaviors and language play, children illustrated again and again their imaginative approach to text and the interactive nature of their involvement with reading. In their very personal stances toward books, these young readers brought *their perspectives* on what it means to be truly literate (Griffin 2001).

SUGGESTIONS FOR TEACHERS

The following suggestions are offered as "ideas," not hard-and-fast rules. What works in one setting, with one class of children, may not work as well in another. No matter what structures or frameworks we put into place, as teachers and guides, we must always remember to step back and listen to what children are telling us about what works best for them.

Getting Started

- Consider pairing children (rather than allowing them to choose their own partners) with partnerships remaining together for at least five to six weeks. This allows time for partners to build collaborative relationships. In pairing students, consideration should be given to reading level (pairing readers of approximately equal expertise) as well as students' social and emotional needs.
- Consider alternating teacher pairing of readers with students' choices of reading partners.
- Observe and offer support and encouragement when partnerships struggle with collaboration. If friction persists, switch partners.

Support for Peer Partnerships

- Provide regular minilessons or discussion sessions where children can share thoughts and ideas about reading with a partner. Such sessions might include the following:
  - Create a wall chart of "Ways to Help My Partner" that can be added to throughout the year. This serves as a review for children at the start of partner-reading time and a visual reminder of the importance of responsible partner behaviors. It is important that this chart be created *with the children, using their words and ideas.*
  - Provide models of supportive partner behaviors such as taking turns reading alternate pages, choral reading, and assisting when a partner struggles. Children typically love to model and demonstrate for classmates.
- Check in frequently during peer-partner reading, highlighting and celebrating positive, supportive behaviors as well as redirecting or making alternative suggestions when partners are struggling.
- Provide a wide variety of texts from which partners choose. These can include, but are not limited to,
  - predictable or patterned texts
  - poetry
  - books based on familiar songs and chants
  - decodable texts
  - familiar stories and folktales
  - picture books

- rebus books
- big books
- charts and stories created during shared writing and modeled writing
- children's own published books

- rebus books
- big books
- charts and stories created during shared writing and modeled writing
- children's own published books

NEXT STEPS FOR TEACHERS: RESOURCES ABOUT PEER PARTNERSHIPS

The list below includes a few journal articles about peer partnerships; two texts that include short discussions of partnerships, *The Art of Teaching Reading* (Calkins 2001) and *Guided Reading: Good First Teaching For All Children* (Fountas and Pinnell 1996); and an upcoming book, *Shoulder to Shoulder: Beginning Readers Move Towards Independence in Peer Partnerships* (Griffin 2004).

Berghoff, B., and K. Egawa. 1991. *"No More 'Rocks': Grouping to Give Students Control of Their Learning."* The Reading Teacher 44 (8), 162–167.

Calkins, L. M. 2001. *The Art of Teaching Reading.* New York: Addison Wesley Longman.

Fountas, I. C., and G. S. Pinnell. 1996. *Guided Reading: Good First Teaching For All Children.* Portsmouth, NH: Heinemann.

Griffin, M. L. 2000. Emergent Readers' Joint Text Construction: A Study of Reading in Social Context. Unpublished doctoral dissertation, University of Rhode Island.

———. 2001. "Social Contexts of Beginning Reading." *Language Arts* 78 (4), 371–378.

———. 2002. "Why Don't You Use Your Finger? Paired Reading in First Grade." *The Reading Teacher* 55 (8), 766–774.

———. 2004. *Shoulder to Shoulder: Beginning Readers Move Towards Independence in Peer Partnerships.* Portsmouth, NH: Heinemann.

MacGillivray, L. 1997. " 'I've Seen You Read:' Reading Strategies in a First-Grade Class." *Journal of Research in Childhood Education* 11 (2), 135–146.

MacGillivray, L. and S. Hawes. 1994. "I Don't Know What I'm Doing—They All Start With B: First Graders Negotiate Peer Reading Interactions." *The Reading Teacher* 48 (3), 210–217.

NEXT STEPS FOR TEACHERS: CHILDREN'S LITERATURE CITED

Aruego, J., and A. Dewey. 1986. *Five Little Ducks.* New York: Crown.

Cowley, J. 1987a. *Long Long Tail.* Bothell, WA: Wright Group.

———. 1987b *Mr. Grump.* Bothell, WA: Wright Group.

———. 1987c. *Noise.* Bothell, WA: Wright Group.

———. 1987d. *Ratty Tatty.* Bothell, WA: Wright Group.

———. 1987e. *Snap!* Bothell, WA: Wright Group.

———. 1987f. *Spider Spider.* Bothell, WA: Wright Group.

———. 1987g. *Tiny Woman's Coat.* Bothell, WA: Wright Group.

———. 1989. *Mrs. Wishy Washy.* Bothell, WA: Wright Group.

Coxe, M. 1997. *Big Egg.* New York: Random House.

Hunia, F. 1977a. *Sly Fox and the Red Hen.* Loughborough Leicestershire, England: Ladybird Books.

———. 1977b. *Three Billy Goats Gruff.* Loughborough Leicestershire, England: Ladybird Books.

Makar, B. 1980a. *Cop Cat.* Cambridge, MA: Educators Publishing Service.

———. 1980b. *The Jet.* Cambridge, MA: Educators Publishing Service.

———. 1980c. *Meg.* Cambridge, MA: Educators Publishing Service.

Waber, B. 1972. *Ira Sleeps Over.* New York: Houghton Mifflin.

Westcott, N. B. 1988. *Down by the Bay.* New York: Crown.

8 | SCAFFOLDING CHILDREN'S IDENTITY MAKING WITH LITERATURE

JANICE HUBER AND D. JEAN CLANDININ[1]

Children are gathering in pairs and small groups throughout the room. Voices rise and fall as children read, talk, discuss, and wonder. Sometimes a burst of laughter breaks through. Corina[2] and I (Janice) are sitting side by side along one edge of the room, next to the computers, beside the puppet theatre. Corina grabbed my hand as soon as she entered the classroom, her face still warmed by outside play and sunshine on this beautiful warm fall afternoon. "Can I read with you?" she asked as she led me toward one of the bookshelves. "Sure," I said, inwardly noting how often she likes to read with us (Jean, Kate, and me) during this shared reading time. Her eyes moved across the rows of books as she searched, bending down to see those on the bottom shelf. "What are you looking for?" *"Allison,"* she answered at almost the same moment as she found it. Today Corina decides we should take turns, each reading a page. She begins.

ENTERING INTO THE CLASSROOM

Summer was beginning to fade as we began a yearlong narrative inquiry (Clandinin and Connelly 2000) at City Heights, a school nestled in a busy multiethnic community on the fringes of a city center. Kate, an experienced teacher and researcher, was beginning her second year in the combined

[1]We acknowledge the support of the Social Sciences and Humanities Research Council of Canada in a grant to D. Jean Clandinin and F. Michael Connelly.

[2]Children, teacher, and school names are pseudonyms.

third- and fourth-grade classroom. As she welcomed back twenty-five returning children and three children new to City Heights School and to Canada, she also welcomed us, Jean and Janice, friends and former colleagues who spent the year with her. We participated in classroom life as both teachers and researchers. This meant we worked alongside Kate and the children on a daily basis in all the ways that teachers do. It was at City Heights School that we first met Corina.

Coming to Know Corina

We met her on our first day of school and came to know her life stories over time, both during our year at City Heights and at the beginning of the following school year in a Grade 5 classroom at Greenville School, also in the city center. As we worked alongside Corina in the classroom, she told stories of living with her father and of her longing for school breaks when she could visit her mother in a place some distance from the city. Corina's father was of Vietnamese heritage, her mother of First Nations heritage. They met and lived in the community around City Heights until shortly after Corina was born. When her parents no longer lived together, Corina lived with her father. By the time she started school, she and her father lived in a house some distance from City Heights.

Beginning school shaped a new storyline in Corina's life as she learned to live with a local family during the week and spend weekends with her dad. We knew from Corina's stories that her life was not always easy in the home of the local family, and we watched as her relationships grew with another fourth-grade boy and his mother. Their comings and goings together from school became a rhythm as the year unfolded. Corina did not seem to talk much about this relationship with other children in the room. It was an identity story woven with other silences in Corina's life, silences we wondered about as we saw her lingering at the edges of conversations and activities, neither in nor out but quietly watching from the fringes. At the beginning of fifth grade, Corina moved to Greenville, a classroom and school where Kate, another teacher, and we worked together as teacher researchers/researcher teachers. Moving to Greenville School meant that Corina was able to live with her dad full time.

Corina loved the richly textured collection of children's literature in the classroom. As the days and weeks passed, we started to attend to Corina's choice of literature. We came to know Corina as a lover of memoir. She read and reread books of stories of people's lives, some fictional, some nonfictional. Allen Say's books *Allison* (1997) and *Grandfather's Journey* (1993) were ones Corina often returned to during the afternoon reading time and in moments throughout the day. Our noticing Corina's returns to these books marked the beginnings of our puzzling through children's identity making in relation with literature. We introduce Corina both here and later in three "literacy moments" as a child who helped us to understand more about scaffolding new identity stories. Our teaching work with Corina is a central thread in this chapter.

As teachers who research teaching, we want to share the possibilities of scaffolding a child's identity. We take a longer view, not one of scaffolding toward an immediate, short-term goal, but as scaffolding across a life composition. In particular, as we trace the interactions among ourselves and Corina in three of what we call literacy moments from across two school years, we explore how a narrative understanding of children's identity making helps us to understand scaffolding as a deeply narrative, relational, experiential, unfolding process. In what follows, we first use field notes to construct a description of experiences lived with Corina in two classrooms. We refer to our descriptions as literacy moments. These three literacy moments comprise a kind of vignette that cuts across different times and places.

Three Literacy Moments with Corina

Literacy Moment One: September 1999

"What are you looking for?" I (Janice) asked. *"Allison,"* Corina answered at almost the same moment as she found it. Today Corina decides we should take turns, each reading a page. She begins. She reads an account of Allison's family, her mother, father, doll Mei Mei, and the kitten outside the window. I read the next page, about the kimono sent by Allison's grandmother. Corina's eyes do not shift from the images around the text we are reading. I wonder what Corina is thinking as we read this story of adoption. The story weaves across Allison's questions of who she is as a Japanese girl with White American parents and of Allison's questions of her classmates: Do they look like their parents? Do they have a mother in another country, "another mommy who gave you away?" (Say 1997, 12). When we finished the book, Corina and I talk. We talk about how the cat becoming part of Allison's family seems to help Allison understand her adoption in new ways. Corina quietly wonders if I know that she, too, has a mom in another place. When I say that I do know, Corina talks about the younger stepsiblings who live with her mom. She wonders if I know that her mom is First Nations and that her mom made her a dream catcher. A few days later when I am back in the classroom, Corina takes me to her desk. From somewhere in the back of her desk, she pulls out a package. It is white paper taped together. She opens up the package. Inside is the dream catcher from her mom.

Literacy Moment Two: March 2000

Corina is a lover of memoir, and she is a child who really caused me (Janice) to think more about Allen Say's books *Allison* (1997) and *Grandfather's Journey* (1993). Together Corina and I have read these books again and again.

Literacy Moment Three: September 2000

I (Jean) sit beside Corina on the floor of this new classroom in this new school. I am back as a teacher researcher/researcher teacher but Janice, Kate, and I are now in a different school. How happy I am that Corina has come to this school. She takes me away to an empty space, a classroom that is, for the moment, not in use. She wants me to read with her, and the book she has chosen (Adler 1993) tells of Anne Frank and draws a bit on her diary. We sit together on the floor, leaning up against each other. The book has many pictures and we look at them carefully, taking turns reading the captions. She asks about being Jewish and wonders why the Jewish people were being taken away to camps to be killed. We begin to talk of difference, of what racism means. She looks at me and I ask if she has ever experienced racism. She nods "yes" and then quickly turns our attention back to the book. I wonder if her fascination with the stories of children who are different allows her to see something else of herself.

We carefully selected these three moments to show Corina's scaffolding of her identity. The moments stretched across thirteen months and two different schools and classrooms. The scaffolding occurs in different relationships, with different books, with different characters, with different storylines.

UNDERSTANDING SCAFFOLDING OF CHILDREN'S IDENTITY MAKING

We use these three literacy moments to illustrate what we mean by scaffolding children's identity making through literature. Wood, Bruner, and Ross' (1976) definition of scaffolding as a process that "enables a child or novice to solve a task or achieve a goal that would be beyond his unassisted efforts" (90) is the starting point for our considerations of using literature to create spaces for children to scaffold new stories to live by, new identity stories. Drawing on Vygotsky's (1962) theories of learning, Dewey's (1938) theories of experience, and Connelly's and Clandinin's (1994, 1999) theories of narrative knowledge and identity, we conceived of children's interactions with a rich diversity of children's literature and conversation as a way to think of scaffolding children's identities. Scaffolding is the intertwining of teaching and learning, and for us, we imagine this intertwining occurring in three ways: in the kinds of spaces we, as teachers, create; in the kinds of literature we offer; and in the conversations and writing we encourage children to engage in.

FIGURE 8–1
*Understanding
Scaffolding of Children's
Identity Making*

Understanding Scaffolding of Children's Identity Making

- attending to the kinds of spaces teachers create
- attending to the kinds of literature available
- attending to the kinds of conversations and writing children engage in

Steiner and Souberman (1978) wrote that Vygotsky, who viewed learning "as a profoundly social process, emphasizes dialogue and the varied roles that language plays in instruction and in mediated cognitive growth" (131). We see Vygotsky's attention to learning as social and as occurring through interaction and expression, being linked with Dewey's (1938) description of experience as occurring through interaction in particular situations. Both Dewey and Vygotsky "were advocating the individual and the situation act together" (Prawat 2002, 19). They both adopted "a transactional approach that views meaning making as something that goes on in the world and not just in the head" (Prawat 2002, 19). Dewey (1938) wrote that

> The conceptions of situation and of interaction are inseparable from each other. An experience is always what it is because of a transaction taking place between an individual and what, at the time, constitutes his environment. . . . The two principles of continuity and interaction are not separate from each other. They intercept and unite. They are, so to speak, the longitudinal and lateral aspects of experience. Different situations succeed one another. But because of the principle of continuity something is carried over from the earlier to the later ones. As an individual passes from one situation to another, his world, his environment, expands or contracts. He does not find himself living in another world but in a different part or aspect of one and the same world. What he has learned in the way of knowledge and skill in one situation becomes an instrument of understanding and dealing effectively with the situations which follow. The process goes on as long as life and learning continue. (43–44)

Dewey's (1938) two criteria of experience, interaction and continuity, shaped Connelly and Clandinin's (1994) metaphorical way of thinking of an educated life. They wrote that "living an educated life was an ongoing process. People's lives were composed over time, life stories were lived and told, relived and retold" (153).

Connecting Vygotsky's (1962) ideas on learning as a socially mediated activity with Dewey's (1938) understanding of experience in teaching and learning shifts our understanding of scaffolding as directed toward an immediate task, toward a sense of scaffolding as unfolding over a life composition. The idea of stories to live by (Connelly and Clandinin 1999) helps us link teaching and learning with the storied lives teachers and children are composing in and out of schools and classrooms. In this way scaffolding can be understood as an unfolding process that enables a child to move from living his or her stories to telling and retelling his or her stories with new insights. In these teaching-learning situations, teachers, too, are learning to tell and retell their stories.

Philosophical Beginnings
• learning is social • emphasizing dialogue • occurring through interaction and expression • experiencing a transaction between individual and environment • adopting two principles: continuity and interaction • viewing lives composed over time • scaffolding unfolding over a life composition • living, telling, retelling, reliving life stories • experiencing stories to live by

SPACES, LITERATURE, AND CONVERSATION AS WAYS TO SCAFFOLD IDENTITY

Earlier we wrote that the kinds of spaces we created with children, the kinds of literature we used, and the kinds of conversations and writing we enabled for children were helpful in scaffolding children's identity stories, that is, in helping them move beyond telling to retelling and reliving their stories with new, more imaginative possibilities. We wanted to allow children to tell their identity stories of who they were and who they were becoming with new insights.

As we thought about the kinds of spaces, literature, and conversation in the classroom, we drew on the five conditions for an educative experience identified by Connelly and Clandinin (in progress) that shape the unfolding of an educated life. In this way we further describe and understand scaffolding of children's identity stories.

In the following section, we explain each condition and suggest how our view of scaffolding might be used by other teachers.

FIGURE 8–3
*Five Conditions for an
Educative Experience*

Five Conditions for an Educative Experience
1. Meeting the other as a person 2. Negotiating meaning 3. Establishing safe places 4. Giving back the story 5. Inquiring narratively (Connelly and Clandinin, in progress)

Meeting the Other as a Person

The first condition of an educative experience, "the importance of meeting the other as a person" (Connelly and Clandinin in progress, 51), requires that we engage in a way that "allows each individual, teacher and child, to bring their wholeness to the experience" (52). It is more than hearing school stories but hearing stories from across their lives. It is about the storied lives children and teachers are composing in all of their complexity. The stories are not just the child's stories, they are the teacher's stories as well. A learning experience is mutual for both teacher and children.

In the three literacy moments we described with Corina, we provided examples of the moments shaped by teachers and the rhythms of classroom life (Connelly and Clandinin 1988). Each literacy moment was shaped by the teacher utilizing shared reading, a time when children shifted from quiet, on-their-own reading to sitting side by side or against one another in groups to read. Additionally, by supporting and allowing the child to select what was to be read, the shared readings often spilled over from the quiet reading as some children brought those books into the small group space of shared reading. Sometimes shared reading picked up on books read or discussed earlier in the day or on previous days. In both the City Heights and Greenville classrooms, shared reading eventually flowed into a time when the teacher gathered the whole class to celebrate the literature they read. The teacher provided a time for the children to talk about ideas; to read pages loved because of language, ideas, or images; to sing; and to act out favorite parts of text.

In our observation, this whole group time provided by the teacher also became a space for children to share stories of who they were and who they were becoming. For example, early in the year, Kate shared *Whoever You Are* (Fox 1997) as an entry point and invitation for children to write, draw, paint, and talk about their similarities and differences. In the months and weeks that followed, Lia, a child refugee from Somalia, often chose *Whoever You Are* as a book to share when the class celebrated literature. Kate's introduction of the book seemed to help Lia scaffold the stories she was telling of who she was becoming in Canada. When she shared in this whole class context, Lia often talked about liking *Whoever You Are* because it included "more than White people." We sensed, in Lia's interactions with *Whoever You Are,* a meeting of her life stories with the characters in the book. We sensed a moment of awakening (Connelly and Clandinin 1994) to who she was becoming, a new possible telling of who she was.

Lia not only learned from Corina, but we learned from Lia. As teachers, when Lia made visible her reason for liking the book, we confronted our dominant position as White teachers and renewed our belief in the importance of diverse children's literature in the classroom. Lia helped us scaffold our own stories as we questioned our cultural dominance and who we were becoming as teachers. We learned that in meeting Lia as a person, we needed to listen, to learn, and to awaken to who we were and might become in Lia's stories of us.

In the literacy moment shaped as Corina and Janice read *Allison* (Say 1997), there was also a sense that interaction with and revisiting Allison's search for belonging shaped a similar narrative scaffolding experience for Corina, a moment of awakening to how she might tell a story of who she was becoming. As we trace this literacy moment, attentive to Connelly's and Clandinin's (in progress) first condition for an educative experience, there is the possibility of a meeting between Corina and Allison as two young girls who share a similar identity story of figuring out who they are in relation with parents. Janice, as teacher, mediated this meeting of child with book character. Although the literacy moment does not describe it, we know that Janice told stories of an adopted brother and that Corina knew this story. This meeting of Corina and Allison was mediated as Corina heard Janice's stories of adoption. Here again Corina's stories also allowed Janice to scaffold new stories of who she was becoming in this classroom context.

In this way, as Corina made her stories to live by visible, she also called forth our stories. It was within this meeting of life stories that mutuality was shaped. Stories were drawn forth for Corina and us as we interacted with the books and with one another's lived and told stories. In Figure 8–4 we offer possibilities for what other teachers might do in their classrooms.

FIGURE 8–4
*How Teachers Can Meet
the Student as a Person*

How Teachers Can Meet the Student as a Person

- Provide time for shared reading
- Support children and scaffold the spilling over of private reading to public sharing
- Use the public sharing to write, draw, paint, and talk about difference
- Observe and promote opportunities when one student can build on the literary selections or conversations of another
- Confront the positions our students ascribe to us as the teacher

---

Negotiating Meaning

A second condition Connelly and Clandinin (in progress) describe as important for an educative experience is the sense that "meaning is being negotiated, not transmitted. . . . Making connections as persons establishes a basis for a relationship in which the possibility for negotiating meaning is created" (52). A sense of relationship among Corina and each of us comes through in all three literacy moments. As we lived in the City Heights multi-age third- and fourth-grade classroom, we often saw Corina lingering at the edges. However, at times such as shared reading, she, for the most part, invited us to read with her.

In the first literacy moment, we see Corina trusting Janice with an identity story as she talks about her mom. When Corina knows that Janice knows she has a mom in another place, Corina threads new stories of herself in their conversation: stories of her stepsiblings, of her mom as First Nations, of an identity artifact she treasures. In these gradual negotiations of who she is, Corina seems to be awakening to the knowledge that she can share these identity stories with Janice. Corina's bringing the dream catcher to school, tucking it away in her desk, and bringing it out to show Janice could also be understood as a transformation of who Janice is in Corina's life. Janice is now someone who knows these stories of who Corina is and who she is becoming. It was their relationship that seemed to help Corina to understand that making meaning of her identify could be negotiated.

The second literacy moment, noting that Janice and Corina often revisited *Allison* (Say 1997) and *Grandfather's Journey* (Say 1993), also tells us something of the relationships Corina and Janice were making. There is in this literacy moment a telling of the kinds of relationships we imagine as linked with the educative qualities of this experience for Corina and for us.

However, there is another relationship at work here. There is a sense that a thread of connection, a narrative relationship, keeps drawing Corina back to *Allison* and *Grandfather's Journey*. In the first literacy moment, we see Corina drawn into the storyline in *Allison,* a storyline of a child puzzling through who she is in relation with adoptive parents. In the second literacy moment, we tell that Corina is drawn back, for many months, to *Grandfather's Journey*. The book tells the story of Say's grandfather, of his leaving Japan for California, and then of his yearnings for Japan. When Say's grandfather returns to Japan many years later, he then yearns for California. From Say's telling of this identity story in his grandfather's life, we learn of his grandfather's sense of dislocation, of never quite feeling at home in any one place. We sense that Corina is drawn to this story as she senses her own dislocation, moving from her two-parent home to living with a local family during the week and her father on the weekends. In the first literacy moment, she tells us of her yearnings for her mother's home when she is with her father. We imagine her, too, negotiating her sense of dislocation in a parallel way to Say's description of the grandfather's dislocation. We see this negotiation of dislocation as an ongoing inner conversation in which Corina lays her shifting story alongside the grandfather's shifting story.

In order to scaffold her identity, we see Corina experiencing meaning as negotiated not only between herself and her teachers but between herself and the characters in the two books. Connelly's and Clandinin's (in progress) second condition for an educative experience helps us think through Corina's returnings to *Allison* and *Grandfather's Journey* as spaces where she could negotiate meaning of her stories of experience. We imagine that in this process of negotiating meaning of who Allison and Grandfather are and who she (Corina) is, that Corina (and we) sense an opening for scaffolding new identity stories. In rereading the books with her and making spaces for her internal conversations with Grandfather, Corina—and we—are scaffolding a new story to live by in which Corina names herself as a child who lives with a sense of dislocation.

In this section, we have described how we observed and participated in Corina's negotiation of meaning. It is difficult for us to give advice to other teachers based on our experiences because much of what occurred depended on what Corina initiated. We do think that teachers can create a classroom that fosters negotiation from students, so we offer some suggestions in Figure 8–5.

FIGURE 8–5
Negotiating Meaning

> ## Negotiating Meaning
>
> - Respond to children's initiatives to read and talk
> - Provide invitations to children to read and talk
> - Build trust
> - Know children's stories. Learn the stories as they are composed
> - Seek texts that seem to match realities children seem to be constructing

Establishing Safe Places

A third condition important for an educative experience (Connelly and Clandinin in progress) "is the notion of establishing a safe place. We talk about the importance of a safe place in making possible experimentation with tellings of the self" (52).

Both classrooms were organized so that children sat in desks grouped with three or four other children. Some time each day was spent working in desks and groups. For the most part, children chose who they wanted to sit with in their desk groups. In addition, there were also spaces in the classrooms where children could move—both during desk and group work and at other times of the day. It was not uncommon to enter into either classroom and to see children working in small groups on the carpeted gathering area, at the picnic table Kate brought into the multi-age third- and fourth-grade classroom, on the floor on either side of bookshelves separating spaces in the classrooms, or at centers around the rooms.

This choice of space often led children into the hallways. Quiet and shared reading time was one of these times. There was, as shown in the third literacy moment, a sense of searching out safe places. We sensed that Corina, at least at the start of the year, did not feel safe with possible experimentations of who she was. In the first literacy moment, she began a possible experimentation of who she was as she shared her story in relation to Allison's. However, for Corina, we often saw her as living a story of who she was as moving along the edges of the classroom community, as moving along the edges of different cultural groups, as moving along the edges of different family possibilities. In the third literacy moment, when Jean and Corina moved to a neighbouring empty classroom to read the Anne Frank book (Adler 1993), we sensed that for Corina, both the empty classroom and conversations with Jean were safe spaces. Together, they read the Anne Frank book, their bodies touching as they leaned up against one another. Corina felt safe to ask Jean questions she was puzzling over, and she felt safe enough to let Jean know that racism was a story she both lived and told of herself. In nodding "yes" that she had experienced racism, we see Corina experimenting, trying out a new story of herself with Jean. In this moment, Corina's sense of safety with Jean allows us to see her telling a previously silent story, the telling of it scaffolded by her sense of safety. As Corina tells this previously untold story, a new story of who Jean and Corina are in relation is scaffolded.

In the literacy moments with Corina, safety was seen as both physical safety and relationship safety. Our interaction with Lia, a child refugee from Somalia, helped us see something else about safety and its place in scaffolding children's identity. In the story we told earlier, we spoke of Lia's fascination with *Whoever You Are* (Fox 1997). Lia's interactions with this book helped us to see that safety is created not only by the freedom to choose where and with whom to be and by the nature of the relationship with another person (both teachers and classmates), but also in relation with the kinds of storylines available. Lia carried this book with her and frequently shared it as she engaged in possible experimentations with who she was. The fact that Lia could find a book which offered a mirror (Florio-Ruane 2001; Galda 1998) of who she was and wanted to be in this classroom created a sense of safety for her. One mirror was being able to see children who physically resembled her. Another mirror was being able to see that all children had similarities and were worthy of love. Lia's experience was of being torn from her homeland and of being transplanted to Canada. Finding *Whoever You Are* gave her a window for what was possible in this new country. That she shared it so often gave her classmates and us a window into knowing how she was experimenting with her story to live by. Over time, these experimentations became new tellings she could scaffold in her identity making.

Some of the concept of "creating a safe place" can be based on organizational procedures, and we have made some suggestions regarding this in Figure 8–6. Obviously, the concept of a safe place is much more intangible than the organization of physical space, so we recommend that teachers reflect on their own classrooms to think about how they might build safety in their own settings.

Establishing Safe Places

- Cluster desks to create groups. Allow considerable student choice in group selection
- Organize instruction utilizing individual, small group, and whole class learning
- Provide transitional areas as a fourth "space"
- Utilize the building as an extended classroom, including the hallway and adjacent empty classrooms when supervisor permits

---

FIGURE 8–6
Establishing Safe Places

Giving Back the Story

A fourth condition for an educative experience "is linked to the notion of response. Response, for us, is the giving back of a story. Response both validates an individual's story and gives a sense of responsible listening. It connects listeners' and tellers' stories in a collaboration that creates the possibility of new interpretations, new stories, for both" (Connelly and Clandinin in progress, 53).

Earlier in this chapter as we described our coming to know stories of Corina's life, we noted that we often saw Corina lingering at the edges of conversations and activities. We also noted Corina's engagement with literature and, in particular, her engagement with memoir. In the third literacy moment there was a sense that, through interaction with the Anne Frank book (Adler 1993), Corina experiences a giving back of stories of her life and Jean experiences a new understanding of Corina's choice of the Anne Frank book. In their reading Corina puzzles over the mistreatment of Jewish people. Jean puzzles over Corina's choice of this book. Based on the strength of a yearlong relationship, Jean tentatively offers a possible giving back when she asks Corina if she has experienced racism. Corina accepts this giving back of her story as she nods "yes." In that moment of response, Jean scaffolds a possible telling of Corina's story to live by, a story that she is a child who lives with racism.

In the first literacy moment between Janice and Corina, the giving back of Corina's story comes from Corina's reading of the text of Allison's life. As the character Allison figures out who she is with her adoptive parents, Corina is given back a story of her own attempts to figure out who she is in relation with her mom. Janice's response that she knows Corina has a mom in another place is a giving back of Corina's story that families are of many kinds, that Janice knows and accepts that and, consequently, accepts Corina. This double giving back seems to scaffold a new possible telling of Corina's story. She now begins to tell a story of seeing herself as a child with a mother in another place. Once Corina and Janice have scaffolded this telling of Corina's story, Corina seems able to scaffold another story by telling Janice who her mother is. This scaffolding of Corina's identity keeps unfolding over time as Corina brings the dream catcher her mom made to school and shows it to Janice. In showing the dream catcher to Janice, Corina is giving her new story of herself back to Janice so that Janice can see that Corina has shifted her earlier identity story of being a child without a mother to being a child with a mother in another place.

In these responses, what seems important is the sense of validation and responsible listening. It was Corina's choice to make the opening that allowed Janice, as a responsible listener, to open the conversation about how children live in relation to mothers. Jean, as a responsible listener, was also able to hear an opening to scaffold a new identity story with Corina.

Corina did not linger at the edges of shared reading but instead was often quite insistent that we read with her. Literature in which the experiences of diverse lives were told drew Corina in from the edges of the classroom. We noted in her choice of literature that she was drawn to plotlines where people struggled with difficult human choices such as interracial adoption, immigration, and genocide. This literature, in spaces of shared reading when conversations opened up about the interlappings between Corina's life and the lives of the characters in the stories, seemed to shape educative spaces where Corina could not only name who she was but also imagine and then live out new stories of who she was becoming. We summarize how teachers might give back the story in Figure 8–7.

Giving Back the Story

- Foster a transactional response to literature
- Validate the experience
- Be a responsible listener

FIGURE 8–7
Giving Back the Story

Inquiring Narratively

The fifth condition important for an educative experience "is a sense of inquiry: narrative inquiry that opens lived and told stories" (Connelly and Clandinin in progress, 53) to other possible livings and tellings, that is, to scaffolding new identity stories.

Creating conditions that allow children to inquire into their stories to live by is no easy matter. As teachers we need to create spaces where children can ask questions about their own life texts and those of their classmates. We need to help them see they are authors of their own lives. In part we do that by the rich literature environment we create, an environment rich in fiction and nonfiction. The literature available needs to offer children and teachers possible ways to see their stories. We do not think it was an accident that Corina found Say's books compelling. She saw Allison as a child who also did not quite fit in a "typical" family, someone else who did not live with two parents and her siblings. She also saw Allison's skin color and different racial heritage; perhaps she saw Allison of Asian heritage as she saw herself. She also saw a "mommy who gave you away," something with which Corina sensed a resonance. It was in the talks with Janice in the first literacy moment that we sensed Janice's careful, gentle scaffolding as Corina began to quietly speak of who she was and of the story she was telling of herself. She awakened to a new way to tell her story to live by in that moment and began, several days later, to live a more confident story as she brought her mother's gift, the dream catcher, to school.

A year after the first literacy moment, Corina is still choosing stories of children whose life stories resonate with hers. In the third literacy moment, she chooses a nonfiction book about Anne Frank (Adler 1993), a child about Corina's age, a child who is killed because of her racial and religious heritage. Corina's choice of this book allows Jean to carefully scaffold a new aspect of Corina's story to live by as she asks about racism. Again this creates a sense of stories to live by as something to inquire into. With Corina we saw her initially on the edges but as she found the Allen Say books, particularly *Allison* (1997) and *Grandfather's Journey* (1993), and the Anne Frank book, she and we saw the possibility for her to begin to tell other stories of who she was, of who she was becoming. We and she began to see the possibility of scaffolding her story to live by from the story to live by cultivated in previous classrooms, in her home outside of school, and in her community.

This fifth condition for an educative experience was created as we, as teachers, made spaces for each child to tell, write, paint, and photograph who they were and who they were becoming. Kate, Janice, and Jean, as teachers, encouraged the use of memory box artifacts as triggers for story-telling of who the children were and who they were becoming. Early in the year we took photographs of each child carefully positioning themselves on playground equipment. This became another way for children to tell their stories. Similar pictures could be taken at several points throughout the year as artifacts documenting children's shifting sense of who they were becoming. Conditions for inquiry were also present in the opportunities we made for children to write their own stories in journals, notebooks, and memoirs. These tellings of their own stories, this awakening to the diverse ways they might tell their stories, also encouraged them to inquire into who they are.

As teachers we created an environment where children could fill their journals and notebooks with narrative fragments of their lives. We made time and space for them to read their own and each others' writings. In each sharing, questions were asked, wonders raised, resonances shared, so that they each came to see there were other possible tellings. These sharings among children gave them an opportunity to scaffold each others' identity stories.

In this space, there was rich literature. (A list of some books used can be found in Figure 8–9.) As children entered the classrooms, a diverse range of genres loosely arranged along genre lines were available to children. Informational books such as books about the natural or human-made world—insects, animals, plants, weather, geography and landforms, skyscrapers, dams, aquariums, and zoos—shaped some classroom spaces. Other classroom spaces were shaped by clusterings such as poetry, fiction, nonfiction, fairy tales, folktales, seasons, memoir, multicultural literature, and book series such as those written by Robert Munsch. Some of the baskets and bookshelves in the classrooms grouped books by life themes such as friendship, family, First Nations, diversity, culture, language, and celebrations. These groupings were not easily distinguishable or separate from one another; for example, *Allison* (Say 1997) could have been placed with diversity books as well as with family books. *Grandfather's Journey* (1993) and books such as *This Land Is My Land* (Littlechild 1993), *The Lotus Seed* (Garland 1993), and *The Other Way to Listen* (Baylor 1978) could have been placed in memoir or cultural groupings. In fact, in both classrooms, there were many times when a book became "lost" and was located by a child who remembered putting it in a place highlighting another of its multiple storylines.

As we sensed a child's interest, we sought out other books that offered connections to scaffolding a new insight into a life telling. As we created these narrative inquiry spaces with children, we were helping them and us become readers of their and our worlds (Calkins 2001). More than that, we were helping them and us become readers of who they were and were becoming in their worlds. Even more than that, we were helping them imagine who they might become. Once again, supporting narrative inquiry is subtle work, but we have suggested some ideas in Figure 8–8.

Inquiring Narratively
• Create spaces where children can ask questions about their own life texts and those of their classmates
• Help students see they are authors of their own lives
• Provide a figurative "space" for children to tell, write, paint, and photograph who they are and who they are becoming
• Take and use photos of children
• Help children to take and to use their own photographs
• Help children fill their journals with narratives of themselves and their experiences

FIGURE 8–8
Inquiring Narratively

AN ONGOING PROCESS OF SCAFFOLDING STORIES TO LIVE BY

Scaffolding of stories to live by is teaching and learning intertwined. We created spaces by meeting each other as people as we ensured there were times for children to read alone in quiet reading and to share read. As teachers we made the books we read aloud to the whole class available for children to read alone or with friends. Celebrating literature was a key time each day when the students gathered together as "whole people" to share those literacy experiences that resonated with them. It was a space for them and us as teachers to share stories. We created spaces where children understood that meaning is always being negotiated. As teachers we made visible our own processes of negotiating meaning with books. We encouraged children to engage in similar negotiations of meaning. We created spaces where the children felt safe to engage in experimenting with multiple tellings of self. We did this, in part, by allowing children to choose with whom they sat and by allowing them freedom to move within the classroom. As teachers we realized that children would come to feel safe both physically and in relational ways in an evolving process. We created spaces through responding to children's lived and told stories. Sometimes as teachers we helped children find books that we thought might be a resonant response with a child's story. Sometimes as teachers we could link possible story threads from particular literature to children's life stories. We linked these four conditions for an educative experience together with a fifth condition, that is, with a strong orientation to narrative inquiry. Our lives as teachers and children's lives were laid alongside the stories children read. As noted above, we created a rich literature environment, filled with fiction and nonfiction, cultural and family diversity, and diverse plotlines. This enabled us as teachers to create spaces where children could find a range of imaginative possibilities for themselves.

As we tried to create educative spaces, we needed to make decisions about whether to help, the amount of help to give, the timing of giving the help, and the end goal of instruction. These were, and are, the questions we ask ourselves as we create spaces, as we choose literature and make it available to children, and as we engage in conversations and writing with children. Our end goal is always to help children and ourselves to compose more educated lives. We know that other teachers may have similar goals, and when we think about our best suggestions, we feel the most powerful thing we can suggest is a list of texts that we have found useful (see Figure 8-9).

**Literature with Possible Spaces for Scaffolding
Children's Identity Stories**

Title	Author
All I See	C. Rylant
All the Colors of the Earth	S. Hamanaka
All the Places to Love	P. MacLachlan
All Those Secrets of the World	J. Yolen
Allison	A. Say
An Angel for Solomon Singer	C. Rylant
Annie and the Old One	M. Miles
The Art Lesson	T. dePaola
Barrio: José's Neighborhood	G. Ancona
The Big Box	T. Morrison with S. Morrison
Black Misery	L. Hughes
The Bracelet	Y. Uchida & J. Yardley
Brown Honey in Broomwheat Tea	J. C. Thomas
Celebrating Ramadan	D. Hoyt-Goldsmith
A Chair for My Mother	V. Williams
Chicken Sunday	P. Polacco
Children of the Earth . . . Remember	S. Schimmel
Chrysanthemum	K. Henkes
The Color of Home	M. Hoffman & K. Littlewood
The Colors of Us	K. Katz
The Composition	A. Skármeta & A. Ruano
Crow and Weasel	B. Lopez
Crow Boy	T. Yashima
Dear Willie Rudd,	L. Moore Gray
December	E. Bunting
Dia's Story Cloth	D. Cha
Do You Believe in Magic?	S. Pirotta
Dreamstones	M. Trottier & S. East
The Elders Are Watching	D. Bouchard & R. Vickers
Encounter	J. Yolen
Everybody Needs a Rock	B. Baylor
The Face at the Window	R. Hanson
Faithful Elephants	Y. Tsuchiya
Faraway Home	J. Kurtz
From Slave Ship to Freedom Road	J. Lester & R. Brown

A Gift for Gita	R. Gilmore
Going Home	E. Bunting
Grandad Bill's Song	J. Yolen
Grandfather's Journey	A. Say
Grandma According to Me	K. Magnuson Beil
A Grandmother's Story	G. Halak
Grandpa, Is Everything Black Bad?	S. L. Holman
Guess Who My Favorite Person Is	B. Baylor
A Handful of Seeds	M. Hughes
Heather Has Two Mommies	L. Newman & D. Souza
Home to Medicine Mountain	C. Santiago
How My Parents Learned to Eat	I. Friedman & A. Say
I Can Hear the Sun	P. Polacco
I Wish I Were a Butterfly	J. Howe
I'm in Charge of Celebrations	B. Baylor
If at First You Do Not See	R. Brown
If Sarah Will Take Me	D. Bouchard
If the World Were a Village	D. J. Smith
In Daddy's Arms I Am Tall	J. Steptoe
In My Momma's Kitchen	J. Nolen
Jambo Means Hello	M. Feelings
Jen and the Great One	P. Eyvindson
Josepha—A Prairie Boy's Story	J. McGugan
The Keeping Quilt	P. Polacco
The Kissing Hand	A. Penn
Knots on a Counting Rope	B. Martin Jr. & J. Archambault
Lights for Gita	R. Gilmore
Lilly's Purple Plastic Purse	K. Henkes
The Long Road	L. Garay
The Lotus Seed	S. Garland
Love as Strong as Ginger	I. Look & S. Johnson
Marianthe's Story—Painted Words	Aliki
Me and Mr. Mah	A. Spalding & J. Wilson
The Meaning of Respect	D. Bouchard
The Memory Box	M. Bahr
The Memory Coat	E. Woodruff
Morning on the Lake	J. Bourdeau Waboose
A Morning to Polish and Keep	J. Lawson
A Movie in My Pillow	J. Argueta
Mr. Lincoln's Way	P. Polacco
The Mud Family	B. James
My Heart Soars	Chief D. George
My House Has Stars	M. McDonald & P. Catalanotto
My Kokum Called Today	I. Loewen
My Mom Is So Unusual	I. Loewen
Nadia's Hands	K. English

FIGURE 8–9
continued

FIGURE 8-9
continued

The Name Jar	Y. Choi
No Mirrors in My Nana's House	S. Saint James
No More! Stories and Songs of Slave Resistance	D. Rappaport
The Other Way to Listen	B. Baylor
Owl Moon	J. Yolen
A Picture Book of Anne Frank	D. A. Adler
Pink and Say	P. Polacco
Plantpet	E. Primavera
The Rag Coat	L. Mills
The Rainbow Tulip	P. Mora
Red Parka Mary	P. Eyvindson
Remember the Butterflies	A. Grossnickle Hines
A River Ran Wild	L. Cherry
Rose Blanche	R. Innocenti
The Roses in My Carpets	R. Khan & R. Himler
Sadako	E. Coerr & E. Young
Sami and the Time of the Troubles	F. Parry Heide & J. Heide Gilliland
Silent Observer	C. MacKinnon
Sister Anne's Hands	M. Lorbiecki
Smoky Night	E. Bunting
So Far from the Sea	E. Bunting
Some of the Pieces	M. Madenski
Something from Nothing	P. Gilman
Something to Remember Me By	S. Bosak & L. McGraw
The Song Within My Heart	D. Bouchard
Stargazing Sky	D. Kogan Ray
A Story of Jean	S. Gaitskell & L. Lafrance
Stranger in the Mirror	A. Say
The Streets Are Free	Kurusa
Stringbean's Trip to the Shining Sea	V. B. Williams
Sunshine Home	E. Bunting
Sweet Clara and the Freedom Quilt	D. Hopkinson
Talking Walls	M. Burns Knight
Tar Beach	F. Ringgold
Tea with Milk	A. Say
Tell Me Again About the Night I Was Born	J. L. Curtis
Thank You, Mr. Falker	P. Polacco
This Land Is My Land	G. Littlechild
Tico and the Golden Wings	L. Lionni
Train to Somewhere	E. Bunting
Under Our Skin	D. Holsclaw Birdseye & T. Birdseye
The Upside Down Boy	J. F. Herrera

The Wall	E. Bunting
Way Home	L. Hathorn & G. Rogers
The Way to Start a Day	B. Baylor
The Wednesday Surprise	E. Bunting
The Whales' Song	D. Sheldon & G. Blythe
What I Believe	D. Holsclaw Birdseye & T. Birdseye
What's the Most Beautiful Thing You Know About Horses?	R. Van Camp
The Whispering Cloth	P. Deitz Shea
White Socks Only	E. Coleman
Whoever You Are	M. Fox
Wilfred Gordon MacDonald Partridge	M. Fox
The Yellow Star	C. Agra Deedy
The Yesterday Stone	P. Eyvindson

FIGURE 8–9
continued

We began this chapter with a sketch of coming to know Corina, a child at City Heights and Greenville Schools. Through three literacy moments we showed how Corina's stories to live by were scaffolded. We described the five conditions necessary for shaping an educative experience: meeting the other as a person, negotiating meaning, establishing safe places for experimenting with the telling of new stories to live by, the place of response (giving back) as windows and mirrors for scaffolding stories to live by, and narrative inquiry as shaping openings for living and telling new stories. In this chapter we tried to map out our understandings of scaffolding children's identity by attending to three literacy moments and by describing how we saw Corina and ourselves in a continuous process of scaffolding stories to live by, of becoming all we might become.

9 | SOME ASSEMBLY REQUIRED
Scaffolding in the Classroom

ADRIAN RODGERS

The chapters in this volume represent a cross-section of approaches to scaffolding literacy in elementary school classrooms. The ideas are provocative and the suggestions grounded in the everyday life of classrooms. While these chapters provide rich and robust ways to think about teaching and learning, they also pose a number of issues for teachers. In this chapter I try to anticipate what some of those challenges might be and suggest ways to deal with them.

DEFINING SCAFFOLDING

When we think about making changes to our existing teaching practices, we naturally think about what problems we might encounter. In the case of scaffolding, we think about problems that might arise as a result of changing the way in which we work with students. The root of these challenges may lie with the difficulty in defining what scaffolding is and how it might be used. Looking across the chapters in this volume, I find that the contributors define scaffolding as a process that

- occurs at the point of difficulty and within the student's zone of proximal development
- operates as a back-and-forth interaction between teacher and student, where the teacher supports, the student responds, and the teacher alters the level or kind of support accordingly
- is informed by careful teacher observation of the student in order to determine the amount of support needed

- occurs at the instructional level so that the student can move forward to more independent learning
- includes a range of possible instructional procedures
- is grounded in theory and in practice

Using scaffolding means that teachers must

- be deeply committed to knowing each child and how to best work with the child
- know what needs to be taught, and how what needs to be taught fits in the bigger body of knowledge
- know the instructional procedures that will assist the student(s) in need
- be flexible in meeting multiple needs simultaneously
- have a clear vision of a desired outcome
- be willing to consider alternatives to the status quo and to undertake some instructional risks in undertaking new practices

These characteristics of scaffolding and of teachers who want to use scaffolding allow teachers to realize goals that are targeted directly at teaching students, rather than just meeting curricular guidelines mandated by a school or a district. Scaffolding instruction allows the teacher to

- work successfully with the most difficult-to-teach students
- develop a structured approach to support students as they learn new or difficult material or procedures
- customize instruction for individual learners or small groups of learners
- economize instruction by targeting assistance where and when it is needed

Although scaffolding can be used to achieve powerful goals, teachers may find it somewhat challenging to do. In the sections that follow, I identify where the challenges may lie, with the aim of helping you, the reader, anticipate difficulty and reasons for that difficulty.

CHALLENGES OF SCAFFOLDING

Scaffolding involves a more targeted approach to teaching, a stark contrast to the more common form of classroom organization in which the teacher leads activities that are directed at the whole class. With this more common instructional approach, teachers often teach to the middle of the class, an approach that favors students achieving fairly easily and quickly at about an average level. Organizing instruction so that the needs of differentiated learners are addressed (because after all, every learner is different) will be a challenge for anyone who is accustomed to teaching to the middle. On the other hand, anyone who is accustomed to teaching to the middle and not satisfied with teaching only some of their students will likely want to invest the time it takes to differentiate instruction.

Compounding the challenge of scaffolding learning is the fact that most curricular materials are designed to support teaching to the middle and do not necessarily help with those students who need extra assistance. This is perhaps not the fault of curriculum developers, since it is difficult to anticipate what a teacher might need to assist the struggling student.

In some cases it is difficult to know how to help students who are having difficulty learning to read. We often know what *does not* work since we may have pulled a number of previously useful tools from our toolbox of instructional strategies and used them without success. Confronted with this failure, we continue to look for what *does* work. At first, we might think that an extra pair of hands might assist us, and we might call in the help of a parent volunteer or perhaps a paraprofessional working in our room. Certainly these individuals might be of assistance, especially after we find out what works, but in the early stages of trying to identify how we might scaffold student learning at the point of difficulty, if the teacher does not know how to assist the student, the parent or paraprofessional will not know.

Although we have a moral and ethical responsibility to teach all of our students, including those finding it difficult to learn, we are daily faced with the realization that there is not just one struggling student in the room. In fact, there may be many struggling students in the room, and we need to meet the needs of each one of them. At the same time, we also have an obligation to meet the needs of the whole class, a class with many students who may not need a more scaffolded approach. Instruction to meet so many needs will be challenging.

Another challenge with scaffolding instruction is that struggling students who might benefit from a more scaffolded instructional approach often have multiple needs. We know that a teacher can scaffold instruction by recognizing the point at which difficulty occurs and then structuring supports at that point to support learning. When students have multiple difficulties, it is hard for the teacher to know what is difficult for the student or what the child is "not getting," because the multiple problems have disguised the point of difficulty.

I have said that teachers who do a good job of scaffolding student learning are able to tailor their teaching within the zone of proximal development. By this I mean that the teacher can follow the Goldilocks principle, offering prompts and directions to the student that are neither too hard nor too easy, but rather are "just right." While this is easy to say, it is difficult to do. Even Goldilocks made mistakes on her way to finding the chair, the bed, and the porridge that were just right. Clearly, having a sense of what a student is presently able to do, so that we can tailor our response, involves a set of much more complex decisions. Suffice it to say, it is all too easy for a teacher to inadvertently make things too easy or too hard, and it is all too difficult to find the prompts that are just right.

Even if a teacher is successful in finding prompts that are "just right" in scaffolding student instruction, the nature of the teacher-student exchange is different from a more typical classroom encounter. Whereas in a more typical classroom encounter the teacher might give directions and await a response, in scaffolding student learning the exchange may be more rapid-fire and the teacher enters into a back-and-forth learning relationship with the student—a relationship where what the teacher does depends on what the student does. Since some teachers are accustomed to talking while students listen, shifting to listening more and observing closely represents a fundamental shift in teaching.

KEY FEATURES OF EFFECTIVE SCAFFOLDING

Having identified why scaffolding may be challenging to undertake, let's turn now to identifying key features of effective scaffolding. Wood and Wood (1996) noted that Vygotsky's definition of the zone of proximal development leaves us with the task of identifying "the nature of the guidance and the collaboration that promotes development" (5). So what is the nature of the guidance and collaboration that promotes development?

A Knowledgeable Teacher

Teachers who have specialized knowledge about teaching early literacy share an understanding about what readers need to be able to do. They teach students what they can try at difficulty, such as rereading, looking at parts of words, using knowledge about letter-sound relationships, or incorporating meaning into attempts. But more significantly, although they agree on what to teach, effective teachers who scaffold learning know that they must tailor the timing of their instruction—when they give help—in response to each student's changing abilities in these areas.

These teachers do not operate from a script that directs them to teach a particular scope or sequence of skills on particular days; it comes out of their heads because they know about teaching. This leads naturally to the conclusion that the best person—the most well-equipped person to scaffold literacy learning, particularly with students having difficulty learning to read—is a trained teacher, not a paraprofessional or parent volunteer.

Provide Opportunities for Errors

Errors are necessary for learning. As Elbers (1996) says, they are "occasions for various suggestions, demonstrations or explanations" (284). They provide opportunities for the student to explore new frontiers in learning, opportunities that are verbally mediated by a tutor (Hoogesteder, Maier, and Elbers 1996, 357).

A key feature of effective scaffolding of literacy performance therefore, seems to be the provision for errors to occur. Texts that are neither too easy nor too difficult provide opportunities to explore new frontiers in problem-solving abilities. The Goldilocks principle again!

Too many errors, however, would likely be counterproductive to the learning process, losing the student's engagement and contribution to the problem solving. Obviously, without the student's contributions, there can be no interaction.

As David Wood points out though, instruction cannot be just right 100 percent of the time (Wood 2003). From time to time, help will be offered at too high a level without enough support or too low a level with too much support. Consider for example, this interaction between Ken and his teacher Sarah when they were reading together and Ken ran into difficulty with the word *lived:*

Ken: In a teeny tiny dollhouse—a ____ [omitted the word *lived*]

Sarah: You can't skip words.

Ken: What is it?

Sarah: What would make sense?

Ken: Mouse. [there's a picture of a mouse on the page]

Sarah: Try the first letter.

Ken: Wind up.

Sarah: What letter does it start with?

Ken: L.

Sarah: What sound does it make?

Ken: Luh.

Sarah: So go back and try it again, and think what would make sense and start that way.

Ken: Wind up.

Sarah: How does it start?

Ken: Luh.

Sarah: What would make sense and start with luh?

Ken: I'm getting there! [said quietly, almost to self]

Sarah: Could it be lived or sat? (Requiring Ken to use some visual information)

Ken: Lived!

Even though Sarah gave successively more help when Ken was unsuccessful, she seemed to start out with giving too little help right at the outset. Ken gamely contributes, but it is easy to imagine the interaction breaking down with another student.

What seems to count, therefore, in effective scaffolding is not necessarily being accurate with the amount of help you give, every single time you give help, but observing the impact of the amount of your help on the student's success. A scaffolding maxim offered by David Wood which fits very well here is to give more help when the student flounders and less help when the student is successful (Wood 2003).

Decide What to Teach

Effective scaffolding also involves making decisions about what to teach. Readers, particularly those just emerging into reading or those having difficulty learning to read, make a variety of types of errors during their reading, some representing, for example, an emerging use of visual information and others representing what seem to be just a slip in control. For example, a student who has brought one-to-one matching under control some weeks previous may still insert or omit a word now and then while reading, even though that student may be able to use visual information in more sophisticated ways, substituting *said* for *shouted* and *got* for *going*. With a student who usually makes these kinds of substitutions but fails to make a one-to-one match on one line of text while reading, which error should receive attention: when the one-to-one matching was off and the student failed to notice, or the error of *got* for *going?* Which teaching decision will lift the student's current ability, and which one will focus the student on a process that represents old learning?

Certainly not the error in which the one-to-one matching was off. Even though it is the more alarming error because it is such a basic skill for reading, it is not at the student's cutting edge of learning; one-to-one matching has already been brought under control. In fact, if you take a student back to that error to fix it, the student will likely be able to fix it quickly and easily, without recalling that the error was even made in the first place. The other errors, though, of using just the initial letter at difficulty are errors at this particular student's cutting edge, and attending to them will lift the student's processing.

The scaffolding process involves first making a decision about whether any attention should be paid to an error. It should not be unusual for a teacher to ignore certain errors because they are not on the student's cutting edge of learning, either because the student will find it too easy or too hard to fix. Wood and Wood (1996) describe this feature of scaffolding as "domain contingency" (7) in that the teacher has to make decisions about what to teach.

Modulating the Level of Help

The amount of help the teachers give at difficulty should also vary from student to student. Wood and Wood (1996) refer to this element of tutoring as "instructional contingency" (7)—or making decisions about how specific the help should be. More or less support can be provided along a continuum that includes telling, demonstrating, directing, or questioning. On this continuum, questioning a student about what to do next will provide the least amount of help ("What can you try?"), whereas telling ("That word is *hat*") or demonstrating (showing the student what to do) offers more support.

Wood and Wood (1996) describe the process of scaffolding as being particularly taxing on "human powers of observation, attention and memory" (10). Their observation seems well justified in the context just described. We might infer that before stepping in to scaffold, or lift learning, a teacher needs to weigh up several decisions, such as "What is this student currently able to do?", "What should I teach now?", "Should I let that error go?", "How much help should I give?", "How much help did I just give?", "How successful was the student when I just helped?", or "Should I give more help?" All of these factors seem embedded in the moment-by-moment teaching decisions made by the teachers who are scaffolding learning.

RECONCEPTUALIZING SCAFFOLDING AS A CONTINUUM

As the reader can see, the way in which teachers might use scaffolded approaches is not an either-or proposition. Instead the teacher can think of scaffolding as a continuum, on which the teacher might move back and forth during the course of the day. Thus, one example of this continuum depicted in Figure 9–1 is the context of support:

FIGURE 9–1
Context of Support

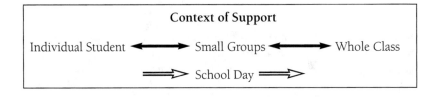

Instructional Choice

Teachers might also work on a different level, not only concerned about in what grouping they will implement the support structure, but also wondering what the principal task will be. For example, a teacher might choose to deal with an issue regarding the content of a lesson (The word *frog* begins with the letter *f*), a concept (*frog* is a word used to describe a kind of animal), or a skill (can you spell *frog?*). This continuum of instructional choice is depicted in Figure 9–2.

FIGURE 9–2
Continuum of Instruc-tional Choice

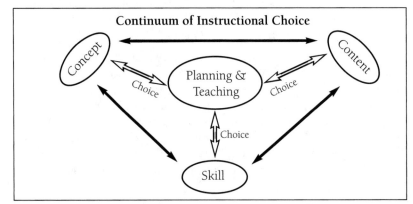

Instructional Support

In addition to the instructional choices the teacher will need to make, the teacher must also make a decision related to how to interact with the child. Will the lesson be governed more by teacher questioning and demonstrating, student responding, or some interrelationship between the two? As further evidence of a continuum, it is likely that during a lesson, this balance will shift depending on how the student responds to the teacher prompts, and therefore at any one time, the teacher will be at a different place on this continuum of interaction. This is depicted in Figure 9–3.

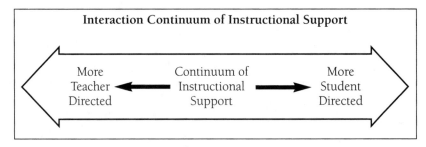

FIGURE 9–3
*Interaction Continuum of
Instructional Support*

Student Need

An additional concern for teachers is the kind of student issue with which they are dealing. In some cases, a teacher might be dealing with a student or group of students who typically respond well to less structured forms of teaching, and the teacher might only need to use a more scaffolded approach on rare occasions. Thus, this intermittent form of scaffolding might be thought of as incidental, occasional, or centered only around one particular learning problem. On the other hand, in a different year the same teacher may have some students who persistently struggle and who benefit from carefully scaffolded lessons. This range of student needs is depicted in Figure 9–4.

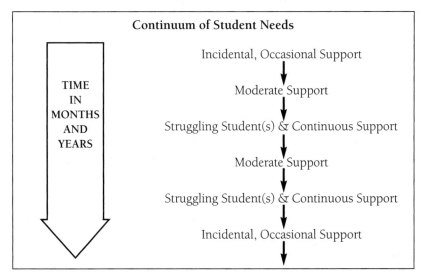

FIGURE 9–4
*Continuum of Student
Needs*

USEFULNESS AND CHALLENGES POSED BY SUPPORTS ON MULTIPLE LEVELS

While it is helpful to think about how scaffolding occurs on a continuum that occupies multiple levels, it is also helpful to think about the usefulness of this continuum and the challenges posed by it. I have depicted these in Figure 9–5.

Usefulness and Challenges Posed by Supports on Multiple Levels		
Continuum of support	Usefulness	Challenges
Context of Support Individual ↕ Group ↕ Whole class	• Tailor instruction to needs of class, group, or individual • Differentiate instruction for different classes taught by same teacher • Right students can get support at the right time, where and when they need it	• Requires teacher to weigh needs of one against needs of the many • Requires teacher to weigh the needs of one student in need versus another student who may be in need simultaneously • Necessitates multitasking
Instructional Choice Content ↕ Concept ↕ Skill	• Supports teacher in instructional choice • Represents an alternative for teachers who feel they only teach "content" • Supports authentic teaching and learning	• Necessitates complex decision making on the part of the teacher • Focus on one can inadvertently turn scaffolding into "skill, drill, and kill" approach
Instructional Support Teacher ↕ Student	• Establishes a to-and-fro approach where the teacher and student interaction changes depending on the student response to instruction	• Can easily become teacher-dominated; teacher moves forward with agenda without attending to student need or understanding • Can easily become student-dominated, highly constructivist, and lacking necessary instructional supports
Student Need Incidental ↕ Ongoing	• Supports right students getting the right instruction at the right time • Supports teacher in thinking about a range of supports	• Difficult to distinguish where to apply scaffolded support • Easy to think of an either-or situation as if there were only two choices rather than a continuum of supports

FIGURE 9–5 *Usefulness and Challenges Posed by Supports on Multiple Levels*

What is significant about Figure 9–5 is that it depicts the range of levels on which scaffolding may take place, and the exciting opportunities as well as the risks posed by such carefully targeted instruction. This duality of possibility and challenge means that it is essential for teachers to use the range of supports, as described in the preceding figures, to be better equipped to provide carefully tailored instruction to students.

Although scaffolding offers a range of opportunities for how a teacher might engage a child or a group of children, it is fraught with many challenges which we must consider.

SLIPPERY SLOPES

Thinking about how we might use a more scaffolded approach to lessons offers a great opportunity to teachers, but there are also some slippery slopes that teachers have to negotiate. By slippery slopes, I mean factors beyond our control that have the effect of pulling us back to the status quo. There are a number of these factors, but if I had to list only three they would be

- standardized testing,
- school and teaching culture, and
- inertia.

Standardized Testing

Let's look at the first slippery slope: standardized testing. There is no reason that standardized testing should itself represent a barrier to scaffolding student instruction, but it may be that in a particular district, school, or grade level, so much emphasis is placed on these high-stakes, one-shot tests that teachers feel the need to teach to the test to the exclusion of everything else. Indeed, it might even be said that these might have been issues formerly thought to be more relevant to secondary or middle school classrooms, but they now are increasingly faced by teachers of the youngest students. This is a difficult slope to climb, and my best advice is that you see scaffolded instruction as a way of augmenting or supporting quality learning, which will in turn create positive performance on things like standardized tests. Another way to think about scaffolding is as a support for some challenged students, and by supporting learning of students who are "on the bubble," we may have impressive outcomes on things such as the pass rate on the standardized test.

Culture

A second slippery slope is the culture of the school and grade level, with particular attention to fellow teachers and their teaching practices. By this I mean that you might be the most innovative teacher in the world, but if your principal pushes a "team" approach and you are the junior teacher on the Grade 2 team, it may be difficult to move initiatives forward. I have even visited schools where a group of thirty-year veteran teachers have referred to one of their colleagues as the "junior teacher" even when that person was a twenty-year veteran! Scaffolding student lessons does offer hope since it should not interfere with the curricular planning of the team, but clearly there are some teams that demand so much of teachers, it is difficult to do anything but follow the vision of the team, which may not necessarily be aligned with the vision of the individual teacher. My best advice in this situation is that an individual teacher might try to articulate how more carefully scaffolded lessons might actually carry the agenda of the team forward, rather than seeing scaffolding as something outside or apart from the efforts of the team.

Inertia

A third slippery slope is the force of inertia: the difficulty of moving ourselves forward when we are pulled back with our own desire to leave things the way they already are. This is a more complicated way of saying "Don't fix it if it isn't broken." Certainly there is a lot to be said for leaving things that currently work the way they are. That said, scaffolding student learning might better be thought of as augmenting quality teaching rather than as a wholesale change in teaching. In other words, if you live in a nice house where everything works well except for the television, which does not receive Channel 6, no one is asking you to buy a new house with a television that works—merely that you change the channel on the television to one that works. Thus, to overcome inertia it can be helpful to think about how scaffolding student learning builds on your current teaching repertoire rather than seeing it as an extra task to be accomplished in an already busy day.

USING SCAFFOLDS TO CONSTRUCT OUR TEACHING

Although teachers have many different ways of defining scaffolding, it can be said that all scaffolding is teaching, but that not all teaching is scaffolding. Scaffolding is a process of interaction designed to lift learning. Teachers' choices of approaches, curricula, or materials can all work toward this end, especially when materials and resources are used to support new understandings.

Scaffolding is not straightforward. Teachers who are effective seem to work from an analytical stance. They account for what the learner has to be able to do, the learner's present abilities, the materials that will lift performance, the amount of help that will be needed, and the kind of help that will be needed so that the child can work as independently and successfully as possible.

Most importantly, in this era of emphasis on what teachers know and can do, conversations regarding scaffolding place students back at the heart of instructional decision making. Since consideration of the student response is a key element of scaffolded instruction, students have a key role to play in scaffolding. By considering how we might better scaffold our instruction, we place students back at the center of our planning and teaching.

BIBLIOGRAPHY

Adler, D. A. 1993. *A Picture Book of Anne Frank.* New York: Holiday House.

Allard, H. 1977. *Miss Nelson Is Missing!* Boston: Houghton Mifflin.

Allington, R. L. 2000. *What Really Matters for Struggling Readers: Designing Research-Based Programs.* New York: Longman Publishing.

Allington, R. L., editor. 2002. *Big Brother and the National Reading Curriculum: How Ideology Trumped Evidence.* Portsmouth, NH: Heinemann.

Applebee, A. N. 1978. *The Child's Concept of Story.* Chicago, IL: University of Chicago Press.

Armbruster, B. B., F. Lehr, and J. Osborn. 2001. *Put Reading First: The Research Building Blocks for Teaching Children to Read: Kindergarten through Grade 1.* Jessup, MD: National Institute for Literacy.

Armstrong, T. 2003. *The Multiple Intelligences of Reading and Writing: Making the Words Come Alive.* Alexandria, VA: Association for Supervision and Curriculum Development.

Arnheim, R. 1991. *Thoughts on Art Education, Occasional Paper 2.* The Getty Center for Education in the Arts. Los Angeles, CA.

Aruego, J., and A. Dewey. 1986. *Five Little Ducks.* New York: Crown.

Ashton-Warner, S. 1963. *Teacher.* New York: Simon and Schuster.

Bader, L. A. 1983. *Bader Reading and Language Inventory.* New York: Macmillan.

Baylor, B. 1978. *The Other Way to Listen.* New York: Macmillan.

Bracey, G. W. 2003. *On the Death of Childhood and the Destruction of Public Schools.* Portsmouth, NH: Heinemann.

Bransford, J. D., and N. S. McCarrrell. 1974. "A Sketch of a Cognitive Approach to Comprehension: Some Thoughts About Understanding What It Means to Comprehend." In *Cognition and Symbolic Processes,* edited by W. B. Weimer and D. S. Palermo, 189–229. Hillsdale, NJ: Erlbaum.

Bodrova, E., and D. J. Leong. 1996. *Tools of the Mind: The Vygotskian Approach to Early Childhood Education.* Englewood Cliffs, NJ: Prentice Hall.

Brown, H., and B. Cambourne. 1987. *Read and Retell: A Strategy for the Whole Language/Natural Learning Classroom.* Portsmouth, NH: Heinemann.

Bruner, J. S. 1974. "Organization of Early Skilled Action." In *The Integration of a Child Into a Social World,* edited by M. P. M. Richard, 167–84. London, England: Cambridge University Press.

———. 1975. "The Ontogenesis of Speech Acts." *Journal of Child Language* 2, 1–40.

Bruner, J. 1986. *Actual Minds, Possible Worlds.* Cambridge, MA: Harvard University Press.

Bruner, J., and N. Ratner. 1978. "Games, Social Exchange and the Acquisition of Language." *Journal of Child Language* 5(1), 391–401.

Calkins, L. M. 1986. *The Art of Teaching Writing.* Portsmouth, NH: Heinemann.

———. 1994. *The Art of Teaching Writing,* revised edition. Portsmouth, NH: Heinemann.

Calkins, L. M. 2001. *The Art of Teaching Reading.* New York: Addison Wesley Longman.

Cazden, C. 1983. "Adult Assistance to Language Development: Scaffolds, Models and Direct Instruction." In *Developing Literacy: Young Children's Use of Language,* edited by R. P. Parker, 3–18. Newark, DE: International Reading Association.

———. 1988. *Classroom Discourse: The Language of Teaching and Learning.* Portsmouth, NH: Heinemann.

———. 1992. *Whole Language Plus: Essays on Literacy in the United States and New Zealand.* New York: Teachers College Press.

Chard, D. J., S. Vaughn, and B. J. Tyler. 2002. "A Synthesis of Research on Effective Interventions for Building Reading Fluency with Elementary Students with Learning Disabilities." *Journal of Learning Disabilities* 35(5), 386–406.

Clandinin, D. J., and F. M. Connelly. 2000. *Narrative Inquiry: Experience and Story in Qualitative Research.* San Francisco, CA: Jossey-Bass.

Clay, M. M. 1966. *Emergent Reading Behavior.* Unpublished doctoral dissertation, University of Auckland Library.

———. 1991. *Becoming Literate: The Construction of Inner Control.* Portsmouth, NH: Heinemann.

———. 1993. *An Observation Survey of Early Literacy Achievement.* Portsmouth, NH: Heinemann.

———. 2001. *Change Over Time in Children's Literacy Development.* Portsmouth, NH: Heinemann.

———. 2002. *Running Records.* Portsmouth, NH: Heinemann.

Collins, D. R. 2000. *Joshua Poole and Sunrise.* Barrington, IL: Rigby.

Connelly, F. M., and D. J. Clandinin. 1988. *Teachers as Curriculum Planners: Narratives of Experience.* New York: Teachers College Press.

———. 1994. "Telling Teaching Stories." *Teacher Education Quarterly* 21(1), 145–58.

———. 1999. *Shaping a Professional Identity: Stories of Educational Practice.* New York: Teachers College Press.

———. In progress. *Narrative and Education.* Unpublished manuscript.

Cowley, J. 1987a. *The Long Long Tail.* Bothell, WA: Wright Group.

———. 1987b. *Mr. Grump.* Bothell, WA: Wright Group.

———. 1987c. *Noise.* Bothell, WA: Wright Group.

———. 1987d. *Ratty Tatty.* Bothell, WA: Wright Group.

———. 1987e. *Snap!* Bothell, WA: Wright Group.

———. 1987f. *Spider Spider.* Bothell, WA: Wright Group.

———. 1987g. *The Tiny Woman's Coat.* Bothell, WA: Wright Group.

———. 1989. *Mrs. Wishy Washy.* Bothell, WA: Wright Group.

Coxe, M. 1997. *Big Egg.* New York: Random House.

Darling-Hammond, L., and P. Youngs. 2002. "Defining 'Highly Qualified Teachers': What Does 'Scientifically-Based Research' Actually Tell Us?" *Educational Researcher* 31 (December): 13–25.

Davidson, J. L. 1982. "The Group Mapping Activity for Instruction in Reading and Thinking." *Journal of Reading* 26, 52–56.

De La Paz, S. 1999. "Self-Regulated Strategy Instruction in Regular Education Settings: Improving Outcomes for Students with and Without Learning Disabilities." *Learning Disabilities Research and Practice* 14(2), 92–106.

Delpit, L. 1988. "The Silenced Dialogue: Power and Pedagogy in Educating Other People's Children." *Harvard Educational Review* 58(3), 280–98.

Dewey, J. 1938. *Experience and Education.* New York: Collier Books.

Dorr-Bremme, D. W. 1990. "Contextualization Cues in the Classroom: Discourse Regulation and Social Control Functions." *Language in Society* 19, 379–402. Cambridge, England: Cambridge University Press.

Edwards, P. D. 1998. *The Grumpy Morning.* Illustrated by Darcia Labrosse. New York: Hyperion Books.

Elbers, E. 1996. "Cooperation and Social Context in Adult-Child Interaction." *Learning and Instruction* 6(4), 281–86.

Englert, C. S., R. A. Berry, and K. L. Dunsmore. 2001. "A Case Study of the Apprenticeship Process: Another Perspective on the Apprentice and Scaffolding Metaphor." *Journal of Learning Disabilities* 34(2), 152–71.

Englert, C. S., and T. V. Mariage. 1991. "Making Students Partners in the Comprehension Process: Organizing the Reading 'POSSE.'" *Learning Disability Quarterly* 14, 123–38.

———. 1996. "A Sociocultural Perspective: Teaching Ways-of-Thinking and Ways-of-Talking in a Literacy Community." *Learning Disability Research and Practice* 11(3), 157–67.

———. 2003. "The Sociocultural Model in Special Education Interventions: Apprenticing Students Into Higher-Order Thinking." In *Handbook of Learning Disabilities,* edited by H. L. Swanson, K. R. Harris, and S. Graham, 450–67. New York: Guilford.

Englert, C. S., T. V. Mariage, M. A. Garmon, and K. L. Tarrant. 1998. "Accelerating Reading Progress in Early Literacy Project Classrooms: Three Exploratory Studies." *Remedial and Special Education* 19(3), 142–59.

Englert, C. S., T. E. Raphael, and L. M. Anderson. 1992. "Socially-Mediated Instruction: Improving Students' Knowledge and Talk About Writing." *Elementary School Journal* 92(4), 411–50.

Englert, C. S., T. E. Raphael, L. M. Anderson, S. L. Gregg, and H. M. Anthony. 1988. "Students' Metacognitive Knowledge About How to Write Informational Text." *Learning Disability Quarterly* 11, 18–46.

Englert, C. S., T. E. Raphael, and T. V. Mariage. 1994. "Developing a School-Based Discourse for Literacy Learning: A Principled Search for Understanding." *Learning Disability Quarterly* 17, 3–33.

Englert, C. S., K. L. Tarrant, and T. V. Mariage. 1992. "Redefining Instructional Practice in Special Education: Perspectives on Good Teaching." *Teacher Education and Special Education* 15(2), 62–86.

Fine, J. C. 1991. "The Effect of Direct Instruction in Story Grammar Using Deep Processing on the Reading and Writing Achievement of Second Graders." *Dissertation Abstracts International* 52(12), 4204A. (UMI No. 9210706.)

Fine, J., and A. Moreyra. 1997, May. "Read and Retell: A Strategic Breakthrough for All Students." Paper presented at the conference of the International Reading Association, Atlanta, GA.

Florio-Ruane, S. 2001. *Teacher Education and the Cultural Imagination: Autobiography, Conversation, and Narrative.* London, England: Lawrence Erlbaum.

Fosnot, C., editor. 1996. *Constructivism: Theory, Perspectives and Practice.* New York: Teachers College Press.

Fountas, I. C., and G. S. Pinnell. 1996. *Guided Reading: Good First Teaching for All Children.* Portsmouth, NH: Heinemann.

Fox, M. 1997. *Whoever You Are.* New York: Harcourt Brace and Company.

Galda, L. 1998. "Mirrors and Windows: Reading as Transformation." In *Literature-Based Instruction: Reshaping the Curriculum,* edited by T. E. Raphael and K. H. Au, 1–11. Norwood, MA: Christopher-Gordon.

Galda, L., S. Rayburn, and L. C. Stanzi. 2000. *Looking Through the Faraway End: Creating a Literature-Based Reading Curriculum with Second Graders.* Newark, DE: International Reading Association.

Gallimore, R., and R. G. Tharp. 1990. "Teaching Mind in Society: Teaching, Schooling and Literate Discourse." In *Vygotsky and Education: Instructional Implications and Applications of Sociohistorical Psychology,* edited by L. C. Moll, 175–205. Cambridge, MA: Cambridge University Press.

Gambrell, L. B., and R. J. Bales. 1986, Fall. "Mental Imagery and the Comprehension-Monitoring Performance of Fourth- and Fifth-Grade Poor Readers." *Reading Research Quarterly* 21(4), 454–64.

Garan, E. M. 2002. *Resisting Reading Mandates: How to Triumph with the Truth.* Portsmouth, NH: Heinemann.

Gardiner, H. 1983. *Frames of Mind: The Theory of Multiple Intelligences.* New York: Basic Books.

Garland, S. 1993. *The Lotus Seed.* New York: Harcourt Brace and Company.

Gibson, S. A. 2002. "The Theory of Practice of Literacy Coaches: Describing the Relationship Between Coaching Sessions and Kindergarten and First Grade Teachers' Beliefs and Instructional Behaviors." *Dissertation Abstracts International* 63(04), 1305A. (UMI No. 3049028.)

Goldenberg, C. 1991. "Instructional Conversation: Promoting Comprehension Through Discussion." *The Reading Teacher* 46, 316–26.

Graham, S., and K. R. Harris. 1989. "Improving Learning Disabled Students' Skills at Composing Essays: Self-Instructional Strategy Training." *Exceptional Children* 56, 201–14.

———. 1994. "The Role and Development of Self-Regulation in the Writing Process." In *Self-Regulation of Learning and Performance: Issues and Educational Applications,* edited by D. Schunk and B. Zimmerman, 203–22. Hillsdale, NJ: Erlbaum.

Graves, D. 1984. *A Researcher Learns to Write.* Portsmouth, NH: Heinemann.

Griffin, M. L. 2000. Emergent Readers' Joint Text Construction: A Study of Reading in Social Context. Unpublished doctoral dissertation, University of Rhode Island.

———. 2001. "Social Contexts of Beginning Reading." *Language Arts* 78(4), 371–78.

Hibbing, A. N., and J. L. Rankin-Erickson. 2003. "A Picture Is Worth a Thousand Words: Using Visual Images to Improve Comprehension for Middle School Struggling Readers." *The Reading Teacher* 58, 758–70.

Hiebert, E. H. 1999. "Text Matters in Learning to Read." *The Reading Teacher* 52(6), 552–66.

Hinshaw, S. P. 2000. "Attention-Deficit Hyperactivity Disorder: The Search for Viable Treatments." In *Child and Adolescent Therapy: Cognitive-Behavioral Procedures,* 2nd ed., edited by P. C. Kendall, 88–128. New York: Guilford.

Holm, L., and C. Horn. 2003. "Bridging the Gap Between Schools of Education and the Needs of 21st-Century Teachers." *Phi Delta Kappan* 84 (January): 376–80.

Hoogesteder, M., R. Maier, and E. Elbers. 1996. "The Architecture of Adult-Child Interaction. Joint Problem Solving and the Structure of Cooperation." *Learning and Instruction* 6(4), 345–58.

Housen, A., and P. Yenuwine. 2000. *Visual Thinking Strategies: Understanding the Basics.* New York: Visual Understanding in Education.

Hunia, F. 1977a. *The Sly Fox and the Red Hen.* Loughborough, Leicestershire, United Kingdom: Ladybird Books.

———. 1977b. *Three Billy Goats Gruff.* Loughborough, Leicestershire, United Kingdom: Ladybird Books.

Idol, L., and V. J. Croll. 1987. "Story-Mapping Training as a Means of Improving Reading Comprehension." *Learning Disabilities Quarterly* 10, 214–29.

Karmiloff-Smith, A. 1979. "Micro- and Macro-Developmental Changes in Language Acquisition and Other Representational Systems." *Cognitive Science* 3, 91–118.

Karpov, Y. V. (2003). "Development through the Lifespan: A Neo-Vygotskyian Perspective." In *Vygotsky's Educational Theory in Cultural Context,* edited by A. Kozulin, B. Gindis, V. S. Ageyer, and S. Miller, 138–55. New York: Cambridge University Press.

Langer, J. A. 1995. *Envisioning Literature: Literacy Understanding and Literature Instruction.* Newark, DE: International Reading Association.

Littlechild, G. 1993. *This Land Is My Land.* San Francisco, CA: Children's Book Press.

Lyon, G. R., J. M. Fletcher, S. E. Shaywitz, B. A. Shaywitz, J. K. Torgesen, F. B. Wood, A. Schulte, and R. Olson. 2001. "Rethinking Learning Disabilities." In *Rethinking Special Education for a New Century,* edited by C. E. Finn, A. J. Rotherham, and C. R. Hokanson. Washington, D.C.: Thomas B. Fordham Foundation and the Progressive Policy Institute.

Lyons, C. A. 2003. *Teaching Struggling Readers: How to Use Brain-based Research to Maximize Learning.* Portsmouth, NH: Heinemann.

Lyons, C. A., and G. S. Pinnell. 2001. *Systems for Change in Literacy Education: A Guide to Professional Development.* Portsmouth, NH: Heinemann.

MacGillivray, L. 1997. "'I've Seen You Read': Reading Strategies in a First-Grade Class." *Journal of Research in Childhood Education* 11(2), 135–46.

MacGillivray, L., and S. Hawes. 1994. "I Don't Know What I'm Doing—They All Start With B: First Graders Negotiate Peer Reading Interactions." *The Reading Teacher* 48(3), 210–17.

Makar, B. 1980a. *Cop Cat.* Cambridge, MA: Educators Publishing Service.

———. 1980b. *The Jet.* Cambridge, MA: Educators Publishing Service.

———. 1980c. *Meg.* Cambridge, MA: Educators Publishing Service.

Many, J. E. 2002. "An Exhibition and Analysis of Verbal Tapestries: Understanding How Scaffolding Is Woven Into the Fabric of Instructional Conversations." *Reading Research Quarterly* 37(4), 376–407.

Mariage, T. V. 1995. "Gaining Insight Into Why Children Learn: Examining the Nature of Teacher Talk in Reading." *Learning Disability Quarterly* 18(3), 214–35.

———. 2000. "Constructing Educational Possibilities: A Sociolinguistic Examination of Meaning-Making in Sharing Chair." *Learning Disability Quarterly* 23(2), 79–104.

———. 2001. "Features of an Interactive Writing Discourse: Conversational Involvement, Conventional Knowledge, and Internalization in Morning Message." *Journal of Learning Disabilities* 34(2), 172–96.

Mariage, T. V., C. S. Englert, and M. A. Garmon. 2000. "The Teacher as 'More Knowledgeable Other' in Assisting Literacy Learning with Special Needs Students." *Reading and Writing Quarterly* 16, 299–336.

Mariage, T. V., and M. A. Garmon. 2003. "A Case of Educational Change: Improving Student Achievement Through a School/University Partnership." *Remedial and Special Education* 24(4), 215–33.

Marshall, J. 1987. *Red Riding Hood.* New York: Dial Books.

Martin, B., and P. Brogan. 1972. *Teacher's Guide, Instant Readers.* New York: Holt, Rinehart and Winston.

Marzano, R. J., and D. E. Arredondo. 1986. *Tactics for Thinking.* Alexandria, VA: ASCD.

McPhail, D. 2000. *Drawing Lessons from a Bear.* Boston: Little, Brown, and Co.

Mehan, H. 1982. "The Structure of Classroom Events and Their Consequences for Student Performance." In *Children In and Out of School: Ethnography and Education,* edited by P. Gilmore and A. A. Glatthorn, 59–87. Washington, D.C.: Center for Applied Linguistics.

Moats, L. C. Spring/Summer 1998. "Teaching Decoding." *American Educator* 22(1-2), 42–49, 95–96.

Moss, J. F., and M. F. Fenster. 2002. *From Literature to Literacy: Bridging Learning in the Library and the Primary Classroom.* Newark, DE: International Reading Association.

Muldowney, C. J. 1995. "The Effect of a Paired Reading Program on Reading Achievement in a First Grade Classroom." ERIC No. ED379634.

National Institute of Child Health and Human Development. 2001a. *Report of the National Reading Panel: Teaching Children to Read: An Evidence-Based Assessment of the Scientific Research Literature on Reading and Its Implications for Reading Instruction. Reports of the Subgroups.* Washington, D.C.: National Institutes of Health.

————. 2001b. *Report of the National Reading Panel: Teaching Children to Read: An Evidence-Based Assessment of the Scientific Research Literacy on Reading and its Implications for Reading Instruction: Summary.* Washington, D.C.: National Institutes of Health.

Nes, S. L. 1997. *Less-Skilled Readers: Studying the Effects of Paired Reading on Reading Fluency, Accuracy, Comprehension, Reader Self-Perception, and Lived Experiences.* Dissertation Abstracts Online. No. AAG9736884.

Ninio, A., and J. Bruner. 1978. "The Achievements and Antecedents of Labeling." *Journal of Child Language* 5, 1–15.

Olby, R. C. 1970. "Francis Crick, DNA and the Central Dogma." *Daedalus* 99.

Palincsar, A. S. 1986. "The Role of Dialogue in Providing Scaffolded Instruction." *Educational Psychologist* 21, 73–98.

Paris, S. G., M. Y. Lipson, and K. K. Wixson. 1994. "Becoming a Strategic Reader." In *Theoretical Models and Processes of Reading.* 4th ed. edited by R. B. Ruddell, M. R. Ruddell, and H. Singer, 788–800. Newark, DE: International Reading Association.

Pavio, A. 1986. *Mental Representations: A Dual-Coding Approach.* New York: Oxford University Press.

Pinnell, G. S., and I. C. Fountas. 1998. *Word Matters: Teaching Phonics and Spelling in the Reading/Writing Classroom.* Portsmouth, NH: Heinemann.

————. *Word Study: Phonics & Spelling Lessons, Buddy Study System.* Developed by Irene C. Fountas. 35–45 min. each. Heinemann, 2002. Videocassettes.

————. 2003a. *Phonics Lessons: Letters, Words, and How They Work, Grade K.* Portsmouth, NH: Heinemann.

————. 2003b. *Phonics Lessons: Letters, Words, and How They Work, Grade 1.* Portsmouth, NH: Heinemann.

————. 2003c. *Phonics Lessons: Letters, Words, and How They Work, Grade 2.* Portsmouth, NH: Heinemann.

Portalupi, J. 1999. "Learning to Write: Honoring Both Process and Product." *Primary Voices K–6: Teaching Young Writers the Elements of Craft* 7, 2–6.

Prawat, R. S. 2002. "Dewey and Vygotsky Viewed Through the Rearview Mirror—and Dimly at That." *Educational Researcher* 31(5), 16–20.

Pressley, M. 1998. *Reading Instruction That Works: The Case for Balanced Teaching.* New York: Guilford.

Pressley, M., A. Roehrig, K. Bogner, L. M. Raphael, and S. Dolezal. 2002. "Balanced Literacy Instruction." *Focus on Exceptional Children* 34(5), 1–14.

Randell, B. 1996. *Sally's Red Bucket.* Crystal Lake, IL: Rigby.

Ready to Read. 1986. *Nick's Glasses.* Huntington Beach, CA: Pacific Learning.

Rodgers, E. M., and G. S. Pinnell, editors. 2002. *Learning from Teaching in Literacy Education: New Perspectives in Professional Development.* Portsmouth, NH: Heinemann.

Roehler, L. R., and D. J. Cantlon. 1997. "Scaffolding: A Powerful Tool in Social Constructivist Classrooms." In *Scaffolding Student Learning,* edited by K. Hogan and M. Pressley, 6–42. Cambridge, MA: Brookline Books.

Root, P. 1998. *One Duck Stuck.* Illustrated by Jane Chapman. Cambridge, MA: Candlewick Press.

Rosenblatt, L. M. 1978. *The Reader, the Text, the Poem.* Carbondale, IL: Southern Illinois University Press.

Roser, N., J. V. Hoffman, C. Farest, and L. D. Labbo. 1992. "Language Charts: A Record of Story Time Talk." *Language Arts* 69, 44–52.

Rozin P., S. Poritsky, and R. Sotsky. 1971. "American Children with Reading Problems Can Easily Learn to Read English Represented with Chinese Characters." *Science* 171, 3977, 1264–67.

Samway, K. D., G. Whang, and M. Pippitt. 1995. *Buddy Reading: Cross-Age Tutoring in a Multicultural School.* Portsmouth, NH: Heinemann.

Say, A. 1993. *Grandfather's Journey.* New York: Houghton Mifflin.

———. 1997. *Allison.* New York: Walter Lorraine Books.

Scharer, P. L., S. A. Gibson, and A. Van Order. 2001, December. "Student Responses to a Kindergarten School-Home Book Project." Paper presented at the annual meeting of the National Reading Conference, San Antonio, TX.

Schlein, M. 2000. *The Year of the Panda.* New York: Scholastic.

Siegel, M. 1994, April. "The Curricular Possibilities of Transmediation: Strategy Framework and Metaphor." In C. Panofsky (Chair): Vygotsky and Beyond: Semiotic Mediation and Its Significance for Literacy Teaching and Performance. Symposium conducted at the meeting of the American Educational Research Association, New Orleans, LA.

Singer, D. G., and T. A. Revenson. 1996. *A Piaget Primer: How a Child Thinks,* revised edition. New York: Plume/Penguin.

Smith, F. 1983. "Reading Like a Writer." *Language Arts* 60(5), 558–67.

Smith, T. E. C., E. A. Polloway, J. R. Patton, and C. A. Dowdy. 2000. *Teaching Students with Special Needs in Inclusive Settings,* 3rd ed. Boston: Allyn and Bacon.

Stein, N., and C. Glenn. 1979. "An Analysis of Story Comprehension in Elementary School Children." In *New Directions in Discourse Processing: Vol. 2.,* edited by R. O. Freedle, 53–120. Norwood, NJ: Ablex.

Steiner, V. J., and E. Souberman. 1978. Afterword. In *Mind in Society: The Development of Higher Psychological Processes,* by L. S. Vygotsky. Cambridge, MA: Harvard University Press.

Stone, C. A. 1993. "What Is Missing in the Metaphor of Scaffolding." In *Contexts for Learning: Sociocultural Dynamics in Children's Development,* edited by E. A. Forman, N. Minick, and C. A. Stone. New York: Oxford University Press.

———. 2002. "Promises and Pitfalls of Scaffolded Instruction for Students with Language Learning Disabilities." In *Speaking, Reading, and Writing in Children with Language Learning Disabilities: New Paradigms for Research and Practice,* edited by K. G. Butler and E. R. Silliman, 175–98. Mahwah, NJ: Erlbaum.

Swanson, H. L. 1989. "Verbal Coding Deficits in Learning Disabled Readers: A Multiple Stage Model." *Educational Psychology Review* 1, 235–77.

Tharp, R., and R. Gallimore. 1988. *Rousing Minds to Life: Teaching, Learning, and Schooling in Social Context.* New York: Cambridge University Press.

Tierney, R. J., and M. Leys. 1984. "What Is the Value of Connecting Reading and Writing?" (Report No. 55.) Urban, IL: University of Illinois Center for the Study of Reading. (ERIC No. ED 251 810.)

Tompkins, G. E., and L. M. McGee. 1989. "Teaching Repetition as a Story Structure." In *Children's Comprehension of Text: Research Into Practice,* edited by K. D. Muth, 59–78. Newark, DE: International Reading Association.

Topping, K. J., and G. A. Lindsay. 1992. "The Structure and the Development of the Paired Reading Technique." *Journal of Research in Reading* 15(2), 120–36.

Troia, G. A., and S. Graham. 2002. "The Effectiveness of a Highly Explicit, Teacher-Directed Strategy Instruction Routine: Changing the Writing Performance of Students with Learning Disabilities." *Journal of Learning Disabilities* 34(4), 290–305.

Troia, G. A., S. Graham, and K. R. Harris. 1999. "Teaching Students with Learning Disabilities to Mindfully Plan When Writing." *Exceptional Children* 65, 215–52.

Tudge, J. 1990. "Vygotsky, the Zone of Proximal Development, and Peer Collaboration: Implications for Classroom Practice." In *Vygotsky and Education: Instructional Implications and Applications of Sociohistorical Psychology,* edited by L. C. Moll, 155–72. Cambridge, MA: Cambridge University Press.

U.S. Secretary of Education. July, 2002. *Secretary's Annual Report on Teacher Quality: Meeting the Highly Qualified Teachers Challenge.* Washington D.C.: U.S. Department of Education.

Vygotsky, L. 1962. *Thought and Language.* Cambridge, MA: MIT Press.

———. 1978. *Mind in Society: The Development of Higher Psychological Processes.* Cambridge, MA: Harvard University Press.

———. 1986. *Thought and Language.* (Translation newly revised and edited by Alex Kozulin.) Cambridge, MA: MIT Press.

Waber, B. 1972. *Ira Sleeps Over.* New York: Houghton Mifflin.

Watson, D., C. Burke, and J. Harste. 1989. *Whole Language: Inquiring Voices.* Ontario, Canada: Scholastic-TAB Publications, Ltd.

Westcott, N. B. 1988. *Down by the Bay.* New York: Crown.

White, E. B. 1952. *Charlotte's Web.* New York: HarperCollins.

Wittrock, M. C. 1983. "Writing and the Teaching of Reading." *Language Arts* 60, 568–606.

Wood, D. 2003. "The Why? What? When? and How? of Tutoring: The Development of Helping and Tutoring Skills in Children." *Literacy Teaching and Learning* 7 (1 & 2), 1–30.

Wood, D., and H. Wood. 1996. "Vygotsky, Tutoring and Learning." *Oxford Review of Education* 22(1), 5–16.

Wood, D., J. S. Bruner, and G. Ross. 1976. "The Role of Tutoring in Problem-Solving." *Journal of Child Psychology and Psychiatry* 17, 89–100.

Yatvin, J. 2002. "Babes in the Woods: The Wanderings of the National Reading Panel." *Phi Delta Kappan* 83(5): 364–69. Reprinted in Allington 2002.

Zigmond, N., and J. Baker. 1994. "Is the Mainstream a More Appropriate Educational Setting for Students with Disabilities? The Case of Randy." *Learning Disabilities Research and Practice* 9(2), 108–17.

CONTRIBUTORS

Emily C. Bouck is a doctoral candidate in the Department of Counseling, Educational Psychology, and Special Education at Michigan State University. Her research interests are in the areas of curriculum and achievement outcomes for students with mild mental impairment. She is also interested in the differential services provided to special education students in rural, urban, and suburban communities.

D. Jean Clandinin is professor and director of the Centre for Research for Teacher Education and Development at the University of Alberta. She is a former teacher, school counselor, and school psychologist. She is the author of several books and many articles and chapters in books. Her most recent book, coauthored with Michael Connelly and entitled *Narrative Inquiry,* was published by Jossey-Bass in 2000.

Joyce C. Fine is an associate professor of reading/language arts at Florida International University. She works closely with teachers and children in schools and has written articles and chapters in books on the topics of literacy development and teacher education. She loves learning, especially with her children and grandchildren.

Irene C. Fountas is professor in the School of Education at Lesley University in Cambridge, Massachusetts, where she directs a comprehensive school-reform project. She has been a classroom teacher, language arts specialist, and consultant in school districts across the nation and abroad, and has received numerous awards for her contributions to literacy. Irene and coauthor, Gay Su Pinnell, have published several books with Heinemann, including *Guided Reading: Good First Teaching for All Children* (1996), *Guiding Readers and Writers, Grades 3–6: Teaching Comprehension, Genre, and Content Literacy* (2000), *Phonics Lessons: Letters, Words, and How They Work, Grades K, 1, 2, and 3* (2002), and *Word Study Lessons: Phonics, Spelling, and Vocabulary* (2004).

Sharan A. Gibson is currently an assistant professor at San Diego State University's School of Teacher Education. She teaches graduate-level courses in literacy research, instruction, and assessment for preservice teachers and teachers working toward certification in reading instruction. Sharan has also worked as a classroom teacher, reading specialist, and early literacy consultant.

Janice Huber is an assistant professor at St. Francis Xavier University in Nova Scotia, Canada. She has taught in elementary classrooms in rural, urban, and international schools. She completed her Ph.D. at the University of Alberta in 2000. She is the author of many articles and chapters in books.

Her most recent publications are in *Curriculum Inquiry*, the *Journal of Curriculum Studies*, and *Reflective Practice*.

Troy V. Mariage is an assistant professor in the Department of Counseling, Educational Psychology, and Special Education at Michigan State University. His research focuses on literacy instruction for students with mild disabilities in elementary classrooms. More recently, he has worked with several of Michigan's most underperforming schools in an effort to reculture the buildings into learning organizations, with a special focus on the role that literacy learning and teaching plays in this process.

Gay Su Pinnell is a professor in the School of Teaching and Learning at The Ohio State University. She has extensive experience in classroom teaching and field-based research and in developing comprehensive approaches to literacy education. She has received the International Reading Association's Albert J. Harris Award for research and the Charles A. Dana Foundation Award for her contributions to the field of education. She is also a member of the Reading Hall of Fame. With Irene Fountas, she has coauthored several books on teaching reading, writing, and phonics, including *Word Matters: Teaching Phonics and Spelling in the Reading/Writing Classroom* (1998) and *Phonics Lessons: Letters, Words, and How They Work, Grades K, 1, 2, and 3* (2002).

Mary Lee Prescott-Griffin is an assistant professor of education at Wheaton College in Norton, Massachusetts. She has published several articles related to her research into social contexts of early literacy and is the author of two books, one on peer partnerships and the other on reading fluency.

Adrian Rodgers has taught literacy and learning for the past sixteen years, first at a Junior and Senior High School in Labrador and then at the college level in Ohio. He has a Ph.D. in Educational Studies with a specialization in English, drama, and teacher education from The Ohio State University. He is currently assistant professor in Teacher Education at The Ohio State University in Newark, Ohio, where his work focuses on literacy and its importance to preservice and inservice teachers. He is the author of "Old Roads and New Paths" in *Learning from Teaching in Literacy Education* published by Heinemann in 2002.

Emily M. Rodgers taught for ten years in Newfoundland prior to joining the faculty of The Ohio State University as an assistant professor in the College of Education. Her research focuses on the professional development of teachers and the nature of effective scaffolding of literacy learning. She received the National Reading Conference Outstanding Student Research Award in 1999. Emily is co-editor of *Learning from Teaching in Literacy Education* along with Gay Su Pinnell, published by Heinemann in 2002.

Barbara Joan Wiley is currently an adjunct professor at The Ohio State University and program coordinator for the OSU Literacy Collaborative project. She works with teachers as they train to become literacy coordinators in their schools. She has been a classroom teacher and reading specialist in school districts across the nation and abroad.

INDEX

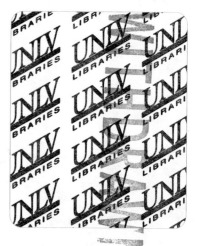